Responsible Data Science

Transparency and Fairness in Algorithms

Grant Fleming
Peter Bruce

WILEY

Responsible Data Science

About the Authors

GRANT FLEMING is a data scientist at Elder Research, Inc. His professional focus is on machine learning for social science applications, model interpretability, civic technology, and building software tools for reproducible data science.

PETER BRUCE is the Chief Learning Officer at Elder Research, Inc., author of several best-selling texts on data science, and Founder of the Institute for Statistics Education at `Statistics.com`, an Elder Research Company.

About the Technical Editor

ROBERT DE GRAAF is a data scientist and statistician from Melbourne, Australia. He is the author of *Managing Your Data Science Projects* and coauthor of *SQL Cookbook, 2nd edition*. He is husband to Clare and father to Maya and Leda, and enjoys playing guitar and learning new languages.

Acknowledgments

First and foremost, we acknowledge the support of Elder Research, Inc., and of John Elder (chairman) and Gerhard Pilcher (CEO) in particular. We have benefited greatly from the technical and philosophical conversations we have shared with our colleagues. Elder Research has been most generous in permitting us to pursue this project. At the same time, this book has not been reviewed or edited by the company, and we, the authors, bear sole responsibility for all opinions, errors, and omissions.

We thank, especially, our coauthors on select chapters. Will Goodrum lent his expertise to the legal issues explored in Chapter 3, "The Way AI Goes Wrong, and the Legal Implications," and Sam Ballerini helped enormously in writing the code for the facial recognition CNN example in Chapter 8, "Auditing for Neural Networks."

Robert de Graaf served as technical editor, raising important points and contributing in many places to a better book. This book certainly would have been incomplete without his input.

Our editorial team at Wiley has been most supportive throughout the process. Jim Minatel, associate publisher, embraced our vision from the beginning. Our editor, Jan Lynn, kept us on track and patiently shepherded the various pieces of the project to all come together. Saravanan Dakshinamurthy handled the production side of things, Louise Watson did the copy-editing, and Pete Gaughan managed the process behind the scenes.

We would like to thank Matthew Dwinnell and Amy Zhang for their tips on working with HTML and CSS, as well as our co-workers Brittany Pugh and Chris Lee for their advice and feedback. Grant would like to thank his professors and mentors, including Edward Munn Sanchez, Lite Nartey, Edward R. Carr, Gregory Magai Patterson, Jennifer Bess, Mark Schaffer, Patrick Jessee, and Brandie Wagner, for their endless support of his efforts and spirit. Peter's appreciation goes to Galit Shmueli, his coauthor on other book projects, with whom he has had lively conversations on ethical issues surrounding the practice of data science.

Finally, we express our appreciation to our students at `Statistics.com` who have made constructive and useful comments on the material presented here.

Contents at a Glance

Introduction   xix

Part I   Motivation for Ethical Data Science and Background
             Knowledge   1

Chapter 1   Responsible Data Science   3

Chapter 2   Background: Modeling and the Black-Box Algorithm   27

Chapter 3   The Ways AI Goes Wrong, and the Legal Implications   49

Part II   The Ethical Data Science Process   71

Chapter 4   The Responsible Data Science Framework   73

Chapter 5   Model Interpretability: The What and the Why   99

Part III   EDS in Practice   135

Chapter 6   Beginning a Responsible Data Science Project   137

Chapter 7   Auditing a Responsible Data Science Project   173

Chapter 8   Auditing for Neural Networks   225

Chapter 9   Conclusion   265

Index   273

Contents

Introduction		xix
Part I	**Motivation for Ethical Data Science and Background Knowledge**	**1**
Chapter 1	**Responsible Data Science**	**3**
	The Optum Disaster	4
	Jekyll and Hyde	5
	Eugenics	7
	Galton, Pearson, and Fisher	7
	Ties between Eugenics and Statistics	7
	Ethical Problems in Data Science Today	9
	Predictive Models	10
	From Explaining to Predicting	10
	Predictive Modeling	11
	Setting the Stage for Ethical Issues to Arise	12
	Classic Statistical Models	12
	Black-Box Methods	14
	Important Concepts in Predictive Modeling	19
	Feature Selection	19
	Model-Centric vs. Data-Centric Models	20
	Holdout Sample and Cross-Validation	20
	Overfitting	21
	Unsupervised Learning	22
	The Ethical Challenge of Black Boxes	23
	Two Opposing Forces	24
	Pressure for More Powerful AI	24
	Public Resistance and Anxiety	24
	Summary	25

Chapter 2   Background: Modeling and the Black-Box Algorithm   27
Assessing Model Performance   27
    Predicting Class Membership   28
    The Rare Class Problem   28
    Lift and Gains   28
    Area Under the Curve   29
    AUC vs. Lift (Gains)   31
    Predicting Numeric Values   32
        Goodness-of-Fit   32
        Holdout Sets and Cross-Validation   33
    Optimization and Loss Functions   34
Intrinsically Interpretable Models vs. Black-Box Models   35
    Ethical Challenges with Interpretable Models   38
    Black-Box Models   39
        Ensembles   39
        Nearest Neighbors   41
        Clustering   41
        Association Rules   42
        Collaborative Filters   42
        Artificial Neural Nets and Deep Neural Nets   43
        Problems with Black-Box Predictive Models   45
        Problems with Unsupervised Algorithms   47
Summary   48

Chapter 3   The Ways AI Goes Wrong, and the Legal Implications   49
AI and Intentional Consequences by Design   50
    Deepfakes   50
    Supporting State Surveillance and Suppression   51
    Behavioral Manipulation   52
    Automated Testing to Fine-Tune Targeting   53
    AI and Unintended Consequences   55
    Healthcare   56
    Finance   57
    Law Enforcement   58
    Technology   60
The Legal and Regulatory Landscape around AI   61
    Ignorance Is No Defense: AI in the Context of
      Existing Law and Policy   63
    A Finger in the Dam: Data Rights, Data Privacy,
      and Consumer Protection Regulations   64
    Trends in Emerging Law and Policy Related to AI   66
Summary   69

Part II   The Ethical Data Science Process   71

Chapter 4   The Responsible Data Science Framework   73
Why We Keep Building Harmful AI   74
    Misguided Need for Cutting-Edge Models   74
    Excessive Focus on Predictive Performance   74

Ease of Access and the Curse of Simplicity   76
The Common Cause   76
The Face Thieves   78
An Anatomy of Modeling Harms   79
The World: Context Matters for Modeling   80
The Data: Representation Is Everything   83
The Model: Garbage In, Danger Out   85
Model Interpretability: Human Understanding for
Superhuman Models   86
Efforts Toward a More Responsible Data Science   89
Principles Are the Focus   90
Nonmaleficence   90
Fairness   90
Transparency   91
Accountability   91
Privacy   92
Bridging the Gap Between Principles and Practice
with the Responsible Data Science (RDS) Framework   92
Justification   94
Compilation   94
Preparation   95
Modeling   96
Auditing   96
Summary   97

Chapter 5   Model Interpretability: The What and the Why   99
The Sexist Résumé Screener   99
The Necessity of Model Interpretability   101
Connections Between Predictive Performance
and Interpretability   103
Uniting (High) Model Performance and Model
Interpretability   105
Categories of Interpretability Methods   107
Global Methods   107
Local Methods   113
Real-World Successes of Interpretability Methods   113
Facilitating Debugging and Audit   114
Leveraging the Improved Performance of Black-Box
Models   116
Acquiring New Knowledge   116
Addressing Critiques of Interpretability Methods   117
Explanations Generated by Interpretability Methods
Are Not Robust   118
Explanations Generated by Interpretability Methods
Are Low Fidelity   120
The Forking Paths of Model Interpretability   121
The Four-Measure Baseline   122

Building Our Own Credit Scoring Model   124
Using Train-Test Splits   125
Feature Selection and Feature Engineering   125
Baseline Models   127
The Importance of Making Your Code Work for
    Everyone   129
    Execution Variability   129
    Addressing Execution Variability with
      Functionalized Code   130
Stochastic Variability   130
Addressing Stochastic Variability via Resampling   130
Summary   133

Part III   **EDS in Practice**   **135**

Chapter 6   **Beginning a Responsible Data Science Project**   **137**
How the Responsible Data Science Framework
    Addresses the Common Cause   138
Datasets Used   140
Regression Datasets—Communities and Crime   140
Classification Datasets—COMPAS   140
Common Elements Across Our Analyses   141
Project Structure and Documentation   141
    Project Structure for the Responsible Data
      Science Framework: Everything in Its Place   142
    Documentation: The Responsible Thing to Do   145
Beginning a Responsible Data Science Project   151
Communities and Crime (Regression)   151
    Justification   151
    Compilation   154
    Identifying Protected Classes   157
    Preparation—Data Splitting and Feature
      Engineering   159
    Datasheets   161
COMPAS (Classification)   164
    Justification   164
    Compilation   166
    Identifying Protected Classes   168
    Preparation   169
Summary   172

Chapter 7   **Auditing a Responsible Data Science Project**   **173**
Fairness and Data Science in Practice   175
The Many Different Conceptions of Fairness   175
Different Forms of Fairness Are Trade-Offs with
    Each Other   177
Quantifying Predictive Fairness Within a
    Data Science Project   179

Mitigating Bias to Improve Fairness   185
    Preprocessing   185
    In-processing   186
    Postprocessing   186
Classification Example: COMPAS   187
    Prework: Code Practices, Modeling, and Auditing   187
    Justification, Compilation, and Preparation Review   189
    Modeling   191
    Auditing   200
        Per-Group Metrics: Overall   200
        Per-Group Metrics: Error   202
        Fairness Metrics   204
        Interpreting Our Models: Why Are They Unfair?   207
        Analysis for Different Groups   209
    Bias Mitigation   214
        Preprocessing: Oversampling   214
        Postprocessing: Optimizing Thresholds
            Automatically   218
        Postprocessing: Optimizing Thresholds Manually   219
Summary   223

Chapter 8   Auditing for Neural Networks   225
Why Neural Networks Merit Their Own Chapter   227
    Neural Networks Vary Greatly in Structure   227
    Neural Networks Treat Features Differently   229
    Neural Networks Repeat Themselves   231
    A More Impenetrable Black Box   232
        Baseline Methods   233
        Representation Methods   233
        Distillation Methods   234
        Intrinsic Methods   235
Beginning a Responsible Neural Network Project   236
    Justification   236
    Moving Forward   239
    Compilation   239
    Tracking Experiments   241
    Preparation   244
    Modeling   245
    Auditing   247
        Per-Group Metrics: Overall   247
        Per-Group Metrics: Unusual Definitions
            of "False Positive"   248
        Fairness Metrics   249
        Interpreting Our Models: Why Are They Unfair?   252
        Bias Mitigation   253
        Wrap-Up   255
Auditing Neural Networks for Natural
    Language Processing   258

	Identifying and Addressing Sources of Bias in NLP	258
	The Real World	259
	Data	260
	Models	261
	Model Interpretability	262
	Summary	262
Chapter 9	**Conclusion**	**265**
	How Can We Do Better?	267
	The Responsible Data Science Framework	267
	Doing Better As Managers	269
	Doing Better As Practitioners	270
	A Better Future If We Can Keep It	271
Index		**273**

Introduction

In this book, we will review some of the harmful ways artificial intelligence has been used and provide a framework to facilitate the responsible practice of data science. While we will touch upon mitigating legal risks, in this book we will focus primarily on the modeling process itself, especially on how factors overlooked by current modeling practices lead to unintended harms once the model is deployed in a real-world context.

Three core themes will be developed through this book:

- Any AI algorithm can have a harmful, dark side: once they are applied in the real world, AI algorithms can cause any number of harms. An algorithm designed to help police catch murderers can later be appropriated by totalitarian states to persecute dissidents; an algorithm that expands the availability of financial credit for the vast majority of people may nonetheless intensify bias against minorities.

- The dark sides of AI algorithms are created or deepened by current modeling approaches. By focusing only on technical considerations like maximizing predictive performance, data scientists ignore the potential for their model to aggravate biases against certain groups, generate harmful predictions, or otherwise be used by other groups in the future for malicious purposes.

- New modeling approaches are needed if we want to use AI more responsibly. If data scientists and their users are going to continue to use AI algorithms to make consequential decisions, then they ought to do so with consideration for a broader range of technical and societal factors than are normally considered.

New U.S. diplomats in training used to be told "not to give unintentional offense." Our primary goal for this book is to tell you a variant of this: that there are a number of specific actionable steps that you, the reader, can begin taking to reduce the risk of causing unintentional harm with your models.

In particular, this book focuses on how to make models more transparent, interpretable, and fair. It will present illustrations and snippets of code in a way that a technically literate manager or executive can understand, without necessarily knowing any programming language.

What This Book Covers

Chapter 1, "Why Data Science Should Be Ethical," provides historical background for the ethical concerns in statistics and an introduction to basic modeling methods. In Chapter 2, "Background: Modeling and the Black-Box Algorithm," we define various types of predictive models and briefly discuss the concepts of model transparency and model interpretability. Chapter 3, "The Ways AI Goes Wrong, and the Legal Implications," reviews the landscape of the types of ethics and fairness issues encountered in the practice of data science (e.g., legal constraints, privacy and data ownership concerns, and algorithms "gone bad") and finishes by distinguishing interpretable models from black-box models. In Chapter 4, "The Responsible Data Science (RDS) Framework," we discuss the desired characteristics of a Responsible Data Science framework, summarize the attempts by other groups at creating one, and combine the lessons learned from these other groups with those presented in the book up until this point to construct our own framework, the aptly named Responsible Data Science (RDS) framework. Chapter 5, "Model Interpretability: The What and the Why," prepares the reader for implementing the RDS framework in later chapters by doing a deeper dive into model interpretability and how it can be achieved for black-box models. We begin setting up a responsible data science project within our framework and performing initial checks on two datasets in Chapter 6, "Beginning a Responsible Data Science Project." In Chapters 7, "Auditing a Responsible Data Science Project," and Chapter 8, "Auditing for Neural Networks," we delve into case studies in auditing conventional machine learning models and deep neural networks for failure scenarios, fairness, and interpretability. Finally, we conclude the book in Chapter 9, "Conclusion," with a look to the future and a call to action.

Who Will Benefit Most from This Book

Much has been written elsewhere about the legal issues relevant to AI; thus, our primary audience is not corporate general counsels. Instead, this book is intended for the following two groups:

- Data-literate managers and executives
- Business-literate data scientists and analysts

Although the focus placed on responsibility in data science is relatively new, many people have been trained in the myriad wonderful things that AI can accomplish. They have also read in the news about the ethical lapses in some AI projects. These lapses are not surprising, because relatively few data scientists are trained in how to adequately understand and control their AI while maintaining high predictive performance in models. Hence, we aim this book at data science managers and executives and at data science practitioners.

Practitioners will learn of the ways in which their models, intended to provide benefits, can at the same time cause harm. They will learn how to leverage fairness metrics, interpretability methods, and other interventions to their model or dataset to audit those models, identifying and mitigating possible issues prior to deployment or result delivery. Through worked examples, the book guides users in structuring their models to have a greater consideration for ethical impacts, while assuring that best practices are followed and model performance is optimized. This is a key differentiator for our book, as most responsible AI frameworks do not provide specific technical recommendations for fulfilling the principles that they lay out.

Managers of data science teams, and managers with any responsibilities in the analytics realm, can use this book to stay alert for the ways in which analytical models can run afoul of ethical practices, and even the law. More importantly, they will learn the language and concepts to engage their analytics teams in the solutions and mitigation steps that we propose. While some code and technical discussion is provided, following it in detail is by no means needed. The overall presentation in the book is at a level that provides managers who are at least somewhat familiar with analytics the ability and tools to instill responsible best practices for data science in their organizations.

Finally, a word to individual data scientists. You may think that your project has no implications in the ethical realm. The real-world context for deployment may seem innocuous, the modeling task may seem harmless, and the content of this book may not seem relevant to your project. Though the ideas and techniques presented in this book are primarily discussed in the context of ethically fraught models, they are still useful as the basis for best practices in other modeling contexts. After all, there is a great degree of overlap between traditional best practices for modeling and best practices for responsible data science. Doing data science more responsibly, in the manner that we lay out in this book, improves understanding of the relationships between a model and its real-world deployment context, improves transparency and accountability through better guidelines for documentation, and reduces the risk of unanticipated biases creeping into models by providing workflows for model auditing. Plus, who knows when that innocuous-sounding project may later turn out to have a dark side?

Looking Ahead in This Book

The responsible practice of data science covers a lot of ground in different dimensions.

- **Formal legal and regulatory requirements:** Clearly, any company or individual developing or implementing data science solutions will want to stay on the right side of the law. The most famous attempt to regulate AI is the GDPR; it runs over 80 pages and is quite detailed. It was developed to meet the demands of a specific point in time, but there is no guarantee that it will be a useful guide in the future. Things change rapidly in the field of AI, and the GDPR is like a boulder placed in the path of a stream—sooner or later, the stream will find ways around the obstacle. There are already a number of publications on this topic, and our audience is not the corporate general counsel but rather the manager and the data science practitioner. So, while this book will touch on key laws in this area, such as the GDPR, it will not do so in great depth.

- **Bad actors:** In many cases, the pernicious use of AI is neither inadvertent nor the result of lack of understanding—it is intentional. Deep learning has been put to malicious use by cyber hacks who can digest and analyze multilayered defense mechanisms to determine quickly where weaknesses lie. When those who are responsible for data science development and implementation have malevolent intentions, a lecture on responsibility and a course on ethics will not have much impact. This book will note countermeasures that can have some effect, but dealing with bad actors, like dealing with regulators, is not the primary focus of this book.

- **AI out of control:** In many cases, those deploying AI are responsible parties, obeying the law, and yet their AI has in some sense "escaped their full control" after deployment. Perhaps it has morphed into something that was not initially intended, or perhaps it has triggered effects and reactions that were unanticipated. Maybe not all decision-makers in the organization that designed the AI, or affiliated stakeholders throughout the project, fully understood or appreciated from the beginning all of the ways that their AI project would operate in a real-world context. The disconnect between the goals of the model and the realities of the real-world context might make it so that even a perfectly accurate model can cause a great deal of harm. This overarching issue is the main focus of the book: how executives, managers, and practitioners can follow best practices in ethical data science—in particular, how they can better understand, explain, and gain control over their AI implementations.

Special Features

DEFINITION   Throughout the book, we'll explain the meanings of terms that may be new or nonstandard.

NOTE   Inline boxes are used to expand further on some aspect of the topic without interrupting the flow of the narrative.

Small general discussions that deserve special emphasis or have relevance beyond the immediately surrounding content are called out in general sidebar notes.

Code Repository

Code referred to in the text of each of the chapters, plus updates and expanded code for generating additional results, can be found in the repositories at `www.wiley.com/go/responsibledatascience` and `github.com/Gflemin/responsibledatascience`. Unless otherwise noted in the text, the code to reproduce the results within each of the chapters can be found by navigating to the appropriately named chapter subfolders at either of the links (e.g., the code for Chapter 6 can be found in the `responsibledatascience/ch6` subfolder.) The README file within the head of the code repository folder provides instructions for setting up your software environment, and the README files within each of the chapter subfolders provide additional information about the code for that chapter.

Part

I

Motivation for Ethical Data Science and Background Knowledge

In This Part

Chapter 1: Responsible Data Science
Chapter 2: Background: Modeling and the Black-Box Algorithm
Chapter 3: The Ways AI Goes Wrong, and the Legal Implications

Responsible Data Science

Data science is an interdisciplinary field that combines elements of statistics, computer science, and information technology to generate useful insights from the increasingly large datasets that are generated in the normal course of business. Data science helps organizations capture value from their data, reducing costs and increasing profits, and also enables completely new types of endeavors, such as powerful information search and self-driving cars. Sometimes, data science projects can go awry, when the predictions made by statistical and machine learning algorithms turn to be not just wrong, but biased and unfair in ways that cause harm. History has shown that the dual good and evil nature of statistical methods is not new, but rather a characteristic that was present from nearly the moment that they were conceived. However, by adjusting and supplementing statistical and machine learning methods and concepts, we can diagnose and reduce the harm that they may otherwise cause.

In popular and technical writing, these issues are often captured by the general term "ethical data science." We use that term here, but we also use the more general phrase "responsible data science." Ethics can refer in some usages to narrow "rules of the road" that pertain to a particular profession, such as real estate or accounting. Our goal here is broader than that: presenting a framework for the practice of data science that is ethical, but not in a narrow sense: it is *responsible*.

The Optum Disaster

In 2001, the healthcare company Optum launched Impact-Pro, a predictive modeling tool. Impact-Pro was an early success for predictive analytics (predating the term *data science*), and a decade later, Steven Wickstrom, an Optum VP, touted its use cases. For healthcare providers, it could "support steerage to appropriate programs" and "identify members [patients] with gaps in care, complications, and comorbidities." Optum termed these *care opportunities* in one document (i.e., opportunities for more revenue), but they are also of interest to those concerned with cost management: the correct early intervention in a health problem can cost significantly less than more drastic action later. For insurers, information on health risks for specific groups and individuals could be used to set premiums more accurately than is possible using traditional underwriting criteria.

DEFINITION   DATA SCIENCE   We use the term *data science* broadly to cover the process of understanding and defining a problem, gathering and preparing data, using statistical methods to answer questions, fitting models and assessing them, and deploying models in an organizational setting. We consider artificial intelligence (AI) to be part of data science, and we also consider the "science" component of data science to be important.

In 2019, though, a research team found that the tool was fundamentally flawed. For one important group—African Americans—the tool consistently underpredicted need for healthcare. The reason? The tool was essentially built to predict future spending on healthcare, and prior spending was a key predictor for that goal. And prior spending is a function not just of need, but also of ability to pay for and gain access to healthcare. Relative to other ethnic groups in the United States, African Americans have been (and continue to be) less insured, are less able to access healthcare, and possess fewer financial resources for covering healthcare expenses. In Optum's data, therefore, African Americans had less prior spending and, hence, less predicted future need. As a result, African Americans were less targeted for preventive intervention and necessary follow-up healthcare than were other people with similar health profiles. Neither the model nor the data provided to it were able to account for the unanticipated and overlooked societal inequities lurking beneath.

Optum was blindsided. The company thought it had built a tool that was a winner on all fronts: improving health outcomes by being smarter about required follow-up care, and managing costs better in the bargain. Instead, it found itself the focus of widespread bad publicity and was pilloried for creating a product that exacerbated racial bias and widened the healthcare gap faced by African Americans. New York state regulators opened an investigation, and the controversy continued into 2020. At the time of writing, Optum continues to market Impact Pro.

In this case, and in many others, the original intent for using the algorithm was good: good for healthcare providers by optimizing the allocation of scarce resources, and good for patients by ensuring that patients with the greatest needs had those needs met. But good intentions plus smart *artificial intelligence* (AI) led to disaster.

DEFINITION ARTIFICIAL INTELLIGENCE   We use the term *artificial intelligence* generally, to cover both statistical and machine learning methods for prediction with structured numeric data and text, as well as image and voice recognition and synthesis. In this book, we think of AI as having underlying algorithms or models. When discussing solutions for reducing the harms of AI, changing these underlying algorithms or models will be one of the main focal points.

Interestingly, the scenario of good statistics being ill-used is not new. In fact, statistics as a field has a long history of being used for nefarious purposes or causing unintended harms.

Jekyll and Hyde

Let's begin with a look back over a century in history to a classic work of fiction that serves as a metaphor for the issues we face with data science today. In his gothic tale *The Strange Case of Dr. Jekyll and Mr. Hyde*, Robert Louis Stevenson describes two characters. Dr. Jekyll is an analytical man of science, a great asset to society, and a doer of good deeds. However, there is a repulsive, cruel side to him in the form of a separate character, Mr. Hyde, who gets "released" from time to time. The evil Mr. Hyde, in his times of release, tramples a young girl, commits murder, and more. The phrase "Jekyll and Hyde" has come to represent something that has two contradictory but inextricably linked natures—one respected and upright, the other base and evil.

The dual nature of humanity—good and evil combined in the same package—is a universal theme in literature. As humans carry their intelligence into the artificial realm, this duality has come with it.

Artificial intelligence has taken on this Jekyll and Hyde character trait. The enormous benefits brought by AI are evident: it has been a major force powering economic growth over the last several decades. Most aspects of life and industry now incorporate AI approaches in some way. Here are just a few examples:

- When you apply for a loan or a credit card, it is an algorithm that judges whether the application should be approved. This speeds the process, lowers the cost of providing credit, and, by making the process more scientific, standardizes decisions and expands access to credit among the truly creditworthy.

- When you use Facebook, Instagram, Twitter, or other social media services, the ads you see are optimized by an algorithm to be those most likely to get you to respond. This "microtargeting" makes them more relevant to you and, more importantly, makes it possible to provide these social media services at no charge to the user.

- Criminals are often caught on camera at or near the scene of a crime, and facial recognition and identification algorithms make it much more likely that they will be identified and caught.

In each of these cases we can point to a related "Mr. Hyde" that lurks in the background.

- Loan approval algorithms, it turns out, are prone to "redlining" just as humans are, blocking whole neighborhoods from credit, rather than making decisions on the basis of individual characteristics. Moreover, unlike humans, algorithms, if they are not transparent, are resistant to moral suasion and are hard to correct.

- The economic efficiencies wrought by microtargeting of ads is offset by the unease many people feel about being "surveilled." What's more, algorithmic curation of content feeds, seeking to maximize user engagement, drives users towards content that is provocative, inflammatory, and often fabricated. Even without actively provoking, these same recommender algorithms that underpin social media companies also enable political extremists to coalesce and take action.

Computer image recognition algorithms that have been so helpful to law enforcement facilitate dramatic erosions of privacy: one company has scraped the Web and built a database of billions of tagged face images, allowing individuals to upload images of people and find out who they are. When these facial recognition approaches are deployed by law enforcement, the harm resulting from erroneous identifications is magnified, *especially* for darker skinned individuals who are more likely to be falsely identified by these approaches. Sometimes, the negative Mr. Hyde aspect is only weakly counterbalanced by a good Mr. Jekyll. The science of image and voice synthesis has introduced the world to destructive "deep fakes": fabricated videos of people (usually political figures or celebrities) saying things they never said. Individuals or organizations bent on sowing discord or disinformation, or inciting violence have already used deep fakes for these aims. The plus side of the technology is comparatively minimal: better avatars for video games and production efficiencies for Hollywood, which needn't hire so many actors. The public has been highly exposed to these failures (possibly more than to the successes) through public controversies and popular science journalism and books. The good and evil sides to AI are now widely recognized, but this is not the first time that statistics has gone over to the "dark side." Indeed, some of the most foundational breakthroughs in statistical methodology were motivated by goals we now recognize as morally reprehensible.

Eugenics

Turn back the clock to 1886, the very year *The Strange Case of Dr. Jekyll and Mr. Hyde* was published. This was also the year that the famous British statistician Francis Galton published his article "Regression Towards Mediocrity in Hereditary Stature," referring to the tendency of very tall and very short parents to have children closer to average height. This phenomenon gave us the phrase "regression to the mean."

Galton, Pearson, and Fisher

Galton, in addition to his seminal work on regression, also made contributions in correlation and survey methods. His half-cousin was Charles Darwin, and Galton was much taken with Darwin's *The Origin of Species*. Galton thought that, with the help of statistical methods, the evolution of humans could be guided in a positive and useful way. He coined the term *eugenics*, focused much of his research and scientific publications on eugenics, and became the Honorary President of the British Eugenics Society.

Karl Pearson, who contributed to statistics the correlation coefficient, principal components, the (increasingly maligned) p-value, and much more, was a protégée of Galton who assumed the Galton Chair of Eugenics at the University of London. Pearson saw the ideal society as:

> an organized whole, kept up to a high pitch of internal efficiency by insuring that its numbers are substantially recruited from the better stocks, and kept up to a high pitch of external efficiency by contest, chiefly by way of war with inferior races.

R.A. Fisher (design of experiments, discriminant analysis, F-distribution) joined official committees to promote eugenics and, in his "Genetical Theory of Natural Selection," focused on eugenics and what he saw as the need for the upper classes to boost their fertility. The guiding philosophy among the first generation of eugenicists was suppression of reproduction among the "unfit" and encouragement of reproduction among the "fit."

Ties between Eugenics and Statistics

The close ties between eugenics and statistics dissolved as statistics branched out in the service of all scientific disciplines, and eugenics itself was discredited through its close association with Nazi Germany. Now, all who study statistics are familiar with regression, correlation, and the various "lettered" tests: the t-test, F-test, and the chi-square test. Few, however, know that the founding fathers of statistics (they were all men) were also the founding fathers of eugenics: the "science" of manipulating society and individuals to produce a superior race.

Many of the statistical methods that were developed in the service of eugenics are sound and have survived the test of time. The genetic theories and social policies that motivated the founding fathers of statistics are but a long-faded shadow in the eyes of modern statisticians, but they remain a jarring reminder that illumination and truth often come bundled with a measure of darkness.

Another popular application of statistics over a century ago was the supposed correlation of physical features with criminal tendencies; this was part of the pseudoscience of physiognomy. At the time, the presumption of such a connection between appearance and criminality was generally accepted. A quick read of some Sherlock Holmes detective stories, the first of which was written in 1892, gives a flavor for how "criminal types" tended to have certain facial features. For example, a sinister criminal in *The Man with the Twisted Lip* has "a shock of orange hair, a pale face disfigured by a horrible scar, which, by its contraction, has turned up the outer edge of his upper lip, a bulldog chin, and a pair of very penetrating dark eyes."

Unlike eugenics, this application of statistics is not dead. AI approaches have recently been used to infer autism, trustworthiness, and even the criminality of individuals from facial images. A recent Chinese study reported the use of AI to successfully distinguish between criminal faces and noncriminal faces. The authors, Xiaolin Wu and Xi Zhang, assembled two sets of photos.

- **Criminals**: One source was a city police department; the other was wanted posters.

- **Noncriminals**: A set of photos taken from the internet of males meeting certain criteria: no facial hair, no markings or scars, etc.

You can see a sample of the faces in their article "Automated Inference on Criminality Using Face Images," published in the Cornell arXiv prepress service (November 13, 2016, revised May 26, 2017) at arxiv.org/abs/1611.04135.

Wu and Zhang reported that four different classifiers that they built—logistic regression, k-nearest-neighbors (KNN), support vector machines (SVM), and convolutional neural networks (CNN)—all performed well in distinguishing the criminal images from the noncriminal images. Considerable controversy ensued, and the authors claimed to have been taken completely off guard by the storm of criticism they received. They felt compelled to issue rebuttals to their critics, which you can read, along with the original article, at the source noted above. Other Chinese researchers have gone about solving similar problems more subtly, publishing a number of research articles in recent years on subjects such as ethnicity detection for minority groups (mainly Uighur people), facial detection for social credit applications, and even research on constructing simulated facial imagery from DNA samples.

Ethical Problems in Data Science Today

The problems with data science and AI today share one common theme with those of statistical eugenics: human bias. In 1900, evidence-based science was in its infancy. Galton, Pearson, and Fisher shared the common prejudice of the day that people's characteristics and capabilities were genetically determined, with race and sex being key factors. The statistical methods they developed helped them explore and quantify this prejudice. At no point did their statistical work cause them to question their beliefs.

Some of the ethical problems with AI today have, at their root, similar prejudices, often unspoken. Rarely are they expressed as a specific intentional feature of a model. More often, they come in via the data used to train a model, which the model then magnifies and perpetuates at scale. We will see later the example of a résumé-rating algorithm that was led astray by training data, in which men were ranked highly while women were not.

We will not attempt a scholarly or legal definition of ethics in data science; to do so with precision would entangle us unnecessarily in endless argument. (The European Union's General Data Protection Regulation [GDPR] is close to 90 pages.) However, we can say that for a data science approach to be responsible and ethical, one or both of the following ought to be addressed:

- **Bias**: An algorithm that makes predictions for people of a certain race (or religion, ethnic group, gender, belief, or other grouping characteristic) systematically differently than for others is considered biased.

- **Unfairness**: An algorithm that makes predictions in ways that deny due process, deprive people of property or liberty (even temporarily) without transparency or human review, or make decisions that appear intemperate or capricious or aid undemocratic governments in oppression is perceived as unfair.

Bias and unfairness overlap, of course. An algorithm that produces biased predictions would usually be considered unfair. On the other hand, an algorithm may produce biased predictions that, due to an innocuous modeling task or the bias working in favor of underprivileged groups, are generally deemed fair. Both bias and unfairness are subjective, though bias has clear-cut legal implications that we will discuss in Chapter 3, "The Ways AI Goes Wrong, and the Legal Implications." Our goal is not to engage in philosophical debate about bias and unfairness and what constitutes either. Rather, we take the view that, whatever your exact definition of bias and unfairness, these issues require much more attention in data science projects than they tend to receive. Our goal is to provide the guidance and tools to facilitate this.

You will note that "making biased or unfair predictions" lies at the center of this description of responsible data science. Let's now look at how algorithms make predictions.

Predictive Models

We've been speaking generally of data science and AI; let's be more concrete.

Before there was AI, there were predictive models—statistical models that predict an outcome (customer spending, whether an insurance claim is fraudulent, whether a loan will be repaid, etc.). The earliest predictive models have their roots in linear regression (we talked earlier of Galton's contributions) and discriminant analysis (likewise, for Fisher).

Most analysts are familiar with the standard linear regression model:

$$Y = a + b_1x_1 + b_2x_2 \ldots + b_nx_n + error$$

In this model, the effect of predictor variables (x_1, x_2, x_n) on the outcome (Y) is reflected in their coefficients (b_1, b_2, $\ldots .b_n$). For example, suppose Y is an individual's spending with a company, and x_1 is their income. The effect that an individual's income, x_1, has on their spending, Y, can be readily seen in the coefficient b_1. This might be useful if you are doing a research study about consumer spending and want to be able to distinguish the different effects of different predictor variables.

From Explaining to Predicting

Historically, the main purpose of regression was as suggested earlier—to shed light on a relationship between predictor variables and an outcome variable. In this case, the emphasis is not on predicting individual cases but rather on understanding the overall relationship. The focus is on the predictor coefficients (the *b*'s in the earlier equation). For many decades, predicting individual outcome values was a secondary goal, though not unheard of (e.g., using regression to forecast a time series such as product demand). However, this focus on using predictive models to examine underlying relationships in the data has since shifted to using predictive models solely to leverage the predictions that they generate.

NOTE SCARCE DATA   The classical statistical methods of regression and discriminant analysis were developed in the era of scarce data. Typically, data would be gathered in a study or experiment and then analyzed. The cost of gathering data was often high, and there might be hard limits on how much data could actually be obtained. Therefore, all the available data would be used in fitting a model, and statistical analysis methods had to squeeze all possible information out of a sample. In traditional statistical methods, information about the variability in the data is used to calculate metrics (e.g., R^2, standard errors, t-statistics, F-statistics) that help us understand how well the model fits the data. But getting a model that better fits the data at hand does not necessarily help you extrapolate beyond those data.

Suppose you catch a bunch of fish in a net and then proceed to make a detailed description of what you've caught. Now, you want to derive from those details a picture of what all fish are like. If the fish in the net were gathered according to a rigorous sampling plan, this will allow inference to the larger population of fish. However, going into too much detail about the fish in the net won't necessarily translate into an accurate picture of the fish beyond the net. In fact, it can distort the picture if you end up modeling random noise rather than meaningful signal.

In the era of plentiful data, however, there is a simpler solution: hold out some of the data where the outcome is known (i.e., refrain from using it to fit the model), and see how well your model predicts those outcomes.

Predictive Modeling

Companies and other organizations now have a wealth of transactional and other data produced in the routine course of business, and many opportunities to capture value from the data. The earliest widespread use of predictive modeling was credit scoring, which is essentially a general-purpose prediction about whether a person will repay a loan.

Credit scores do not require predictive models. The credit score company Equifax started in 1899 as Retail Credit Company. Founded by the Woolford brothers, it collected data on individuals in a community, information that could be used to determine whether to offer a person credit. In the age of computerized statistical modeling, automated predictive models allowed credit scoring to scale. In the predictive modeling process, a model (e.g., linear regression) is fit to (or "trained on") data where the outcomes, the Ys, are known. The model is then applied (or "scored") to additional "holdout" data where the outcome is known and is used to predict those outcomes. Note that the model is fit only to the training data; when it is scored to the holdout data, it is not refit to those data. The performance of the model is then assessed on the holdout data where we know the actual outcomes: how well did it do?

The analyst can choose among many different model types and can also choose different ways of implementing those models. With linear regression, for example, the analyst chooses which predictor variables to include and whether to include derived variables that account for interaction among the predictor variables. Different models and different implementations of the same model can all be trained and assessed on the holdout data, and the best-performing model can be the final model for deployment (see Figure 1.1).

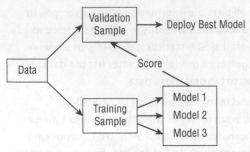

Figure 1.1: The use of data partitions to assess different models

Setting the Stage for Ethical Issues to Arise

When the goal of statistical analysis was to understand relationships among variables, the resulting model and its interpretation could be reviewed and vetted at comparative leisure. One can imagine analysts in a government office poring over regression printouts, or professors in a seminar picking apart a colleague's proposed model. The conclusions of the model might guide public policy or further research but were not to be implemented as decisions at an individual level.

When the statistical model moved into the realm of prediction, as opposed to explanation, the implications of a model became immediate and consequential for individuals. If you were issued a low credit score, it affected your life materially. If you were not told why you received the low score, it made matters worse by providing little opportunity for recourse.

While public concern surfaced about the transparency of credit scores and lack of recourse, the development and tuning of statistical algorithms to make these decisions was not considered much more than the employment of a tool. Back in the 1980s, when these methods saw wide adoption in credit scoring, little thought was given to developing a "responsible approach" to predictive models.

The first step in developing a responsible data science framework is to review the different types of statistical and machine learning models. Various types of models are handled differently, in particular transparent models versus black-box models.

Classic Statistical Models

Linear regression is a transparent model. As shown earlier, the effect of predictor variables on the outcome can be read from the coefficients. Linear regression is only one of a number of popular statistical and machine learning models. Let's briefly review the others, starting with the older classical statistical models.

Logistic Regression. While linear regression tries to predict a numeric value, logistic regression tries to estimate the probability that an observation belongs to a specific class or category. Most logistic regressions deal with binary outcomes, usually coded as 0 or 1. We can use a linear model to do this but not directly. A probability must lie between 0 and 1, and a standard linear regression does not assure this. With a couple of steps, though, we can get there. (Note, we're not showing all the math here.)

1. Instead of probabilities, we deal with odds, which are familiar to bettors. If the probability of an event is 25%, a bettor would say the odds are 1 *to* 3, or 1 *in* 4. Mathematically, we use 1 to 3, so a 25% probability equates to 33%:

$$\text{odds} : \text{odds} = p / (1 - p).$$

2. It turns out we can use odds in a linear model, if we take the natural log of the odds, or the logit:

$$\log(\text{odds}) = a + b_1 x_1 + b_2 x_2 \ldots + b_n x_n + \text{error}$$

3. The predictor coefficient estimates—the *b*'s —can get us back to a probability via exponentiation:

$$\text{probability of outcome} = 1 / \left(1 + e^{-(a+b_1 x_1 + b_2 x_2 \ldots)}\right)$$

Logistic regression remains a workhorse of predictive modeling. The coefficients it produces can illuminate the effects of individual predictors on the odds of the outcome, which makes generating explanations for humans relatively simple.

Discriminant Analysis. Discriminant analysis is the oldest classification technique, dating back almost a century to the work of R.A. Fisher. It was used in early credit-scoring algorithms, and, though it has been eclipsed somewhat in the data science field, it is very computationally efficient, so it can be used where rapid model-fitting is important.

Discriminant analysis calculates functions that, when applied to the predictor values, do the best job of separating the records into their different classes (i.e., classes that are very homogeneous and differ the most from one another). These functions have coefficients that reflect the contribution of individual predictors in separating the classes. They also yield a *classification score* for each record for each class. The classification scores for a record reflect how close a record is to the average predictor values for a class—the higher the score, the closer it is. The scores are based on "statistical distance," a standardized version of the squared difference between a record's predictor values and the predictor value average for the class.

Naive Bayes. Naive Bayes works only with categorical predictors. Returning to the concept of closeness, naive Bayes starts with the idea of finding records whose predictor categories match those of the record to be classified. Whatever class the majority of those records have is the predicted class for the new record. When there are more than a few variables, however, finding exact matches on predictor values is next to impossible. So, instead of this "exact Bayes" algorithm, we work with a "naive" version that considers overall probabilities of predictor values in the outcome classes. Roughly, the algorithm starts as follows:

1. Given a record to be classified for each outcome class, find the probability that each predictor value in the record to be classified occurs in the class. For example, among the outcome class "loan fails to pay," the category of "prior personal bankruptcy yes" likely has higher probability than among the outcome class "loan is current."

2. Multiply those predictor category probabilities together and by the proportion of records belonging to that class.

3. Repeat for the other outcome classes.

Each record gets assigned to whichever class has the highest such product of probabilities.

Naive Bayes is computationally efficient and, alone among predictive algorithms, has the ability to handle categorical variables directly. This is an advantage in cases where data have numerous categories that otherwise would require the creation of many dummy variables.

Black-Box Methods

K-Nearest Neighbors (KNNs). KNN is intuitively simple. The KNN algorithm predicts outcomes for a given record by a two-step process:

1. Find records that are closest to (most like) the record to be predicted.

2. Find the average outcome among those nearby records, or find the majority class—*this is the prediction.*

"Nearness" between two records is typically measured using Euclidean distance (square root of the sum of squared differences) between the two vectors of predictor values, though other measures of distance should be used when the predictor values include categorical as well as numeric data.

For example, if you have two houses with the predictor attributes as listed in the table for Rooms, Acres, and Square Feet, with Value as an outcome, the Euclidean distance between House 1 and House 2 is the square root of 4.56 (considering only the predictor variables).

	ROOMS	ACRES	SQ. FEET (000)	VALUE ($000)
House 1	8	1.5	3.2	450
House 2	10	1	3.8	670
Difference	−2	0.5	0.6	
Difference^2	4	0.25	0.36	Sum = 4.56

Now consider House 3, with 12 rooms, 2.5 acres, and 3,700 square feet. If you do the calculations, you will see that House 1 is closer to House 2 than to House 3. One important note: You can readily see that the Rooms variable dominates the calculation because its scale is greater. This is typically corrected for by converting each variable to a standardized counterpart (e.g., how many standard deviations it is away from the mean for that variable).

How many neighbors should you look at when calculating their mean (or predominant class)? The user sets this number, k. The larger k is, the less variable the predictions are, and the more they will come to resemble the overall average. A smaller k results in predictions that are more responsive to local conditions in the data, but are also more prone to fitting noise.

Decision Tree Ensembles. Tree methods produce a set of rules that are applied to predictor variables to yield predictions. For example, a rule for predicting whether a bank customer will apply for a new loan might look like "IF income > 110.5 and Education level ≤ 1.5 AND Family ≤ 2.5, THEN predict as nonapplier." These rules do not come from humans applying commonsense business judgment, but are derived by an algorithm that determines which rules yield the best predictions (i.e., do the best job of dividing customers into those who applied for the loan and those who did not). Tree algorithms generally proceed as follows:

1. Pick a predictor variable value (a "decision node"), say income = $61,000, and then divide the data into records where Income > $61,000 and records where Income ≤ $61,000. Measure how homogeneous the two partitions are in terms of loan application. Are those above the split mostly "appliers" and those below mostly "nonappliers"?

2. Repeat for all other values of the predictor, and record the split that yields the greatest homogeneity (also called *purity*) in the two partitions. Note that if Income ends up being the best discriminator, which it does, this yields an initial rule of "IF Income ≤ 110.5, classify as 1; otherwise, classify as 0."

3. Repeat for all the other predictors, noting which variable and split yields the greatest homogeneity, and implement that split.

4. In each of the two resulting partitions, repeat the previous process.

5. Keep going until you have fully pure final partitions (called *leaves* or *terminal nodes*).

Figure 1.2 shows the beginning of this process. The algorithm decided on Income = 110.5 as the optimal initial split (out of all possible splits of all predictor variables), and Education = 1.5 as the next split.

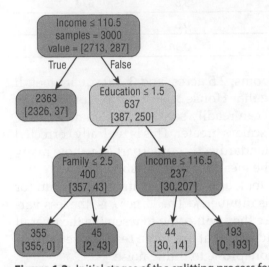

Figure 1.2: Initial stages of the splitting process for the bank customer data

Data Mining for Business Analytics by Shmueli, Bruce, & Patel, © 2020 John Wiley & Sons, Inc. Used by permission.

You can see that this process, carried to the end, yields increasingly meaningless rules for small segments of the data—rules that are fitting the detailed noise in the data, not the signal. One type of remedy is to stop the tree growth, or "prune" the tree back to a point where its rules generalize effectively to the holdout data. A popular twist to this is to use cross-validation, or sequential segregation of different parts of the data as holdout sets, so as not to be biased by the particularities of a single holdout set.

Another remedy is to forget about fine-tuning tree growth and simply to average the predictions of lots of different trees in an "ensemble" approach, taking advantage of the "wisdom of the crowd" (see note). This approach generally performs extremely well, but it loses the advantage of producing simple rules that can be presented effectively to non–data scientists. Ensembled trees have among the best performance of all predictive algorithms and are more popular than their simple tree counterparts.

Although simple trees produce easily interpretable rules, we classify decision trees here as a black-box method, due to the dominance of the ensembled version.

NOTE   WISDOM OF THE CROWD AND THE OX   In his book *The Wisdom of Crowds*, James Surowiecki recounts how Francis Galton attended an event at a country fair in England where the object was to guess the weight of an ox.

Individual contestants were relatively well informed on the subject (the audience was farmers), but their estimates were still quite variable. Nonetheless, the mean of all the estimates was surprisingly accurate—within 1% of the true weight of the ox (over half a ton). On balance, the errors from multiple guesses tended to cancel one another out. The crowd's average was more accurate than nearly all the individual estimates; hence, the name of Surowiecki's book. Diversity of estimates was a strength, not a drawback.

Artificial Neural Networks (ANNs). ANNs initially were an attempt to mimic neural processes in the brain. A useful introduction to neural networks is to reconsider linear regression, in which the coefficients are calculated via a formula that minimizes the squared differences between the predicted values and the actual values. Now imagine an algorithm that randomly chooses the coefficients, uses them to make a prediction, finds the error in the prediction, changes the coefficients to improve the prediction, finds the error again, and keeps repeating that process. Neural networks are an extension of that process.

Consider a simple neural net to predict whether a consumer will like or dislike a new food product. The manufacturer has made a number of samples, all with different combinations of salt and fat (the two ingredients deemed key to consumer acceptance), and has had them rated by consumer panels.

Neural networks are configured in different ways. This one starts with two small random numbers, one for each input (the input layer in the diagram), that are then each multiplied by, say, three weights—the w's in Figure 1.3. The three products for input 1 (Salt) are added to the three products for input 2 (Fat), which yields three "nodes" (neurons) in a "hidden layer" (the choice of three weights being somewhat arbitrary). The process is that the outputs of the three nodes within the hidden layer are then multiplied by three additional weights and summed in the output node, which is compared to a cutoff threshold to assign a classification. (Some additional steps have been omitted for brevity's sake; see Chapter 8, "Auditing for Neural Networks," for more details.)

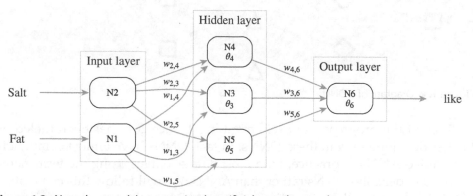

Figure 1.3: Neural network layout: a simple artificial neural network

To this point, predictions from this process are largely random and not worth much. However, the network then reverses itself (*back propagation*): the "error" in the final layer becomes an input and flows through the network in reverse, but with a slight adjustment in the weights. The cycle repeats, with the weights repeatedly adjusted in a way that causes the overall prediction error to continuously diminish.

Deep Neural Nets (Deep Learning). Neural nets have been through several peaks and valleys of popularity since they were first introduced in 1967. However, their popularity has skyrocketed ever since the advent of the "deep learning revolution," which began in 2012 when deep learning and deep neural nets (DNNs) shattered state-of-the-art performance records in image prediction and biomolecular target prediction. What makes a DNN distinct from an ANN? Depth, obviously, is one of the main characteristics. Unlike an ANN, a DNN will have multiple hidden layers (see Figure 1.4).

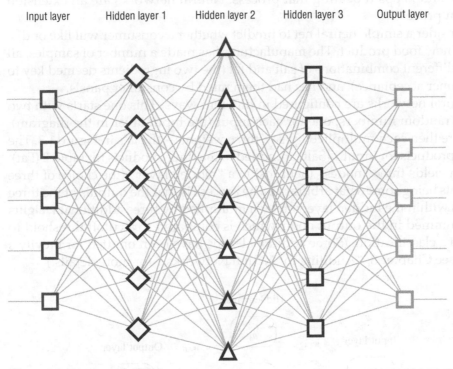

Figure 1.4: Diagram of a DNN

Much of the progress and excitement in AI since 2012 has been fueled by further developments in these DNNs. In fact, DNNs have almost completely supplanted ANNs in practice, with most data scientists using the term *neural networks* to describe DNNs rather than ANNs. We will follow this convention in this book and will confine discussion of ANNs to the technical reviews in the current chapter and the one following. DNNs differentiate themselves from their shallow counterparts in that they contain more than one hidden layer. Each of these hidden layers creates an intermediate representation of the input data, with later layers creating progressively more abstract representations prior to making a prediction. This ability allows DNNs to learn progressively more abstract features from raw data, making them especially useful for modeling tasks that use unstructured data such as image or text data.

Consider the case of deep learning using a convolutional neural network (CNN), a popular variant of DNNs used for image recognition tasks. The many individual pixel values input into a CNN are repeatedly consolidated into larger conceptual groups in a lengthy and complex iterative process. The consolidations that are effective in correctly identifying labeled images (say, "car" as opposed to "person") are saved and used to help classify new images. Those consolidations, it turns out, are highly similar to the higher-level features (edges, shapes, textures, etc.) that humans see in images.

A CNN that learns the features in an image, however, lacks the deep breadth of human knowledge. While a well-trained CNN may achieve remarkable results within specific tasks, it can also easily go haywire when predicting on data that differ even slightly from the data it was trained on. In one case, a CNN was trained to distinguish between malignant and benign skin moles. The CNN did a very effective job with the labeled training data, but what it really did was distinguish between images that had a ruler next to the mole and images that did not. Dermatologists were more likely to place a ruler next to a mole they considered malignant, and the presence or absence of a ruler turned out to be the best predictor of whether a mole was malignant or benign.

In this case, the DNN's mistake was obvious from a quick review of the images, and it is only our surmise, albeit a strong one, that it was a mistake. The presence or absence of a ruler was not specified as a variable; it was something the net learned on its own. There are no readily apparent coefficients and variables that allow us to quickly learn what the net was basing its decision on. We discuss DNNs and how to audit them for these sorts of issues in Chapter 8, "Auditing for Neural Networks."

Important Concepts in Predictive Modeling

Having reviewed the landscape of statistical and machine learning methods used in prediction, let's now review some additional concepts that are key to the predictive modeling paradigm.

Feature Selection

The key to success in prediction is identifying variables (features) that successfully predict an outcome of interest. Both traditional statistical models and machine learning models are driven by the proper selection of predictor variables. Data, such as those drawn from company records of customers and transactions, are most often recorded in a tabular form, in which rows are cases (customers, transactions, patients) and columns are variables. Early on in the evolution of data mining, it was the analyst's job to examine these data and select useful predictor variables. For example, in predicting whether a loan will be repaid, useful variables are things like prior loan repayments, income, job status, age, etc.

As data mining evolved and began to be called data science or data analytics, methods and models also evolved, in which features began to play a much less transparent role in the modeling process. The increasingly widespread use of image and text data necessitated this change, as the high dimensionality of these data made creating handcrafted features practically infeasible. This is most evident in image recognition, in which the "features" are nothing but pixel values (integers) arrayed in a matrix. These must be reinterpreted as higher-level features such as edges and shapes, and even higher-level features such as eyes. Requiring a human to label the relevant features within every image or sentence in a text corpus defeats the whole purpose of machine learning. This task is now done with remarkable accuracy by DNNs.

Model-Centric vs. Data-Centric Models

Earlier, we grouped predictive modeling methods into classical statistical models and black-box machine learning models. A related classification scheme categorizes methods as model-centric or data-centric. Linear and logistic regression and discriminant analysis are all model-centric in the sense that they calculate a formula that is applied globally across all the data to make predictions. Of course, the models are derived from data, but we consider them model-centric due to the global formula. KNN, naive Bayes, classification and regression trees, and neural nets make predictions based on more local characteristics of the data. They are also referred to as *models*, but we put them in the data-centric category because the predictions are more responsive to characteristics of the data that are not global. Data-centric algorithms are more complex and flexible and are more prone to pay attention to random noise in the data.

Holdout Sample and Cross-Validation

To test how well a model predicts, we typically evaluate its performance with a holdout sample, which is a randomly selected sample of data drawn from the same source as the data used to fit the model. The holdout sample, also termed a *validation* or *test sample*, is not used in fitting the model. The data used to fit the model are termed the *training data*.

In some modeling processes, the holdout sample can be used sparingly to get a good idea how the model will perform with new data. In other processes, the holdout sample can be used iteratively to tune the model and to improve its performance. In such a case, it is common to use a modified holdout sample in a process called *cross-validation*.

In cross-validation, the holdout process is repeated for nonoverlapping partitions of the data until all the data have been used in validation. *K*-fold cross-validation involves taking multiple different divisions of the data into training and validation partitions such that *k* different nonoverlapping validation partitions are created and used. The training partitions are overlapping.

Overfitting

The use of a separate sample to evaluate model performance has an important benefit: it helps avoid overfitting, also known as "fitting the noise" instead of the signal. Consider the data shown in Figure 1.5 on advertising expenditure and sales revenue for different periods.

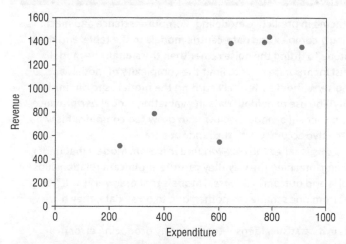

Figure 1.5: Advertising expenditure and revenue for different periods

Data Mining for Business Analytics by Shmueli, Bruce, & Patel, © 2020 John Wiley & Sons, Inc. Used by permission.

As advertising spending rises, so does sales revenue, in general, though the relationship does not closely follow a straightforward line or curve. We could fit a mathematically complex curve to the data, as shown in Figure 1.6.

This model fits the data perfectly—there is no error. We would have little confidence, however, that it would be a good fit to future data. We have fit the noise, not the signal.

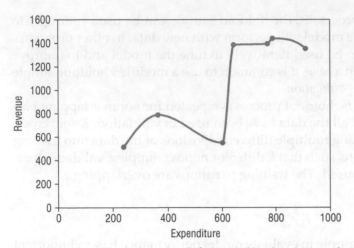

Figure 1.6: Smoothed curve closely fitting to the advertising and expenditure data

Data Mining for Business Analytics by Shmueli, Bruce, & Patel, © 2020 John Wiley & Sons, Inc. Used by permission.

OVERFITTING AND THE BIAS—VARIANCE TRADE-OFF

Overfitting is a constant theme in predictive modeling. Computer science and machine learning brought increasingly complex and data-centric models to the table, and these models are particularly prone to fitting the noise rather than the signal. The model-building process itself must incorporate ways to limit the complexity of models and curb the tendency to fit noise, without so severely curbing the model as to diminish useful predictive capability. The use of holdout data in evaluating model performance is often key to this balancing act—if a model is allowed to grow too complex, this will show up in decreased predictive accuracy with the holdout data.

In more technical terms, this is called the *bias-variance trade-off*. Models that under-fit do a poor job of predicting, meaning the way they capture significant relationships between predictor variables and outcomes is *biased*. Models that are overfit will "jump around" in their estimates from one sample to another, due to noisy data; they have high *variance*.

Note: This use of *bias* is in its statistical sense—consistently producing error in a particular direction.

Unsupervised Learning

The models discussed to this point are supervised learning algorithms, where the goal is to make predictions based on learning from data where an outcome is known. There are other widely used data science algorithms that do not focus on learning to make predictions from labeled data.

Clustering

Clustering algorithms group together records that are similar to one another. The result is a limited number of clusters that are relatively homogeneous and unlike other clusters. Identifying customer segments is a popular application of clustering.

Recommender Systems

■ Virtually all consumers are familiar with the results of recommender systems, which can be seen in product recommendations on Amazon and other digital merchants. They also operate less visibly in social media to display ads and content that you are most likely to be interested in. These recommender systems tailor the content feeds for individuals, seeking to maximize user engagement. Engagement is generated by content that is provocative and inflammatory, and that speaks to a user's concerns and biases. It may often be fabricated. Even without actively provoking, these same recommender algorithms that underpin social media companies also enable political extremists to coalesce and take action.

Our focus in this book is on models that make predictions, because it is in this area that so many concerns about ethical implementation and transparency have arisen, particularly as machines take over the decision-making process.

The Ethical Challenge of Black Boxes

With the arrival of big data and data mining (now commonly referred to as data science), the ability to make real-time automated decisions has also arrived. Knowing how a variable (e.g., income) affects an outcome (e.g., spending) has become comparatively less important—just being able to predict the outcome is often considered sufficient. The black-box methods described earlier share one attribute: They make it hard to discern the effects of individual predictor variables (features) on outcomes. Their impact on the outcome variable lies hidden inside the black box (see Figure 1.7).

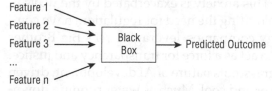

Figure 1.7: The black-box model conceals the effects of features.

Two Opposing Forces

Less than a generation ago, AI and machine learning consisted mainly of clever but still relatively prosaic extensions of traditional statistics in service of business goals—models that would predict the ability to repay loans or propensity to buy a product. Now, AI and machine learning are finally moving into realms that we would have considered science fiction less than a generation ago: cars that drive themselves, machines that carry on adaptive and seemingly intelligent conversations with you, algorithms that create videos of you saying things you never said, and much more.

Pressure for More Powerful AI

This quasimagical aspect of AI acts as an accelerant to the development of even more clever algorithms. Young data scientists and their visionary funders are more motivated by the prospect of developing something disruptive and exciting than they are by the possibility of contributing an extra 2% to a company's margin. This motivating pressure takes on a life of its own, widening and deepening the roles that these cutting-edge AI and machine learning models play in our economic and personal lives. Of course, the widening scope of AI approaches, along with the increased trust placed in them, can be harmful. Taken to the extreme, these models act in service of what researchers like AI Now Institute co-director Meredith Broussard refer to as *technochauvinism* and *technosolutionism*, or the belief that technical approaches alone are capable of solving complex social issues.

Public Resistance and Anxiety

At the same time (and perhaps as a result of increasing backlash against techno-solutionism), the public's anxiety and wariness grow about AI's role in society with each new story of violations of privacy, due process, fairness, or the social compact. Regulatory countermeasures, such as the GDPR within the European Union or the recently introduced Algorithmic Accountability Act in the United States, have come about as a result. This anxiety is exacerbated by the ways in which governments like that in China, citing the need for regulation, have comprehensively constrained technology companies, leveraging AI's Big Brother capabilities while limiting its ability to act as a force for transparency and justice.

It is important to understand the grassroots nature of AI development, driven by the need to do things that are clever and cool. Much as water running downstream in a creek will easily outflank large boulders, advances in AI will not remain bottled up for long. Both the development of new AI technologies and the public's wariness of AI's ill effects will continue in opposition to each other.

Resolving that tension is not something that can be solved with a single decisive action. Finding the right "balance" of when, where, and how AI methods ought to be used is an ongoing issue that will require constant attention and management.

To prepare for a discussion on how this issue can be navigated, we will use the next chapter to dive deeper into the statistical and machine learning modeling methods that we have outlined so far.

SUMMARY

We began this chapter with a review of how a well-intentioned algorithm to predict an individual's need for healthcare services ended up significantly underpredicting this need among African Americans, whose access to healthcare as a group is already limited. We saw how statistics and data science have led a Jekyll and Hyde existence for more than a century, dating from when modern statistical methods were born, joined at the hip with eugenics. Good and bad are often combined in the same package.

Nowadays, automated decision-making and lack of transparency are the sources of danger associated with AI models. We introduced the distinction between interpretable models and black-box models that are not interpretable. Finally, we began our tour of predictive models, a tour that will continue in Chapter 2, "Background: Modeling and the Black Box Algorithm."

Background: Modeling and the Black-Box Algorithm

We reviewed the basics of standard supervised predictive algorithms in Chapter 1, "Why Data Science Should Be Ethical." In this chapter, we build upon that base level of understanding by doing the following:

- Reviewing several important unsupervised algorithms, i.e., algorithms where there is no known outcome to train a model
- Discussing how to assess the performance of prediction models
- Exploring issues of interpretability, and how the inability to interpret black-box models can pose ethical challenges

Assessing Model Performance

Let's review traditional ways of assessing model performance. Measuring how well a predictive model performs depends on which of two categories a predictive model falls within.

- Predicting class membership and predicting the probability of belonging to a class (classification)
- Predicting a numerical value (regression)

Predicting Class Membership

The most common model type is one that predicts class membership—an image could be a dog or a cat, a loan could default or pay off, a web visitor could purchase or not, body tissue in an image might be malignant or benign, etc. Less commonly, the choice might fall among multiple categories (e.g., an auto accident might involve fatalities, injuries only, or property damage only). The most intuitive measure of a such a model is accuracy—what percentage of the predictions are accurate. In the typical binary classification case, the predictions versus actual outcomes are summed up in a 2×2 table termed a *confusion matrix*. For example, consider a training set of loans that have either defaulted or been paid off. Here the model's aim is to predict, on the basis of predictor variables, whether an observation has been paid off or defaulted. We can show the model's results, compared to reality, in the confusion matrix shown in Table 2.1.

Table 2.1: Confusion Matrix for 3,000 Loans

	LOANS PREDICTED PAID OFF	LOANS PREDICTED DEFAULTED
Actual paid off	2,849	25
Actual defaulted	85	41

The accuracy for this model is (2849 + 41)/3000 = 96.33%.

Put another way, the error rate is (85 + 25)/3000 = 3.67%.

However, by lazily predicting all loans as "paid off," the model would do almost as well: it would have accuracy of (2849 + 25)/3000 = 95.8%.

The Rare Class Problem

The loan model is an example of the rare class problem: one class occurs with much less frequency than the other. Generally, the rare class is the one of interest: the loan that defaults, the web visitor who actually purchases, the insurance claim that is fraudulent. We are primarily interested in how well the model separates out these unusual cases from the others; we are less interested in the fact that the model correctly classifies cases overall because most of them are of minimal interest. Two such measures for measuring performance in an unbalanced classification problem are *lift* (and its close relative *gains*) and *area under the curve* (AUC; meaning under the receiver operating characteristic [ROC] curve).

Lift and Gains

Lift and *gains* measure the boost that a model provides in identifying a class of interest. For example, suppose you identify the 10% of loans the model says are most likely to default, and you find twice as many actual defaulters as you would just by searching randomly. This model has a *lift ratio* of 2 for that top 10%. (*Gains* measures the boost from the model in terms of absolute numbers, rather than a ratio.) Gains and lift are often visualized in a chart that shows gains or lift decile by decile, as illustrated in Figure 2.1.

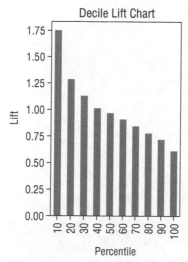

Figure 2.1: Decile lift chart

To construct and interpret the lift chart, we take these steps:

1. Array the cases by their order of probability of being a 1 (i.e., taking up the loan offer).

2. Count the actual 1s in the top 10%.

3. The ratio of that count to the average number of 1s in the dataset is 7.8.

The model in this example is clearly effective: for the predicted top 10%, it identifies nearly 8 times as many loan acceptors as would a random search.

Area Under the Curve

The curve in the metric AUC is the Receiver Operating Characteristics or ROC curve. To understand the ROC curve, we must first understand two additional metrics used to assess binary classification models.

Sensitivity: The proportion of 1s correctly identified

Specificity: The proportion of 0s correctly identified

Most models allow you to adjust the probability cutoff that determines whether a case is predicted as a 1 or a 0. Hence, there is a trade-off. The lower that cutoff, the more 1s you correctly capture, but the more 0s you misinterpret as 1s. The higher the cutoff, the more 0s you correctly identify, but the more 1s you fail to capture.

This trade-off is depicted in the ROC curve shown in Figure 2.2.

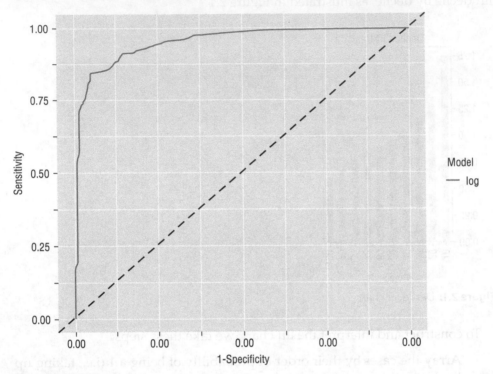

Figure 2.2: ROC curve

The ROC curve is drawn as follows:

1. Array the cases by their order of probability of being a 1 (i.e., taking up the loan offer).

2. Considering only the topmost case, plot sensitivity (y-axis) versus 1-specificity (x-axis).

3. Considering only the top two cases, plot sensitivity (y-axis) versus 1-specificity (x-axis).

4. Continue through the data as shown earlier, plotting sensitivity versus 1-specificity.

NOTE RECEIVER OPERATING CHARACTERISTIC CURVE The term *receiver operating characteristic curve* was originally used to describe the propensity of radar systems to correctly identify targets (sensitivity), as opposed to generating false positives (1-specificity; see Figure 2.3). The radar's discrimination threshold could be lowered to be sure to capture all targets but producing more false positives, or it could be raised to reduce false positives at the cost of losing more real targets. This same concept is now used in medicine (to describe the characteristics of diagnostic procedures) and in machine learning (to describe the ability of models to separate out cases of interest).

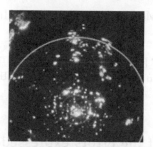

Figure 2.3: A radar receiver shows blips from aircraft and noise (such as ground echoes).

The overall performance of a model can be summed up in the area under the ROC curve (AUC). A model effective in discriminating between 1s and 0s will have an ROC curve that hugs the upper-left corner. As you move down the ranked cases, you encounter mostly actual 1s (y-axis) and few false positives (x-axis). Continuing to move down through the cases, the supply of 1s is mostly exhausted, and the curve remains near the top of the y-axis as more false positives (x-axis) are tagged.

A perfect model would have an AUC of 1; a model that is no better than random selection would have an area of 0.5 (the diagonal).

AUC vs. Lift (Gains)

AUC is a widely used metric in the AI community; it is an overall measure of the discriminatory power of a classification model. Lift, because it focuses on the incremental power of a model for the top-ranked cases, is used in marketing and other applications (e.g., fraud, churn) where targeting is important.

Predicting Numeric Values

Measuring the performance of models in predicting numeric values (generally termed *regression models* in the machine learning community) starts with the difference between the predicted value and the actual value—the *error*. The following are commonly used metrics:

- **Root mean squared error (RMSE):** Square root of the mean of the squared errors
- **Mean absolute error (MAE):** Mean of the absolute values of the errors
- **Mean absolute percentage error (MAPE):** Mean of the absolute values of the errors expressed as percentages

By taking absolute values (or squaring), all of the previously mentioned metrics convert the errors into positive values before averaging. These two other metrics retain the original signs:

- **Mean error:** Mean of the errors
- **Mean percentage error (MPE):** Mean of the errors expressed as percentages

All these metrics are measures of overall model performance.

To home in on "top-value" cases, lift (gains) is used, similarly to how it is used in classification.

1. Array the cases in order of predicted outcome value.
2. Take (say) the top 10% of the cases and measure the total predicted value for that decile.
3. Calculate the average value of the outcome variable.
4. The ratio (excess) of #2 over #3 is the lift (gains) for that decile.

Goodness-of-Fit

There is no equivalent to AUC for numeric prediction. (Correct or incorrect classifications, the basis for AUC, don't exist in a regression context.) However, you will see metrics that measure how well the model predictions fit the data; these are used mainly with linear models.

R^2 (R-squared) and adjusted-R^2 are perhaps the best known; they measure proportion of variability in the data that is explained by the model's predictions. Two other commonly used metrics are Akaike Information Criterion (AIC) and Bayesian Information Criterion (BIC). AIC and BIC (for which calculations are more complex than for the other metrics discussed here) are used mainly in reaching optimal decisions on how many predictors to include in a model.

Holdout Sets and Cross-Validation

Whenever possible, model metrics are calculated on holdout data, also called *validation data*. These are data, selected randomly from the same original source, that were set aside and not used to train (fit) the model. Measuring how well the model performs on the training data yields an overly optimistic estimate of how well the model will do with new data. Measuring performance on the holdout data eliminates most of the bias.

NOTE USE OF HOLDOUT DATA VS. IN-SAMPLE METRICS

You might wonder, "Why would you measure a model's performance using the training data (in-sample data), rather than holdout data?" The answer is largely historical. Regression models were originally developed primarily as a research tool to help answer questions about a set of data, not as a practical tool to predict future data. Metrics for this research goal focused on how well the model explained—fit—the data in question. Plus, datasets were not usually large enough to allow the analyst to spare chunks for holdout samples. The advent of big data brought two things:

- Lots of data to use in holdout sets, without depriving the model of ample training data
- A shift in focus toward prediction, as opposed to explanation

If prediction is the goal, then prediction accuracy with holdout data is the appropriate metric. However, metrics such as R^2 and AIC are still widely encountered, partly because small sample analysis has not disappeared and partly because these metrics have been engineered into software.

Cross-validation carries the idea of holdout data one step further. The use of a single holdout sample carries bias as well—the measurement is held hostage to the particularities of that particular sample. Cross-validation repeats the process, sequentially choosing a different segment of the data to train the model and validating the model on the remaining data. In *k-fold* cross-validation, each pass takes 1/k of the data and sets it aside for use in model validation.

Cross-validation is often included by default as part of the model-building process for certain classes of models. With random forests, for example, cross-validation is used to determine how far to build a tree and avoid overfitting.

Avoiding overfitting, in fact, is a key benefit of holdout validation and cross-validation. With data-driven methods like trees and neural nets, there is no natural limit to the extent to which the model will go in fitting the data, and it will end up fitting noise in addition to signal. Cross-validation and holdout samples can be used to determine how far to let the model-fitting process go so that it has a better chance of optimizing the balance between overfitting and underfitting.

Optimization and Loss Functions

The metrics outlined here are all different views of the performance of a model. Once you've measured how well a model performs, how do you decide which model is best? The generalization of measuring model performance and the incorporation of decision-making make up the process of optimization—choosing the optimal model.

Optimizing the choice of model intersects with the world of operations research, in which you seek to make decisions that achieve the best value of some *objective function*, say profit or revenue, subject to certain constraints (e.g., not exceeding limits of raw materials or person-hours).

DEFINITION OBJECTIVE FUNCTION   Goodfellow et al., in *Deep Learning*, define the objective function: "The function we want to minimize or maximize is called the objective function, or criterion. When we are minimizing it, we may also call it the cost function, loss function, or error function. In this book, we use these terms interchangeably, though some machine learning publications assign special meaning to some of these terms."

In most cases, the objective function in a predictive model will have the goal of maximizing one the metrics described earlier, for example:

- Maximize accuracy
- Maximize recall (sensitivity)
- Maximize AUC
- Maximize lift for the top decile
- Maximize likelihood
- Maximize RMSE (for predicting numeric response)

Loss functions for classification models address the flip side of measures of accuracy. They may be as simple as "proportion misclassified," or they may incorporate situation-specific considerations. However, they all refer to a value to be minimized. For example, assigning different costs to misclassified 0s and 1s is a common way of dealing with the rare-class problem, where identifying one class that is typically uncommon (e.g., frauds, sales, etc.) is more valuable than identifying the more run-of-the-mill cases (e.g., nonfraudulent transactions, prospects who look but don't buy).

In a manual world, whichever model/configuration achieves the maximum value of the objective function with holdout data would be selected. With some algorithms, an iterative optimization process is part of the tuning of the model. In some random forest algorithms, for example, the accuracy of different sized trees is repeatedly measured on cross-validation partitions to select the best tree size. In neural nets, the accuracy (or other metric) is repeatedly measured and factored back into the iterative process of learning.

The term *optimization* is less commonly encountered in data science than in operations research. While the idea is often employed within the lower levels of modeling function calls, the process is often not explicitly thought of in optimization terms or made transparent to the user. However, we find optimization and particularly the idea of constraints useful concepts when it comes to remedying and guarding against bias and unfairness in models. We will discuss those topics in greater detail in Chapter 7, "Auditing a Responsible Data Science Project," and Chapter 8, "Auditing Neural Networks."

Intrinsically Interpretable Models vs. Black-Box Models

While we go into more detail about what interpretability means in coming chapters, for now we illustrate its meaning with an example that we touched upon in the introduction: a linear regression model.

$$Y = a + b_1 x_1 + b_2 x_2 \ldots + b_n x_n + error$$

In this model, the coefficients tell us, in plain terms, how the model thinks a predictor affects the outcome. As an illustration, consider the issue of predicting students' grades in the Student Performance dataset. This dataset records the grades of a cohort of Portuguese students across two different classes, as well as a number of predictor variables about each student. After performing variable selection on and preprocessing the raw data, we were left with 395 observations and the following 7 variables:

VARIABLE	TYPE	DESCRIPTION
G3	Numeric	Final grade (0 to 20)
guardian	Factor	Guardian of student (mother, father, or other)
failures	Numeric	Number of past class failures (0 to 4)
schoolsup	Factor	Extra educational support (yes or no)
absences	Numeric	Number of past absences (0 to 93)

(Collected by Prof. Paulo Cortez and available at `archive.ics.uci.edu/ml/datasets/Student+Performance`). Predictor variables in the Cortez data include numerous demographic, social, and economic factors (e.g., family size, parents living together or apart, parents' employment, internet access, etc.).

The following code uses the *parsnip* package in R to fit a multiple linear regression on a standardized version of this data and generate predictions on the test set:

```
fit_model = linear_reg() %>%
   set_mode("regression") %>%
   set_engine("lm") %>%
   fit(G3 ~ ., data = train_data)
```

```
preds = fit_model %>%
  predict(new_data = test_data) %>%
  bind_cols(test_data) %>%
  select(G3, .pred)
```

Translating the fitted model coefficients into an equation, we get the following:

```
G3 = 11.3 - 0.11(guardianmother) - 0.40(guardianother) - 1.81(failures)
        - 1.44(schoolsupyes) + 0.02(absences)
```

Using this equation, we can interpret exactly how the model made each of its predictions. All we must do is understand how the coefficients relate to the values of the target variable. For example, the 1.44 coefficient for the schoolsupyes variable implies that students who receive extra academic support from the school have a predicted GPA that is 1.44 points higher than it would have been without such extra support.

Logistic regression to predict binary outcomes also produces coefficients that show how a predictor affects the outcome. Considering the same Student Performance data, let's suppose that students with a final grade equal to or above 10 pass their course, making the target variable binary rather than numeric. We can otherwise predict the probability of passing or failing using the same predictor variables.

Using *parsnip*, we can again write modeling code like the following:

```
fit_model_log_class = logistic_reg() %>%
  set_mode("classification") %>%
  set_engine("glm") %>%
  fit(G3 ~ ., data = data_classif[[1]])

preds_log_class = fit_model_log_class %>%
  predict(new_data = data_classif[[2]],
          type = "prob") %>%
  bind_cols(data_classif[[2]]) %>%
  select(G3, .pred_1)
```

This produces a fit logistic model with an equation like so:

```
log(odds of passing) = 1.35 - 0.06(guardianmother)
                        - 0.53(guardianother) - 0.86(failures)

-0.79(schoolsupyes) - 0.03(absences)
```

The coefficients here are interpreted similarly to the way that linear regression coefficients are, just with different units. For example, the -0.06 coefficient for guardianmother indicates that students who have listed their mother as their primary guardian have a 0.06 decrease in their log(odds of passing) than students whose primary guardian is their father or "other." We can get from log(odds) to odds or probability with a couple of steps, but the most immediately interpretable models is at the level of log(odds).

Another example of an interpretable model is a single decision tree. Figure 2.4 illustrates the use of a decision tree to predict whether a bank customer will accept the offer of a loan or not.

The tree in Figure 2.4 could be interpreted as follows:

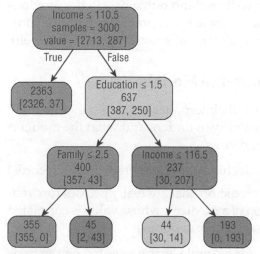

Figure 2.4: Tree for bank loan data

If the customer's income is less than or equal to $110,500 (condition = "True"), they are immediately classified as "non-accept." There are 2,363 such customers, out of the original 3,000 at the top level. For customers whose income is greater than $110,500, there are additional decision nodes to be considered. Looking at the bottom-right node, we see that those customers whose income is greater than $110,500, whose education is above level 1.5, and whose income is also above $116,500 are predicted as loan acceptors.

The tree is derived through an iterative process of dividing the data into smaller and smaller groups.

1. Starting with any predictor and any value of the predictor (the "split" value), measure the homogeneity of the outcome class (acceptor or non-acceptor) for those above the split value and those below.

2. Settle on the predictor and the split value that yields the greatest homogeneity among outcomes in the two splits. This becomes the top-level split.

3. Repeat this process for each of the partitions that result from the top-level split.

4. Continue to split the partitions until some tree-stopping criterion is reached. Note that if no stopping criterion is established, the tree will continue to grow until all final partitions ("leaves") consist entirely of one class or the other.

You can see that the splitting process yields a set of rules that define the predicted class of an outcome variable—these rules are the epitome of interpretability. A complete newcomer to statistics and machine learning could tell you what the relationship is between predictors and outcomes. In the previous illustration, for example, you learn that Income is the predictor with the most influence, as it appears at the top-level split (and at some lower splits as well).

Ethical Challenges with Interpretable Models

Ethical problems may arise with intrinsically interpretable models, though these problems are typically not due to an inability to understand what the model is doing. Rather, they arise due to the following:

- Incompleteness (i.e., the failure to include important predictors or records)
- Inclusion of innocent-sounding predictors that are really proxies for "red-flag" predictors (e.g., the inclusion of a predictor whose value is correlated with race, gender, or similar disallowed categories)

The Scholastic Aptitude Test (SAT), for example, was promoted on the basis of early models that showed it to be an effective predictor of academic success. Later research indicated that this simple analysis left out key predictors—family income and socioeconomic status—that were correlated with both SAT scores and academic success. An example of the inclusion of an inadvertent predictor is the occasional use of "financial shopping propensity" as a variable in setting interest rates. Consumers who can't or don't shop around for favorable loan rates are more likely to pay higher rates, as they are buying in a market that is, in effect, less competitive. Consumers who live in "financial deserts" are likely to have low "financial shopping propensity"; they are also more likely to be African American or Latinx. (It should be noted that the advent of AI-enabled loan processing, in general, has made loans more widely available and less dependent on local knowledge.)

Another example of a missing variable was in a 2007 released study of the drug aprotinin, used to prevent excessive bleeding during heart surgery. Patients who were given the drug were 48% more likely to die during the five years after surgery. However, the surgery's complexity was not accounted for in this estimate. It was known that the sicker patients (perhaps those requiring more complex surgery) were more likely to be given aprotinin.

Black-Box Models

Black-box models present the same ethical challenges of incompleteness and inclusion, however, these challenges are multiplied by the fact that black-box models offer no easy way to understand how the model relates the predictor features to the outcome.

- How can you tell whether you have included all relevant predictors, if you don't know what predictors the model really considers to be important?

- By the same token, how can you tell if an inappropriate predictor has been included?

- If you are feeding a black-box model voluminous low-level predictors (pixel values, say, or lots of text), the relevant predictors may be developed by the model itself and not known to you in the first place.

Let's review different types of black-box models.

Ensembles

We discussed in Chapter 1 Francis Galton's account of the English county fair where a contest was held to estimate the weight of an ox. The average of all the estimates was more accurate than nearly all the individual estimates. In the same way, predictions from different models (or different configurations of the same model) can be averaged, yielding predictions that are more accurate than most of the individual models themselves. For example, suppose you randomly select 10 different training sets from the same overall dataset and fit 5 linear regression models and 5 decision trees to predict house prices; then you apply (score) each model to a new record. The *average* predicted house price for the new record will generally be more accurate than most of the *individual* predicted prices. If you are working with models to make binary classifications, the *majority vote* of the predicted classifications will generally be more accurate than the individual classifications. While ensembles can be applied to any model type, their most common use is with decision trees.

Bagging and Random Forests

A common form of an ensemble is to take multiple bootstrap samples (see "The Bootstrap" note) from the data and fit a model to each, then average the resulting predictions (or take a majority vote). This process is known as *bagging*, which is short for *bootstrap aggregating*. The most common implementation of bagging occurs with decision trees, where it is termed a *random forest*. A random forest is a collection of decision trees, whose predictions are averaged in an ensemble. The process is simple.

1. Select a bootstrap sample of records and a random subset of predictors; then fit a decision tree. Record the prediction.

2. Repeat the previous step B times (where B is selected by the user or set in the software), thus collecting a "forest" of trees.

3. Average the predictions (if numerical values), or take a majority vote (if classifications).

NOTE THE BOOTSTRAP   A *bootstrap sample* is a sample selected randomly and with replacement from the original sample. It can be of any size, but typically it is the same size as the original sample. The bootstrap sample is then used to refit a model or recalculate an estimate. Often, it is used to estimate variability or bias in the estimate; here, we are using it to generate additional samples to leverage the power of ensembles. First suggested by J. Simon in his 1969 book titled *Basic Research Methods in Social Science* and then independently named and elaborated by Bradley Efron in his 1979 paper titled "Bootstrap Methods: Another Look at the Jackknife," the method was met with widespread and sustained skepticism. To understand why it works, it helps to visualize the original sample as being replicated millions of times as a "stand-in" for the larger population from which it came. Then you sample in normal (nonreplacement) fashion from this huge synthetic population to assess variability and derive multiple estimates. Keep in mind that this key step—having the sample stand in for the larger population—is the same conceptual step taken in standard formula-based statistics. (It is simply obscured by the application of formulas.) The bootstrap is now regarded as one of the major statistical advances of the late twentieth century.

Boosting and Boosted Trees

Boosting is a slightly different approach to ensembling, one which focuses on the difficult-to-predict cases. It is rather like learning a passage of music: with practice time limited, repeated practice of the easy parts is of little value. Rather, you want to focus your practice on the difficult bits. The boosting algorithm is as follows:

1. Fit a model to the data.
2. Draw a sample from the data that assigns a higher selection probability to those cases that had the highest prediction error.
3. Refit the model to the new sample.
4. Iterate steps 2 and 3 multiple times.
5. Score the model that emerges from multiple iterations.

Like bagging, boosting is a general procedure but is typically applied mainly to trees. Popular approaches or software packages that use boosting for trees include XGBoost, Light GBM, and catboost.

Nearest Neighbors

Nearest neighbors is perhaps the simplest of the black-box models. Given a record to be predicted, you must find other records that are similar to it and then find their average value or majority class. Despite its simplicity, it is considered a black-box method because there's no structural link between predictors (overall) and predictions. For one record, predictors a, b, and f might be the important variables linking it to its similar neighbors. For another record, it might be predictors b, c, e, and g.

Several popular metrics exist for the distance between, or similarity of, records. A popular one is Euclidean distance: subtract one record from the other, square the differences, sum them, and take the square root. There is one parameter to tune: the number of neighbors to compare.

Clustering

Clustering techniques are a set of unsupervised methods, meaning there's no outcome variable to predict. Rather, clustering uses similarity among records to segment records into clusters of similar records. Several methods exist to do this, with the most popular being hierarchical clustering and k-means clustering. The concept of distance between records gets expanded so that we can measure, in several ways, the distance between clusters and the distance between a single record and a cluster. In this connection, the measure of a cluster's center, the *centroid*, is used.

In hierarchical clustering, records are clustered as follows:

1. Start with each record as a singleton cluster.
2. The two closest records are merged.

3. The process continues as the two clusters that are closest together are merged at each stage, until you are left with a single all-inclusive cluster.

At any stage of the process prior to the end, you have multiple clusters, with the number of clusters diminishing until the end. The user can view cluster membership and how tight the clusters are and then decide how many clusters to use in analysis or decisions.

In *k*-means clustering, records are clustered as follows:

1. Randomly split up the records into *k* groups.
2. At each step, each record is reassigned to the closest cluster.
3. Recompute the centroid of each cluster whose membership changed.
4. Continue repeating the reassignment process until any further reassignment would increase cluster dispersion.

In *k*-means clustering, of course, the user sets *k*, the number of clusters, a-priori.

Association Rules

Association rules deal with transaction-level data, e.g., a list of the products purchased in a transaction, or similar data. Applied across large numbers of transactions, it yields rules of "what goes with what." Retail stores use it to guide the placement of products on shelves and in special displays. For online merchants, it is one of the algorithms used to suggest additional products for you, after you have selected one or more initial products. When used in retail, association rules are also called *market basket analysis*.

Collaborative Filters

Collaborative filters also produce recommendations and deal with user- and item-level data. User-based algorithms answer the question "What have users like me purchased that I have *not* purchased?" The "like me" is determined by web behavior: products purchased, items rated, and items viewed. These algorithms are useful in exploiting similarity in unique tastes. Rather than simply recommending items that are popular overall, the algorithm will recommend items that appeal to other people like you. In that sense, they are helpful in slowing the overall homogenization of tastes and promoting diversity and uniqueness.

When the number of users is much larger than the number of items, the user-based algorithm is computationally expensive, which is important in serving up rapid recommendations in real time. A faster, though less personal, alternative is to base similarity on items rather than users. If an item is selected or viewed by the user, identify other items that share the same profile of "approving users."

Artificial Neural Nets and Deep Neural Nets

Neural networks are the "mother of all black-box models" for two reasons.

- They automatically develop multiple intermediate feature representations from raw data, making them particularly well suited for highly dimensional data (e.g, text or image data).

- They are highly complex and rely upon multiple levels of iteration and randomization, making it almost impossible to directly understand the relationships between inputs and predictions.

We can distinguish between the original artificial neural network (ANN) and deep neural nets (DNN). The latter, also known as *deep learning*, are neural nets with great complexity (i.e., layers and nodes), as well as operations on subsets of low-level predictors (e.g., pixel values) that aggregate them into more useful features. The simplified depictions of an ANN and DNN that were shown in Chapter 1 are repeated in Figures 2.5 and 2.6 for reference.

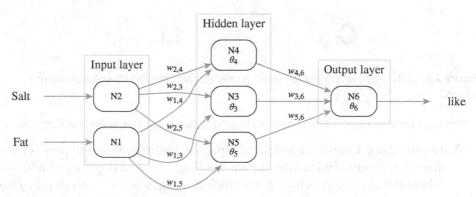

Figure 2.5: ANN with one hidden layer

However, there is more to the deep learning revolution than just the addition of layers to an ANN. For one thing, the continued increase in available computing power, coupled with the use of graphical processors (whose structure is particularly suited to the types of computations required in DNNs), facilitated the complexity of adding layers to DNNs. This added network complexity could now accomplish significant additional learning, rather than simply bogging down the network.

Another factor is the increasingly wide availability of labeled datasets, which can be used to train DNNs. The ImageNet dataset, for example, contains more than 1.5 million images, each matched to one or more words or phrases. (There are thousands of such phrases.)

Input Layer   Hidden Layer 1   Hidden Layer 2   Hidden Layer 3   Output Layer

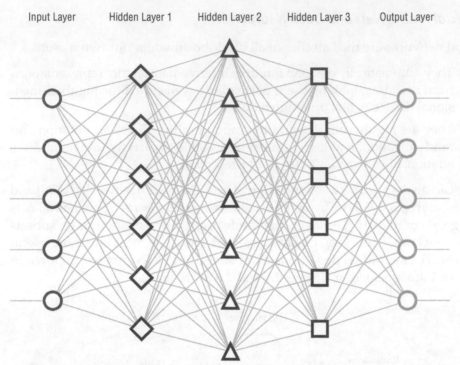

Figure 2.6: DNN with multiple hidden layers. (Other complexities like convolution are not shown.)

Several innovations in neural net structure have also proven revolutionary.

Auto-encoding: One of the seemingly magical features of neural nets is their ability to group objects into like classes (e.g., cats and dogs) even without labels (i.e., without being given labeled images of cats and dogs). This *unsupervised feature extraction* is made possible by the mirror trick of auto-encoding. With no label, the network uses the original input as the target to reproduce, having first gone through a convolution process to develop high-level features (see below). At this point, the network reverses the process and constructs its best guess about the target, based only on the high-level features. The network structure that does the best job of learning to reconstruct its input in the mirror is deemed to have done a good job of learning the high-level features and is returned as the trained network.

Convolutional neural networks (CNNs): In a simple ANN, all input variables go through the same process at each stage. In a *convolutional neural network* (CNN), overlapping subsets of variables are selected at each stage. For each subset, a summary value is calculated and stored. This is repeated for all the data using overlapping subsets, yielding a matrix of reduced dimension that can now serve as an input for further operations that may involve further convolutions and dimension reduction. It is this consolidation of low-level features (e.g., pixel values, text, sound wave amplitudes) that facilitates higher-level feature extraction: starting with individual pixel values, then moving to edges between intensities or colors, then to shapes, and finally to highly recognizable forms (e.g., eyes).

Recurrent neural networks (RNNs): The discussion so far has presumed that inputs are independent of one another. What if they are time-dependent (i.e., sequenced)? RNNs, as well as further architectural advancements of them like Long Short-Term Memory (LSTM) and Transformers, are a type of neural network that are capable of processing sequences of dependent inputs. A common application we are all familiar with is the prediction of the next character in a sentence or phrase that we are typing. The initial "prediction" is null because the network has nothing to go on before we start typing. As we add letters, the network recalculates at each stage, remembering what it was predicting at the prior stage. Having seen us type "the quick brown fox j...", the network will incorporate what it was "thinking" at that point into a recalculation, once it sees us type "u."

DNNs shine in situations of great data complexity. Computer vision and voice recognition are the popularly known implementations of deep learning, but it is also widely applied in other situations; here are some examples:

- Text mining and natural language processing
- Messy data with numerous variables of multiple types that normally require considerable human time for cleaning and feature extraction

We discuss deep neural nets in greater detail in Chapter 8, "Auditing for Neural Networks." From now on, any mention of neural networks refers to deep learning–based approaches.

Problems with Black-Box Predictive Models

The hidden nature of black-box models renders them vulnerable across several dimensions, most notably:.

- Technical issues
- Deployment and communication issues
- Bias and fairness issues

Technical Issues

On the technical side, we cannot know what the model is really doing if we can't see the important predictors. It might achieve stellar performance with training data that can't be duplicated in deployment. Previously, we mentioned the case of the skin mole classification algorithm that did well due to the presence of a ruler in the more serious cases: the dermatologist would not place the ruler in situations where the mole was clearly benign. Our own firm found that a fraud detection model did extremely well at an early stage, but only because the phrase "opened investigation" was one of the available predictors. This variable would not be available in deployment, where the whole point of the model is to determine whether an investigation should be opened.

The analyst might also not know how robust their model is to changes in predictor values. Perhaps you have seen the example, described in Goodfellow, Schlens, and Szegedy's *Explaining and Harnessing Adversarial Examples*, of how a minor injection of noise into an image classification (i.e., an *adversarial attack*) can dramatically change the result, as with the movement from *panda* to *gibbon* shown in Figure 2.7. Ironically, while the model attached only 57.7% confidence to its panda classification, it attached 99.3% confidence to its gibbon classification. (The panda image is from the ImageNet dataset, described in www.image-net.org/papers/imagenet_cvpr09.pdf.)

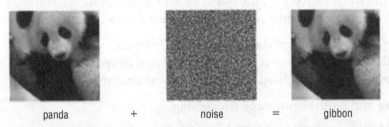

panda   +   noise   =   gibbon

Figure 2.7: A small amount of noise fools the DNN into thinking the panda is a gibbon.

If the important predictors are shielded from view in a black-box model, it will take longer to discover such problems and correct them. It is also more likely that a faulty model will make it into deployment. We will discuss in Chapter 5, "Model Interpretability: The What and the Why," how the application of interpretability methods can help to address these issues.

Deployment and Communication Issues

Being able to explain how a black-box model makes its predictions is important for a data scientist in a number of situations.

- If you are building a model for a client who is not a deeply trained data scientist, confidence is enhanced when you can explain how model predictors are related to outcomes.

- Being able to explain models is also important for building confidence within the organization. This might be for a sales prioritization model that needs buy-in from the sales organization. It might be for a loan approval model that needs the support of the underwriting and general counsel offices. It might be for any model that must be presented to senior management.

- If you have to defend the model in a legal context, for example with regulators, legislators, or civil litigators, being able to understand and explain the model is essential.

- Even in working with other data scientists or experts who provide information and assistance in developing the model, understanding how it works enhances the development process.

Bias or Fairness Issues

Bias and fairness are the issues that have driven most of the bad press about AI. The book jacket for Cathy O'Neil's popular critique of data science models, *Weapons of Math Destruction*, is an illustration of this bad press.

> The models used today are opaque, unregulated, and uncontestable, even when they're wrong. Most troubling, they reinforce discrimination. . . . Models are propping up the lucky and punishing the downtrodden, creating a "toxic cocktail for democracy."

If you don't know what the important predictors are for a model or how they relate to the outcome, you won't know if you have any "red-flag" predictors (e.g., race in loan approval), or predictors that work in an unfair fashion. We will discuss addressing bias and fairness issues in Chapters 7 and 8.

Problems with Unsupervised Algorithms

Because unsupervised algorithms typically do not facilitate decisions about individuals based on predictions, the ethical issues with them tend to be less acute. However, these issues are important from a societal perspective. The main ethical challenges arise from the use of recommender systems to foster communities of like-minded individuals. They are shown postings and images from others when the algorithm determines that these would be of interest, based on the similarity of user profiles. The increased engagement builds and reinforces the user base, which is good for advertisers. Ads are targeted in the same way, which increases their value to the advertiser, and hence their price, compared to ads that are distributed to a more general audience. This is a useful thing, for the most part. Consider data science itself as an example. Most data scientists have benefited substantially from the free flow of useful on-point information from various overlapping online communities. The field would not have prospered as it did without this facility.

However, these same algorithms, operating on auto-pilot, can foster communities motivated by hate and violence. The Charlottesville, Virginia, "Unite the Right" rally, which attracted white supremacists and sparked a violent confrontation, had an active Facebook page until it was removed by Facebook.

Ironically, the very AI that spawned the era of virtual community building and ad targeting has also forced social media companies like Facebook to devote thousands of man-hours to manually review content so they can make human judgments about suitability. And, it is not simply a matter of time. Social media companies are not comfortable with what is, in effect, a censorship role. In a 1964 case where an agreed definition of obscenity was elusive, Supreme Court Justice Potter Stewart said, "I know it when I see it," but this can be a difficult rule to implement for widespread human review, let alone algorithmic review.

Summary

In this chapter, we took a quick tour of the main algorithms used in predictive modeling and AI. This tour was primarily intended as a reference guide to the AI landscape, useful for those who have been exposed to AI methods at some point but who may have moved on to other areas of focus. It may be helpful as well for technical experts who have dived deeply into just one or two aspects of AI. We distinguished between supervised methods (e.g., predictive modeling), where models are trained on data with known outcomes of interest so as to be able to make predictions with new data where the outcome is not known, and unsupervised methods, where models uncover patterns and relationships in data that do not have a defined outcome of interest.

The predictive modeling (supervised) category has the ready capacity to make automated decisions, replacing human judgment, so it is a focus of concern. We saw the difference between intrinsically interpretable methods and black-box methods. Intrinsically interpretable methods like linear or logistic regression yield output where the analyst can readily determine the role that individual predictors play in predictions. Black-box methods like random forests or neural nets are too complex to allow such determinations.

In the next chapter, we develop in greater detail the relevant legal, regulatory, and overall ethical drivers of ethical data science that have become relevant in the last decade.

The Ways AI Goes Wrong, and the Legal Implications

Coauthor: William Goodrum

If we want to understand why cases of "AI gone wrong" occur, we must first understand that they do not occur at random. Rather, harms caused by AI models can arise either as an intentional result of an AI model accomplishing a harmful objective or as an unintended or unanticipated consequence of an AI model accomplishing an otherwise useful objective.

In Chapter 1, "Why Data Science Should Be Ethical," and Chapter 2, "Background—Modeling and the Black-Box Algorithm," we discussed a brief history of ethical concerns about the use of statistics and introduced the technical topics necessary for the remainder of the book.

Now, we delve deeper into the quagmire of irresponsible AI in the present day. In this chapter, we present illustrations of the harms arising from both intentionally malicious uses of AI and honest uses of AI that nonetheless end up causing harm. We develop an understanding of the various different contexts and forms in which these harms occur as well as who experiences these harms. We then transition to a discussion of how these harms are viewed internationally in legal and regulatory contexts. We do not attempt to comprehensively cover the law on the subject, but instead focus on providing some familiarity with the legal considerations that should inform our quest to better understand and control our own use of such powerful algorithms.

AI and Intentional Consequences by Design

The twenty-first-century development, productization, and free distribution of extremely potent AI tools has empowered not just legitimate institutions but "bad actors" as well. These might be criminals, malicious individuals, or, in the most insidious cases, institutions of the state itself.

Deepfakes

Perhaps the most infamous cases of AI working toward a harmful goal involve *deepfakes*. A deepfake is an image, video, or audio track in which a real person is combined with synthesized elements of another imaginary or real person (see Figure 3.1).

Figure 3.1: Deepfake in which Amy Adams's face (left) is swapped out with that of Nicolas Cage (right)

Rights: `en.wikipedia.org/wiki/File:Deepfake_example.gif`

The most notable malicious use of deepfakes has been to swap the faces of (primarily) female celebrities onto pornographic images and videos. Other instances involve political figures—substituting the face of Adolf Hitler, for example, onto the image of the president of Brazil. Audio components can be forged as well if there is a repository of audio from which to learn a person's speech tones and patterns. Resemble.ai claims to be able to clone your voice, enabling you to create scripts that are then read in your voice. University of Washington researchers were able to learn and then synthesize lip movements to match speech patterns, supplying the video side of the equation.

Deepfakes leverage image and/or voice recognition technology to superimpose the face or voice of a specific person onto already existing media. The use of deepfakes to date has been primarily malicious or, at best, innocuous and created primarily for humor. Deepfake creators know that they are, in some cases, violating or skirting the law, and their express intent in these cases is largely to create mischief. Providing them with the ability to explain and interpret their algorithms does not deter them, making this a problem that belongs in the realm of public policy, not responsibility on behalf of the individual practitioner.

The methods outlined in this book, because they assume an algorithm's developer is seeking to avoid causing harm (or at least is not actively seeking to cause it), are of little value in cases like these. Public opprobrium, new regulation, or heightened legal consequences are the only way of controlling such harms. Such was the case with deepfakes for revenge porn in Australia, where a deepfake attack on a law student triggered the passage of specific anti-revenge porn laws.[1]

Supporting State Surveillance and Suppression

Another controversial use of AI working as intended in the furtherance of harmful goals is government use of AI tools to control their citizenry, for example, the Chinese government's use of algorithmically derived "social credit" scores. The concept of social credit is an extension of the idea of an individual's financial creditworthiness, which has been tracked for more than a century. Financial creditworthiness is embodied in the familiar credit score, which is calculated for an individual by an algorithm that purports to predict the likelihood that money lent to the person will be repaid. Banks and other financial institutions can then use the credit score to help make lending decisions.

In China, the credit score has been extended beyond financial questions to social behavior issues, including:

- Failure to clean up after your dog
- Failure to pay traffic fines
- Failure to dim your high beams for oncoming traffic
- Failure to visit elderly parents regularly
- Failure to properly sort your waste and recycling

All these infractions can get factored into your social credit score in China, which, if it drops low enough, can result in consequences including restrictions on air travel, getting loans, pet ownership, and more.[2]

Using AI to track down and punish these offenses may not seem like a harmful goal; you might know some folks who would be happy to have a similar sanctioning regime in the United States or Europe. In China, though, it forms part of the scaffolding of the surveillance state. These social credit scores are an important component of on overall AI effort that also includes facial recognition algorithms and comprehensive data collection. The effort is particularly vigorous in provinces like Xinjiang that are inhabited by Uighurs, who are predominantly Muslim, serving at least in part to suppress that minority.

---

[1] You can read more here at www.mondaq.com/australia/crime/845796/ deepfake-porn-the-dark-side-of-the-web.

[2] You can read more about these consequences on Wikipedia at en.wikipedia.org/wiki/ Social_Credit_System#Examples_of_policies.

While deepfakes are a specific AI deployment that has no current purpose other than humor, mischief, or harm, the algorithms that lie behind the surveillance state also have more standard and legitimate purposes (e.g., maintaining local or national security). Nonetheless, the intent behind the usage of these tools as well as the balance of possible harms and possible benefits are relevant here. While cultural norms of the appropriate role government should take in securing peace and security may differ from country to country, we take the view that using the power of AI to abet ethnic repression or suppression of peaceful political dissent is an irresponsible use of the technology that ought to be curtailed.

Behavioral Manipulation

The Cambridge Analytica scandal is a famous example of standard AI algorithms deployed intentionally in furtherance of dubious goals. In a slick video presentation before a large audience at the Concordia Summit in 2016, Alexander Nix, Cambridge Analytica's CEO, reported how the company had gathered an enormous dataset on U.S. voters that characterized them in psychological and social terms. The data were sourced from public voter records, Facebook profiles, and other sources. Nix then described how the company was able to define individual voters in terms of their dominant personality traits and craft individually targeted political messaging that tapped into the motivations governed by those traits. In his talk, Nix implied that the messaging need not be true: for fear-motivated individuals, a "sharks sighted" sign would be more effective in warding off trespassers than a "private beach" sign, without regard to whether there were sharks present.

Cambridge Analytica was employed by the 2016 Trump campaign. In a *60 Minutes* interview, Brad Parscale, the digital media director of Trump's campaign at that time, described how he supervised a massive message-testing and deployment campaign in which tens of thousands of Facebook ad experiments were conducted daily in an AI-driven search for the message that best produced the desired result (clicking the ad). Attributes like color, different photographs of Hillary Clinton, headlines, and various calls to action were continuously modified in an automated fashion. An algorithm tracked who responded to what combinations and learned what to present to given individuals to maximize a response. This was not something Parscale thought up on his own; it was the same technique Facebook used to maximize responses to commercial advertising.

There is nothing particularly new, or necessarily irresponsible, about personality-driven advertising; Madison Avenue has employed it since the 1950s. The automobile industry has used personality information in crafting car models and the ad campaigns that support them. The use of microtargeting in political campaigns is newer but still more than a decade old: Ken Strasma, who teaches political targeting methods at Statistics.com, pioneered its use as long ago as in the 2004 Kerry presidential campaign. Microtargeting combined with psychological manipulation *is* new and acquires even greater potency when combined with automated experimentation to maximize response. The combination of these three elements with a fourth, deception, is where trouble lies.

Automated Testing to Fine-Tune Targeting

Guided by Facebook staff, Parscale introduced a third element to the Trump campaign's advertising toolkit: continuous testing and optimization. Based in part on the statistical methodology termed multi-armed bandits, continuous testing and the optimization of ads is an important part of the Facebook business model. The more effective an ad is, the more it can be sold for. For important clients, i.e., those with large Facebook advertising budgets, Facebook will embed ad-targeting specialists with the firm to set up and tweak the AI algorithms. In his interview with *60 Minutes* on CBS, Parscale reported that Facebook did this for the Trump campaign, and he came close to crediting Facebook's sophisticated AI-driven advertising strategy for the Trump victory.

DEFINITION MULTI-ARMED BANDITS   In a traditional A/B test, a sample of subjects is gathered, and two treatment options are offered, say medical therapies. Typically, results from the entire sample are anticipated, and a *statistical significance* threshold must be reached to determine that a treatment really is superior and not the product of chance. This can mean that many subjects receive an inferior treatment. In digital marketing, though, there are hundreds, if not thousands, of potential "treatments" (digital ad variants) and millions of potential subjects. A *multi-armed bandit* experimentation process (see Figure 3.2) makes continuous decisions about the "winning treatment" to balance exploitation (rolling ahead with a winning treatment) with learning (continuing to try different options to see how they perform). Various optimization algorithms are used, depending on how much you value speed and are willing to risk losing out on a treatment that might ultimately be a winner but is an early underperformer.

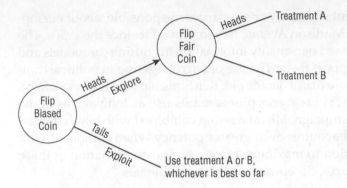

Figure 3.2: A continuous testing algorithm randomizes options (e.g., web page A or B) with a biased coin flip. With the "explore" outcome, another coin flip decides between A or B, this time 50/50. With the "exploit" outcome, the best-performing treatment so far is chosen. For the next case, the biased coin is flipped again. The bias on the coin (the chosen percentage heads, e.g., 30% heads) determines the balance between exploit and explore.

A key feature of the continuous testing process is its huge number of automated experiments and decisions not requiring human review. The real basis for success or failure of an ad, say the presence or absence of particular ethnic groups in a photo, might be hidden. Parscale reported that he was conducting tens of thousands of ads daily at the height of the Trump 2016 campaign.

It remains uncertain how successful the psychographic aspect of targeting was. A competing Democratic digital marketer doubted its effectiveness and also doubted that Cambridge Analytica really had all the Facebook data that Nix claimed it did. Facebook, he said, would not allow this. As it turned out, Nix did have Facebook data from more than 80 million users, data that was scraped illicitly through the Facebook app This is Your Digital Life. That app was developed by Aleksandr Kogan, a research associate at Cambridge University, for the express purpose of collecting data. The user filled out a short quiz, which enabled the app to access not just their own data but the data of all their Facebook friends as well. It was this unauthorized theft of personal data from Facebook that ultimately got Cambridge Analytica into trouble more than the behavioral manipulation it enabled.

Does psychographic behavior manipulation work? Two researchers, Chris Sumner and Matthew Shearing, conducted a study of digital ads aimed at more than 2,000 internet users who were scored either high or low for the personality trait of authoritarianism. They then crafted ads with a call to action to support mass surveillance. The ads came in two flavors.

- Messaging designed to appeal to authoritarians
- Messaging designed to appeal to anti-authoritarians

They found that the messaging flavor mattered. This is an extension of the well-known phenomenon in survey design where it matters how you word a question. What Sumner and Shearing found was that flipping the messaging tone would flip the person's position on the surveillance question.

Statistics and machine learning have brought important new dimensions to the long-standing practice of mass consumer and voter manipulation:

- Massive experimentation, which, coupled with big data, can lead to effective microtargeting at the individual level

- Concealing or obscuring the basis on which particular ads are targeted at particular individuals

Is there anything wrong with this? After all, truth has never been of paramount importance in commercial and political promotion. However, in the old regime of mass advertising, at least messaging was exposed to everyone on a wide basis and available for public viewing and broad judgment. Microtargeting and experimentation with thousands of messaging combinations have given deception and outright lies hidden pockets in which to operate out of sight. Moreover, the focus on individuals as targets can allow broader bias to prevail: The *Washington Post* reported on September 29 that the Cambridge Analytica database prepared for the Trump campaign ended up disproportionately targeting African American voters for messaging aimed at deterring voting.

These three preceding examples illustrate a range of cases where the intent is ill. Why then would the methods we discuss in this book help? In the case of a lone wolf who is an expert coder with mischievous or malicious intent, they might not. But many of the examples of harmful use arise from the development and/or implementation of AI in an organizational context. A data scientist trained from a perspective of transparency, interpretability, and ethical auditing is more likely to spot the potential misuse of the AI they are asked to develop and spread that perspective within the organization. Some individuals concerned with the Cambridge Analytica scandal now say they regret having developed the tools that later led to the company's ruin. A data scientist who is engaged with the broader ethical and societal implications of their work, as embodied in the Responsible Data Science framework we outline in the next chapter, and not simply with the "cool factor" of data science, is less likely to contribute to its misuse. They are also more likely to imbue their data science colleagues, as well as those in their organization who are less technical, with the same ethos.

AI and Unintended Consequences

Let's now turn to cases where the processes that we lay out in the next chapter can be much more helpful: cases where algorithms developed with good or benign intentions produce harmful outcomes (sometimes in spite of otherwise reasonable results). In those circumstances, developers and users of algorithms would have benefited from a process to render the AI models they are working on more transparent and interpretable. This would have provided them the knowledge and tools to anticipate such problems and take steps to reduce the risk of harm.

Healthcare

We already saw, in Chapter 1, the case of Optum, whose algorithm for predicting the need for follow-up care or rehospitalizations boomeranged and ended up discriminating against African Americans. Optum did not set out to discriminate against African Americans; the discrimination was an unanticipated by-product of the algorithm.

The Optum case is not unique. It just happened to generate a lot of attention. According to a study from the Society of Actuaries,[3] more than two dozen risk scoring models are used by healthcare providers and insurance companies. The purpose of the risk score is to predict future health. A research team led by Ziad Obermeyer studied these algorithms and found that, for any given risk score, African American patients consistently experienced more chronic health conditions than did white patients (see Figure 3.3).

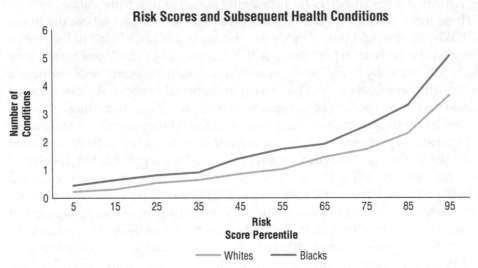

Figure 3.3: Algorithmic risk scores and subsequent chronic health conditions for African American and white subjects

---

[3] www.soa.org/globalassets/assets/Files/Research/research-2016-accuracy-claimsbased-risk-scoring-models.pdf

Another example comes from the field of genetic testing. Hypertrophic cardio-myopathy is a condition in which the heart wall thickens, impeding its ability to pump blood. It affects roughly 1 in 500 people. There is a genetic component to the disease, which can be useful in diagnosis and also in the screening of relatives of a confirmed patient. A person diagnosed with hypertrophic cardiomyopathy may be prescribed treatments ranging from medication to surgery. For African Americans, though, the predictive power of the genetic screening was very low compared to others. The reason? The genetic data used to train the model had practically no gene sequence data from African Americans. Without this data to train on, the model missed the fact that African Americans were far more likely than other groups to have a *benign* version of the genetic mutation asso-ciated with the disease. Hence, they were more likely to be referred for further testing and for treatments that carried at least some degree of unnecessary risk.

Interestingly, bias based on race is still *explicitly* included as part of medi-cine. In June 2020, the *New England Journal of Medicine* catalogued a number of treatment scenarios where race is explicitly included as a risk factor. For example, guidelines promulgated by the American Heart Association assign lower cardiac risk scores to African American patients than to white patients. This means that an African American patient presenting with a given medical history and condition is likely to be assigned a less proactive therapy than a white patient with the same history and condition. Similar examples were cited in nephrology, obstetrics, urology, and other areas. These race-based risk scores most likely are derived from minimally adjusted population estimates and reflect long-standing beliefs in a genetic basis for race covering many biological facets. The scores probably do not reflect sophisticated statistical analysis that allows for adjustment based on "other things being held equal."

Finance

In 2019, Apple introduced a new credit card in conjunction with Goldman Sachs. Shortly after the launch, prominent software developers started to complain publicly on social media that the card was biased against women in setting credit limits. David Heinemeier Hansson, the creator of Ruby on Rails, reported that he had been granted a credit limit that was much greater than that of his wife, Jamie Hansson, although she had a better credit score. On Twitter, he stated:

> **My wife and I filed joint tax returns, live in a community-property state, and have been married for a long time, yet Apple's black-box algorithm thinks I deserve 20x the credit limit she does.**

Steve Wozniak, cofounder of Apple and coinventor of the original Apple computer, chimed in with a similar complaint:

> **The same thing happened to us. I got 10x the credit limit. We have no separate bank or credit card accounts or any separate assets. Hard to get to a human for a correction, though. It's big tech in 2019.**

If Steve Wozniak finds it hard to get Apple's attention to correct this problem, we can be sure that the issue is not simply with algorithmic bias alone. Here, we are dealing with an issue of power, where users are denied the due process or recourse to appeal a decision made about them by an automated black-box algorithm.

Law Enforcement

A notable example of AI bias in the law enforcement arena is the Correctional Offender Management Profiling for Alternative Sanctions (COMPAS) algorithm to predict recidivism (propensity for a convicted criminal to re-offend). Courts have started relying increasingly on AI recidivism algorithms to inform decisions on sentencing. The COMPAS algorithm is among the most prominent of them, and its advocates point to its overall good predictive performance. They have responded to allegations of bias by noting that this predictive performance, as measured by the area under the ROC curve, is similar for African American and white defendants. The trouble is, the errors made are quite different.

- African American defendants are overpredicted to re-offend (leading to tougher sentences).
- White defendants are underpredicted to re-offend (leading to lighter sentences).

The errors are decidedly unfavorable to African American defendants, but they balance out the ones made in favor of white defendants, so the overall error rate is the same for both. We discuss more about the specifics of this case in Chapter 6, "Beginning a Responsible Data Science Project," and Chapter 7, "Auditing a Responsible Data Science Project."

There are other examples of obvious algorithmic predictive bias based on race or gender, but there are also interesting examples of more subtle unintended effects of AI in the area of law enforcement.

Around 2016, undocumented immigrants from Mexico in the Washington State town of Nahcotta, a shellfishing center, began disappearing. Boat workers had occasionally been picked up and deported before, but the pace picked up dramatically in 2016. The political climate had changed, and the tools of big data and AI were being brought to bear.

In the first decade and a half of the 2000s, US immigration policy was highly polarized between those favoring a relaxed, more open-door policy and those favoring a more restrictive policy. The general consensus, though, was that the 10 million people who had lived large portions of their lives here in the United States, albeit without documentation, should not be subject to roundup and deportation. Such a policy might be considered law enforcement in a technical sense, but it would have been seen by most Americans, a quarter of whom have at least one foreign-born parent, as excessive and draconian. Of particular concern was the fate of children who had lived nearly all their lives in the United States but who were technically undocumented aliens.

In the 2013 debate over proposals for immigration reform, the status of undocumented aliens was a principal point of contention. Open-door advocates favored a rapid path to citizenship. Some restrictionists favored ultimate citizenship, while others supported legalized status but not a rapid path to citizenship. Still others opposed nearly all legalization efforts. *No* significant political voice, however, advocated rounding up long-term undocumented aliens and deporting them.

The advent of AI-powered law enforcement techniques disrupted the consensus on this latter point and allowed the US Immigration and Customs Enforcement Agency (ICE) to pursue a more aggressive policy of finding and deporting undocumented aliens, even longtime US residents. Deportations in the first 14 months of the Trump administration tripled from the previous 14 months. Big data and multiple AI tools played an important role.

- Computer vision has contributed two key components: facial recognition and license plate readers.

- Location prediction algorithms can help predict where someone is going to be.

- Entity resolution algorithms enhance identification efforts by bringing together multiple disparate sources of identity data (e.g., ICE files, driver's license records and photos, tax records, utility bills, social media postings, etc.).

All this is not to suggest that law enforcement is unethical. But laws and regulations are not hard formal concepts that exist in a vacuum. Discretion, judgment, and cultural factors are part of the equation that can make laws either part of an agreed consensus-based social compact or the legal basis for a police state. AI and big data have given immigration enforcement a giant push away from the consensus "live and let live" approach to longtime US residents and toward an aggressive pursuit of undocumented people, even those who have been living peacefully in the United States for decades.

On a smaller scale, consider the doorbell camera. A neighbor of one of the authors recently heard a squealing of brakes, the sound of an impact, and then a car accelerating away. A doorbell camera recorded a video of the immediate aftermath: the car accelerating away, followed by a figure staggering into the frame from the left and then out again on the right. Amazingly, the young man who was hit was not seriously injured.

Doorbell cameras feature high-definition video recording and motion-detecting algorithms. Some record continuously, saving the video for a few seconds and then discarding it unless motion is detected. They are popular as personal security devices, enabling residents to see who's at a remote door and preserving evidence of intrusions. As in the escaping auto case, they can also provide useful information for police. Where do ethical considerations come into the picture?

In November of 2019, the online publication *The Intercept* claimed to have seen Amazon internal documents that discussed adding facial recognition capabilities to its entrant in the smart doorbell competition, Ring. The publication said the introduction of facial recognition would lead to the development of "neighborhood watch lists" of suspicious or undesirable people. An attorney for the American Civil Liberties Union (ACLU) raised the alarm that enabling watch list features on Ring would widen the scope of existing government watch lists and exacerbate the denial of due process associated with such lists. And, it is not hard to imagine a consumer-enabled watch list capability taking on a life of its own and leading to algorithm-enabled vigilantism. To be sure, Amazon denied that it had plans to implement facial recognition technology in Ring, though it admitted that it had thought about it. However, technology once developed is hard to keep bottled up. Like water running downhill, it will eventually find its way around obstacles. Pure intentions of the original inventor are no guarantee of long-term protection.

Technology

In 2015, it came to light that Google Photos was mistakenly labeling some dark-skinned people as gorillas. Google's AI had gone down the same path that crude racists had trodden for decades, in referring to African Americans as gorillas or other types of apes. Data scientists at Google, horrified at what was happening, tried to fix the problem. To prevent such offensive mislabeling in the future, they dropped the label "gorilla" from their algorithm's lexicon. After that, the algorithm would either mislabel gorillas as something else or simply throw up its hands and say, "I don't know." For good measure, Google included other terms, such as chimpanzee, chimp, and monkey in the ban. The offensive mislabeling problem was solved by "disappearing" certain animals.

Google's Vision missteps are not limited to Google Photos but underlie the technology itself. The publication *AlgorithmWatch* conducted an experiment with the image of a hand holding a thermometer gun. When the hand was dark-skinned, Google came back with the label "gun." When the hand was colored with a lighter overlay, Google's label changed to "monocular."

In one sense, Google's action on Google Photos was laudable: immediate correction of grossly offensive behavior by its algorithm. In another sense, though, it revealed arrogant presumption. Its algorithm couldn't label people correctly, but instead of discontinuing the labeling (which was hardly an essential service), it elected to alter the reality with which the algorithm was working to eliminate the possibility of offense.

This was a trivial example, perhaps: the addition of more training data will no doubt improve Vision's algorithms over time. Google's behavior should be seen in a context in which managing and altering the popular understanding of reality has long been at the center of totalitarian government behavior. When Joseph Stalin died in 1953, his key lieutenant, Lavrentiy Beria, lost favor and, in the spirit of Stalinism, was executed. The keepers of the Soviet Encyclopedia, mindful of their political duties, "erased" Beria from the books, sending owners a four-page spread on the Bering Sea and Admiral Bering to replace the lavish portrait of Beria. AI can rewrite reality much more effectively, requiring neither paper nor scissors.

The Legal and Regulatory Landscape around AI

In his book *How Will You Measure Your Life?*, Harvard Business School professor Clayton Christensen notes that none of his HBS classmates *intended* to go to prison when they graduated from business school. However, one of those classmates was Jeffrey Skilling, the former CEO of Enron, who went to prison for his role in that company's scandal. While Christensen can offer only speculation for Skilling's specific circumstances, the general theory he offers to the rest of us who would like to avoid a similar fate revolves around how we handle mundane everyday decisions.

> Most of us think that the important ethical decisions in our lives will be delivered with a blinking red neon sign: CAUTION: IMPORTANT DECISION AHEAD. . . The problem is life seldom works that way. It comes with no warning signs. Instead, most of us will face a series of small, everyday decisions that rarely seem like they have high stakes attached. But over time, they can play out far more dramatically.

Data science projects are replete with myriad mundane decisions just like the ones that Christensen alludes to. Which variables should we include in the training dataset? How will we calculate the performance of the model relative to known baselines? Which algorithms should we test for this particular problem?

What should we include in documentation regarding our assumptions? There are no flashing red neon signs to alert us when an important ethical question will arise in our projects, and sometimes those decisions carry legal consequences.

If ethics establish the maximal standard for our behavior, the law establishes the floor.[4] While the technical aspects of data science training are becoming increasingly formalized, most practitioners of data science have little to no education in the law. Complicating matters further is the fact that the legal and regulatory landscape around data science and AI are dynamic and not standardized across localities. As public opprobrium around the harms of these methods begins to result in regulatory action, data science practitioners may soon find themselves bound by a complex web of geographically varying laws and/or regulations where none existed before.

While we cannot provide legal advice, we can provide a guide to the categories of the legal landscape that a data science project might encounter.

1. At the most general level, there's the overarching principle that "if it's illegal for you as a human, it's illegal for an algorithm." This tends to be most true in industries that already have a high degree of preexisting regulation (e.g., financial services).

2. At the next level, there are city, state, national, and supranational laws (e.g., the California Consumer Privacy Act [CCPA], Australia's Privacy Act of 1988, and the EU's General Data Protection Regulation [GDPR]) that regulate the use of data related to citizens or individuals. This includes municipal facial recognition bans in localities like San Francisco, California, and Portland, Oregon.

3. At the administrative level, there are regulations and guidance either to implement laws or to address AI issues in the absence of laws (e.g., the US Defense Department's "Five AI Principles.")

4. In the absence of specific laws or regulations, law enforcement authorities and judges can still invoke the provisions of nonspecific laws or common law, so the risks of working in new areas like AI may not be fully defined until precedents are set. There may also be civil liability for the consequences of AI, e.g., medical malpractice for AI diagnosis or product liability for harms caused by the AI embedded in products. Penalties from civil lawsuits need not involve criminal violations, but can be substantial.

These laws and regulations operate in three main arenas.

- Consumer privacy and the ownership and control of data
- Bias and unfairness that may result from the deployment of algorithms
- Rights to explanation and appeal/recourse

---

[4] See ethics.org.au/ethics-morality-law-whats-the-difference / from the Ethics Center for a discussion of the differences between ethics and the law.

In this section, we provide a brief overview of laws and regulations that govern data and AI. As shown in Figure 3.4, we begin by looking at industries that already have laws and regulations on the books governing AI in practice. We then move out one horizon to consider regulations that have recently come into effect to provide additional safeguards to consumers, particularly around data privacy. Finally, we advance to the frontier and summarize emerging trends in AI law to help you as a practitioner or manager to gain a greater appreciation for the professionalization of our field around the globe in the form of legal standards for behavior.

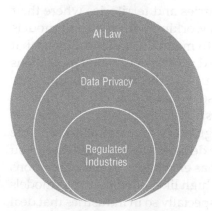

Figure 3.4: The nested categories of laws related to AI

Ignorance Is No Defense: AI in the Context of Existing Law and Policy

Although AI technology has begun performing tasks with near-human or super-human skill, it is not above the law where such laws may apply. If an AI or ML system takes an action that is illegal or recommends an illegal action that is subsequently taken by a human, that is a violation of the law. For example, the Federal Trade Commission (FTC) has prosecuted numerous companies for violations of the Fair Credit Reporting Act of 1970 for discrimination by automated decision-making systems.[5] We have already highlighted some extreme examples of this earlier in the chapter within cases where the form of AI was working as intended, yet working toward a goal that was actively harmful. While much press is devoted to new frontiers of AI application that may lack laws or regulations (such as facial recognition systems), there are some domains where laws already exist and provide means of redress.

---

[5] For a good summary, check out www.ftc.gov/news-events/blogs/business-blog/2020/04/using-artificial-intelligence-algorithms.

For example, some industries that have long leveraged algorithmic decision-making, such as financial services in the Equal Credit Opportunity Act and software-based medical devices, are subject to laws and regulations that extend to algorithmic/quantitative decision-making to ensure transparency and fairness in their applications. For example, in banking, it is illegal in the United States to deny credit to a customer on the basis of their sex, race, or ethnicity. This is true regardless of how the loan decision is made, and banks currently have highly developed internal frameworks for auditing their own models (AI or otherwise) for fairness to ensure compliance with existing regulations. Companies (and by extension their data scientists and modelers) who create algorithms in these industries are subject to the laws of the countries and territories where their models are applied. Similarly, data scientists working with data and models in a classified environment are still required to maintain classification of that information. So, while the technology behind AI may be new, many protections already exist against its criminal or negligent uses in the form of existing laws and regulations in industries where the misuse would follow old patterns.

What does this mean for data science practitioners? Basically, algorithmic decisions are subject to the same or greater degree of regulatory coverage as those made by humans or previously existing quantitative decision support systems. If you are working as a data scientist in a field that has existing laws and regulations that are meant to protect consumers, there is a high likelihood that your models may already be subject to regulation. This is especially so in industries that deal with sensitive personal information, such as medicine, banking, and insurance. In those cases, you might be required to show the basis for an algorithm's decisions, which means an interpretable model must be used.

A Finger in the Dam: Data Rights, Data Privacy, and Consumer Protection Regulations

Apart from those in already regulated industries, up to the beginning of the twenty-first century, there were few if any laws or rules that applied to businesses relying on access to personal information. Personal data were increasingly monetized by digital marketers, internet service providers (ISPs), and search and social media companies.

Concerns over the aggregation, use/misuse, and sale of personal data and information by corporations led in the latter part of the 2010s to significant attention from international lawmakers. This was particularly true in Europe, where citizens were guaranteed an explicit right to privacy by law (Article 8 of the Charter of Fundamental Rights of the European Union). It was clear that the impacts of the internet economy had rapidly outstripped any nascent protections that were put in place at its founding. As the costs of large-scale data breaches at companies such as Adobe, Equifax, and LinkedIn and rising identity theft became apparent, these costs were also being borne primarily by consumers.[6] Lawmakers recognized that regulation may be required to ensure adequate protection of consumer information and sufficient punishment for a failure to safeguard sensitive data.

The most prominent and influential of the regulations to emerge from this period was the General Data Protection Regulations of the European Union (GDPR). Adopted in 2016, the GDPR went into effect in August 2018. The EU enacted GDPR in line with the Right to Privacy enshrined in the 1950 European Convention of Human Rights, one of the founding documents of the supranational union. GDPR provide sweeping, albeit generic, protections to European citizens including (but not limited to): a right to "be forgotten" in terms of online presence, as well as a requirement that any technology companies provide mechanisms by which EU citizens can have their data removed entirely from online platforms.

Because the GDPR were one of the first and most comprehensive frameworks for data regulation, these regulations have become an archetype for other consumer data protection laws and regulations at US state levels. For example, the California Consumer Protection Act (CCPA) was inspired by GDPR, especially in the degree and manner by which personal data are pseudonymized.[7] As of September 2020, other states like Massachusetts and Oregon are considering or enacting laws similar to CCPA for their citizens.

At the national level, Canada enacted its Personal Information Protection and Electronic Documents Act (PIPEDA), which is broadly similar to CCPA in terms of who is protected, what rights they hold to their own data, and the responsibility of businesses that transact in personal information. The influence of GDPR has also spread to non-Western countries of the world that are all too often left out of the tech policy conversation. In Africa, Kenya recently passed its own data protection laws as inspired by the GDPR mold. Brazil's General Law for the Protection of Data (Lei Geral de Proteção de Dados [LGPD]) went into effect in August 2020 and is heavily influenced by GDPR. Southeast Asian nations have a patchwork of data protection regulations, including comprehensive GDPR-like regulations planned in Indonesia and Vietnam. In the last 10 years, the online world has gone from largely unregulated to some form of regulation in most of the world.

What does this mean for data science practitioners? Regulations like GDPR have raised real questions about what data can and cannot be rightfully included in a model by data scientists. For example, if a person has requested that their

---

[6] See the following link for further details: www.csoonline.com/article/2130877/the-biggest-data-breaches-of-the-21st-century.html),

[7] There are key differences between the CCPA and GDPR in who is protected under the law and who is regulated by it; see the handy comparison chart at www.bakerlaw.com/webfiles/Privacy/2018/Articles/CCPA-GDPR-Chart.pdf.

data be forgotten, must a model trained using that person's information now be retrained? According to GDPR, the answer is likely yes, given restrictions not just on the storage of personal information but also its processing. Other regulations like CCPA do not necessarily extend to the analysis and processing of personal information, but focus primarily on levying penalties against companies that fail to adequately safeguard consumer data. Regardless, as data residency and localization laws have begun to build upon the frameworks laid by GDPR and other data privacy regulations, data scientists must be careful whose data they are accessing, and when and how, when building training datasets.[8] This is not just a question of ethical transparency or fairness, but also may increasingly be a question of law, depending on where those data reside.

Trends in Emerging Law and Policy Related to AI

At a recent panel on Data and Privacy at the University of Virginia, one of the authors was asked by students from the School of Engineering and Applied Sciences and the recently formed School of Data Science what he saw as being the most important development in AI in the next five years. The response was quick and, at least from the perspective of the students, unexpected: *regulation*. While it's important to remain abreast of the state of technical art in a field like AI or machine learning, the direction that development takes can be significantly influenced by laws or regulations that make further advancement along a particular path illegal. Facial recognition technology seemed like a solid technological bet as a business 18 months ago; now, companies that made that bet are seeing Dr. Hyde emerge from the laboratory in the cellar.

The advanced technological nature of AI means that large information asymmetries exist between developers/producers of AI and the general public. As in other professional fields, such as medicine, law, and finance, this asymmetry can create a significantly increased potential for harm. As with data privacy issues, governments around the world are moving at different rates to respond to the potential legal issues posed by AI with respect to their citizens. If regulation is to govern the data—the raw field material—by which AI algorithms are trained, so must it also govern the more powerful technologies built on that data.

What is distinct about potential AI laws from the two aforementioned categories of law in this chapter is that governments, in addition to being both the prime customers and adopters for AI, are also charged with being responsible for ensuring the appropriate and ethical use of the technology by their citizens. The end result for data scientists is that the legal and regulatory landscape around

---

[8] See: www.mcafee.com/blogs/enterprise/data-security/data-residency-a-concept-not-found-in-the-gdpr/ for more information.

AI is likely to become an increasingly dynamic environment as governments attempt to balance their deepening investments in AI with the needs of their civil societies. Because of the highly dynamic nature of the AI legal landscape, we focus here on emerging trends, rather than specific or forecasted laws.

Perhaps no country in the world is as broadly concerned with the legal and ethical ramifications of AI as Australia. As early as 2004, Australia had set out 27 best-practice principles for the application of automated decision-making to questions of administrative law to ensure transparency and fairness in adoption. More recently, an active and public debate around automated decision-making in government has arisen as a consequence of the "robodebt" scandal.[9] The Australian government adopted a machine learning technology to validate social welfare payments and assess individuals who had collected more than they were due, only to discover that the system reinforced deep and systemic biases, particularly against minorities. Following this embarrassing deployment of machine learning, legal scholars in Australia began calling for more comprehensive protections against the misuse of AI. The Law Council of Australia has proposed an ethical framework for the development and implementation of AI, along with processes to support implementation.

Elsewhere, there is ongoing discussion and debate about AI ethics and draft legislation. In Europe, serious questions are being raised about the proper use of algorithms in government and assuring the public a right to due process. The European Commission's (EC) recent whitepaper on AI highlighted specifically that the opaque nature by which AI algorithms arrive at decisions poses unique risks to ensuring their fair and just application. Simultaneously, the EC recognizes that any law regulating AI must be sufficiently flexible to encompass future innovation in the rapidly evolving technical domain.

In the United States, federal executive agencies are issuing guidelines for the use of AI in advance of expected laws (e.g., the DoD's Ethical AI Principles). Legislation has also been proposed on the floor of Congress (specifically, the Algorithmic Accountability Act of 2019) that would require companies as well as federal agencies to assess the potential impacts of their AI algorithms on citizens and consumers.

What does this mean for data science practitioners? Industry-specific regulations and privacy rules may not be created specifically with AI in mind but do impinge on the work of data scientists. In some industries, e.g., healthcare, employers may require data scientists to at least be familiar with these industry-specific regulations. Laws specifically aimed at governing AI or other algorithmic decision-making systems, by contrast, lie at the core of data science. Depending on where data scientists work or where their algorithms may be deployed, governments are increasingly looking at whom to hold accountable for the outcomes of AI

---

[9] Readers interested in learning more about robodebt should read: pursuit.unimelb.edu .au/articles/what-is-the-law-when-ai-makes-the-decisions.

models and how. This is a highly dynamic area with significant geographic variability. Governments, to some extent, have been prevaricating or avoiding laws and regulations that would have a hard and specific impact on the practice of AI. Governmental actions have focused more on issuing ethical principles and guidelines. With the legal landscape less than clear, sometimes the only thing data scientists can do is to minimize the harm caused by their own actions. This leaves it to data scientists and broader project teams to translate those ethical principles and guidelines into actual procedural and technical steps (which is why we need the tools presented in this book). Most recently, these efforts have centered on optimizing models to meet specific fairness metrics.

NOTE BIAS, FAIRNESS, AND UNFAIRNESS   What are the definitions of bias and unfairness from a legal standpoint? One is tempted to say that bias and unfairness are self-evident. The problem, though, is that different people see bias and unfairness differently.

Nearly everyone would agree that a social club with an explicit prohibition against membership for certain religious groups shows bias. Now, change the situation slightly—suppose there's no explicit prohibition, but the implicit preferences of the membership committee result in the same groups being excluded? Most people would still contend the club is biased. Consider next an engineering college that selects the highest-scoring applicants for an incoming class, and the result is an overrepresentation of students from affluent families. Some might contend that the selection process itself is implicitly biased, perhaps as a result of a narrow focus on criteria (like test scores and extracurriculars) where high-income groups have more opportunities. Suppose now the selection process is a random selection instead of score-based, and owing to an imbalance in who applies, there's still an overrepresentation of high-income students being admitted. Some schools consider the lack of diversity resulting from these issues to be a bias problem, albeit of society as a whole, and undertake its correction. Others then contend that this correction itself is a form of bias.

Such questions are an unending source of debate in society and within the legal profession itself. Legal scholars Ronald Dworkin and Richard Posner have each written 500-page tomes on the subject of equality and rights, from different perspectives, with each coming to differing conclusions. We will not attempt to contribute to this debate. Each organization must at least grapple with the question and come to its own judgments, and data scientists must think for themselves on the matter. In this book, though, we bring forth tools that can be used to help control the development and deployment of AI projects, not only bringing them into compliance with legal and regulatory requirements but also aligning them with the ethical principles of the organization or the individual.

Similarly, there is little consensus on what constitutes (nonstatistical) bias and fairness within a data science context. In Chapter 7, we will go more into the specific metrics that have been proposed to quantify fairness. However, it will suffice for now to say that fairness is subjective and depends on the context of the modeling task at hand.

Summary

In summary, the legal and regulatory landscape around data science and AI is as diverse and varied as the myriad applications of these technical disciplines themselves. In certain contexts, if it would be illegal for you as a person, it's illegal for an AI algorithm as well. This is most clearly the case in regulated industries like finance or healthcare's medical devices. Outside of industries with high degrees of extant regulation, increased data privacy and security legislation and regulation are leading to real penalties (including fines and jail time) for the misuse of data. However, the very definition of that misuse is in flux, as new laws come into effect. Finally, AI is a powerful tool. The general public is wary of it. Consequently, governments are responding, and laws are or will be changing quickly in the near future (at least as fast as the law changes). Remember, wherever you are and in whatever field you may practice, the law is only the floor. Aspire and adhere to a higher ethical standard, and no laws, regardless of how dynamic the legal landscape around AI is, should oppose your success.

The Ethical Data Science Process

In This Part

Chapter 4: The Responsible Data Science Framework
Chapter 5: Model Interpretability: The What and the Why

The Responsible Data Science Framework

Rather than being confined to some dystopian sci-fi future, the harms of AI methods (and the older statistical methods that gave rise to them) existed in the past and exist in the present. Such harms to personal rights, livelihoods, and lives result from data scientists not understanding their data, their model, or the broader societal context in which their model operates. After spending the previous chapter discussing *what* can go wrong when AI methods veer off track, we now must develop an understanding of *why* AI so often goes astray if we want to avoid causing harm ourselves.

In this chapter, we identify motivations in data science that are associated with creating harmful AI. These motivations will be grounded in discussions around real-world examples of facial recognition technology gone wrong to give us an intuition of what characteristics ought to be encompassed within a responsible data science framework. Afterward, we consider how researchers, corporations, and governments have responded to the AI harms with proposals to make AI more transparent, accountable, and ethical. Finally, we propose a unifying framework for responsible data science that provides an actionable, consistent framework for readers to follow within their own AI projects.

Why We Keep Building Harmful AI

By now, we have seen that the absence of harmful intentions alone is not enough to prevent models from producing harmful predictions. If we want to begin combatting the production of harmful models within our own work, we first must be more conscious of the conditions that make their creation more likely. We have found three motivations to be indicative of situations where incorrect, if not downright harmful, models are more likely to be produced.

Misguided Need for Cutting-Edge Models

Media coverage, corporate press releases, and academic research all give the impression that experimenting in modern data science is synonymous with using cutting-edge neural networks. While neural-network approaches are necessary for completing certain image analysis or natural language processing (NLP)–related tasks, they are often overkill for tabular data and prone to overfitting. Relative to building traditional intrinsically interpretable models or black-box models, building useful neural networks requires notably more data, specialized software knowledge, and greater computing resources. Similar restrictions apply to pretrained neural networks or networks built on transfer learning. Though both methods reduce computational resource needs for using neural networks, they still tend to be harder to implement than other black-box methods, while only achieving marginal increases in predictive performance.

Excessive Focus on Predictive Performance

Progress in data science is measured primarily by improvements in the state-of-the-art (SOTA) prediction performance for a task. And why shouldn't this be the case? After all, groups that beat the current SOTA metric for a computer vision or NLP benchmark are showered with positive media coverage and other advantages.[1] Moreover, predictive performance matters because modeling harms *are* often the result of incorrect predictions. For example, it would be highly dangerous if a model meant to estimate a child's risk of abuse within their home consistently underpredicted that abuse. Most recommendations for such cases center around technical interventions to increase the model's predictive performance. This logic seems sound enough initially—improving the model's predictive performance ought to reduce the amount of incorrect

---

[1] Users interested in tracking the SOTA performance for common modeling tasks can visit paperswithcode.com/sota and sotabench.com.

predictions and the harm that they cause as a result. Why shouldn't everyone follow suit and focus all their efforts on maximizing predictive performance for every modeling task?

Unfortunately, reality is often more complicated. Focusing solely on maximizing predictive performance can aggravate any of the following behaviors:

■ **Overconfidence due to relying on a single aggregate performance metric:** Optimizing for a single metric of interest may not lead to an optimal model. Consider an unbalanced binary classification task, such as predicting whether a particular transaction is fraudulent or legitimate. Because fraudulent transactions are very uncommon (5% or less of all transactions), we could easily reach high levels of accuracy or sensitivity by predicting that every transaction is legitimate. If we are only paying attention to these metrics, we might even think that we have found a good model! Avoiding issues like this begins with considering multiple performance metrics that are appropriate for our task rather than a single one-size-fits-all metric across all tasks.

■ **Discounting of between-group differences:** Even if we are tracking more than one performance metric (or the appropriate single metric), an improvement in a model's overall performance can mask drops in performance for certain groups of observations. When dealing with people, as in the earlier child-abuse risk example, this might mean that an improvement in estimating the risk of abuse for a majority group, for example, inner-city children, masks a dangerous increase in error for rural children. When group information is available in a prediction task, the differences in performance between groups should always be compared to avoid similar situations.

■ **Ignoring the relative importance of some observations:** Business pressures or societal factors might make correct predictions for certain observations more important than correct predictions for other observations. This relative importance is not a characteristic commonly encoded in datasets. It goes beyond looking at multiple performance metrics or differences in performance across groups. To explain, consider a case where a subscription snack company wants to create a model to determine the best location to host an event and maximize revenue from new subscriptions. Should the model simply predict the location with the most foot traffic and (likely) highest number of customer interactions? This option might seem reasonable if we assume that the product appeals equally to a wide range of demographics. However, assume that the company knows that their snacks are keto-friendly, making them substantially more appealing to an audience of gym goers and other highly active individuals. The company may be better off choosing a location with less foot traffic overall but with a higher number of people who fit this demographic. For this snack company, observations from the active group are relatively more important than those from other demographic groups. A tabular dataset typically would not convey this information.

Ease of Access and the Curse of Simplicity

Building a functioning model in 2020 requires nothing more than internet access and a computer. Docker-based virtualization platforms like Binder and Google Collaboratory allow anyone with internet access to click a link and, with no other setup, remotely train or execute state-of-the-art models using Python or R. If that's too much effort, people can source pretrained models directly from technology companies like Amazon or Microsoft, rather than building one of their own. Tools like Google's AutoML even give users the ability to supply a dataset and leave the rest of the model fitting, tuning, and performance metric calculation to software. On the one hand, the increasing availability of these tools is undoubtedly a good thing. They have greatly improved the ease of performing data science and have lowered the barriers for breaking into the field, especially for those located outside of the United States or those who cannot afford a traditional education.

Unfortunately, the ease of use allowed for by these tools often operates at odds with the need to understand how a model works and consider whether it has the potential to do harm. Individuals or organizations new to using AI are much more likely to find resources showing how easy AI is to use, rather than resources teaching about how hard it is to get right. Abstracting away details about the underlying model and data from the user is useful, as long as the user is generally aware of what their software is doing behind the scenes. However, giving underprepared users a click-to-run AI solution that "solves" all of their complex business or organizational problems is a recipe for unanticipated harm—the "curse of simplicity."

The Common Cause

Working through each of the previous three motivations forces us to consider how factors beyond those addressed by traditional data science frameworks, such as the Cross-Industry Standard Process for Data Mining (CRISP-DM; see Figure 4.1) or Microsoft's Team Data Science Process (TDSP) affect our models.

These frameworks present the modeling process as nothing more than posing a question and gathering data, followed by building, tuning, and deploying a model. By not considering factors beyond those encoded directly in the dataset

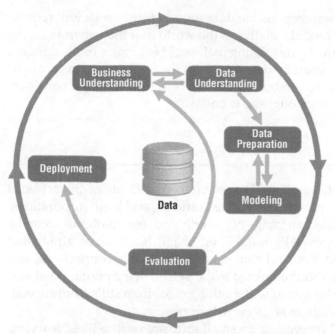

Figure 4.1: A diagram depicting a typical CRISP-DM process

Source: `en.wikipedia.org/wiki/Cross-industry_standard_process_for_data_mining#/`
`media/File:CRISP-DM_Process_Diagram.png`

or in the initial definition of the modeling task, both frameworks force models to live in a vacuum—one where technical approaches alone are enough to prevent, diagnose, and fix any issues that arise within the modeling process. This lack of consideration for the broader real-world context that a model operates in, and the implicit assumption that all information relevant to a modeling task can be captured within the technical aspects of the modeling process, is the primary cause for why people keep building harmful AI models.

We are far from the first people to note that AI is too often used as a blunt technical solution for complex social issues. Researchers across academia and industry, including Ruha Benjamin, Safiya Noble, Timnit Gebru, Rediet Abebe, Joy Buolamwini, Abeba Birhane, Cathy O'Neil, Meredith Broussard, Kate Crawford, Megan Mitchell, Emily Denton, Solon Barocas, Deborah Raji, Rumman Chowdhury, Rachel Thomas, William Isaac, Shakir Mohamed, and Irene Chen (among many others), have written about how inclusivity, power, and participatory design approaches are too often ignored by data science practitioners.[2]

---

[2] Works from each of these researchers are referenced either in this book or in the resources.pdf file within the repositories at www.wiley.com/go/responsibledatascience or www.github.com/Gflemin/responsibledatascience.

Clearly, building our own responsible data science framework will require us to first understand our models relative to the world that they operate in. We will start exploring this now by discussing real-world examples of the dangers of facial recognition technology. By engaging with the different harms brought about by these examples, we can build our own intuitions of what considerations responsible data science ought to encompass.

The Face Thieves

In 2016, a company called Clearview AI began marketing a state-of-the-art facial recognition service to law enforcement, elected officials, and large corporations. The pitch was simple: upload an image of anyone, and, in a matter of seconds, find other images in Clearview AI's multibillion-image database containing that person. The searcher could then find names, addresses, social connections, and all manner of other information connected to the person in the photo. Dead-end criminal cases could now be solved with nothing more than stills from surveillance camera footage or shots of large crowds of people.

How was this possible? Where could a small software startup like Clearview AI have obtained all its images? After all, the main difficulty in building a facial recognition model isn't actually designing the model itself but rather "teaching" the algorithm to identify a diverse set of faces. While there are a number of popular publicly available facial recognition datasets, like the Celeb-Faces Attributes dataset (CelebA) and Google Facial Expression Comparison datasets, the vast majority of these datasets are released for academic use only. Relative to using one of these datasets, creating a purpose-built facial recognition dataset requires massive investments of time and money.

Clearview AI did not have access to these resources. Instead, it resorted to scraping (downloading via algorithm) millions of people's information from all over the internet. This scraping was probably an outright violation of the hosts' terms of service. The app that Cambridge Analytica used to collect Facebook data was a similar case. Facebook claimed that collecting data not just from the app user but from the user's friends was a violation of its terms of service (and yet Facebook made it possible to obtain that data). Scraping like this is widespread and legally murky. Perhaps those doing the scraping figure that if information is published on the internet, it is freely available to use. Or perhaps they obtain permission under false pretenses, which includes "lies by omission" (e.g., not disclosing the full story). Or perhaps the terms of service are not adequately spelled out. In any case, the admittedly difficult standard to which the responsible data scientist should aspire is to consider the following question: "Would the owner and the subject of the data be comfortable with my projected use of the data?" If the answer is likely no, then a wider discussion with colleagues, stakeholders, and, perhaps, attorneys is in order.

Using data from user accounts on social networks such as Twitter, Facebook, and Instagram, Clearview AI built a database containing more than three billion images of faces tagged with names. Despite numerous cease-and-desist orders from the social media companies affected, Clearview AI has continued to scrape their data. Nobody outside of the Clearview AI and an unidentified "independent panel of experts" has been able to validate how the facial recognition algorithm works, ensure that it's accurate, or conduct other tests on it.

Today, Clearview AI's service is still actively used by US law enforcement agencies. Though the company states that it no longer sells its service to customers outside of law enforcement, these restrictions apply only to its domestic market within the United States. We have no way of knowing whether this powerful facial recognition technology is being used abroad by private corporations, oppressive governments, or malicious entities.

An Anatomy of Modeling Harms

The Clearview AI example is undoubtedly problematic; however, we need to disentangle the many reasons why. We can use the diagram in Figure 4.2 as a useful device to develop an understanding of the "anatomy" of modeling harms in a way that approximately maps to the stages in a modeling pipeline. Each stage reveals how information about the world is shaped, augmented, or ignored.

The different stages of the telescope in Figure 4.2 represent, in simplified form, the following:

- **The World:** All of the information in the real world that might be relevant to the modeling task. Recording all the relevant information about the real world as data for a modeling task is often impossible, necessitating some form of sampling.

- **Data:** Certain facts about the world that have been encoded to become suitable for modeling.

- **Models:** Algorithms that leverage statistics and mathematics to find and describe relationships among a set of input data.

- **Model interpretability:** A state whereby the explanations produced by a model are sufficient for humans to meaningfully understand how and why the model makes its predictions.

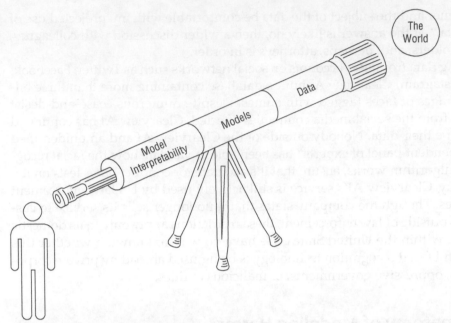

Figure 4.2: Visualizing an information flow diagram as a person using a compound telescope to see details of a far-off world; the different stages of the telescope are analogous to the different stages of the modeling process.

Just as telescopes focus, reflect, and bend light to enable us to see a far-off object, modeling pipelines, through data and algorithms rather than light and lenses, focus information about the real world into a form that humans can utilize (if not fully understand). While these intermediate changes to information from the real world are necessary, they often manifest as harmful predictions because some critical factor is distorted, ignored, or discarded. By becoming more cognizant of how information is changed or lost within each stage of this process, we can better understand how to avoid making dangerous assumptions about our modeling pipelines in practice. Let's examine the Clearview AI example, and facial recognition more generally, in the context of the diagram in Figure 4.2. At each stage, we record takeaways that we will later integrate into our final responsible data science framework.

The World: Context Matters for Modeling

The capabilities of AI have evolved at lightning speed. In the last two years alone, cutting-edge AI approaches have, for the first time, beaten medical professionals at successfully diagnosing conditions in medical images, surpassed human reading comprehension, and gained the ability to produce photorealistic images of imaginary animals and people (as shown in Figure 4.3).

Figure 4.3: Four handpicked examples of photorealistic imaginary faces generated by Nvidia's StyleGAN2 in 2019

However, the ability of an AI approach to solve a task is not sufficient justification for solving that task using AI. Some tasks are so ethically fraught due to real-world circumstances that even an extremely accurate model can cause great harm. To think otherwise is a prime example of "techno-chauvinism."[3]

For example, consider the rollout of surveillance cameras in public locations to automatically scan the faces of all individuals within an area in search of wanted individuals. As of 2020, numerous UK localities have begun to employ these devices. For police, these cameras represent a real advance in crime-solving: the difficult and often fruitless work of tracking down criminals is now entirely automated. All the officers need do is wait for an alert that a match was made. Obviously, incorrect facial matches can inconvenience or harm the people who are matched. To be clear, these false positives often happen, with independent reviewers finding that less than 20% of matches made end up being true positives. However, even a perfectly accurate camera of this sort could be greatly harmful. If people have had their faces included in this system as a result of an

---

[3] Term coined by Meredith Broussard in her book *Artificial Unintelligence* (mitpress.mit .edu/books/artificial-unintelligence).

unjust criminal charge, these cameras would actually serve to magnify injustices and further abuse. If placed in the hands of authoritarian or nationalist governments, they could become an excellent tool for suppression of dissent or for ethnic oppression.

In the past few years, we have seen how this transition can occur. Recall the example in Chapter 1, "Responsible Data Science," of researchers developing a facial recognition algorithm to predict criminality from faces. The authors of that study claimed it was simply an academic exercise designed to advance the state of knowledge. Regardless of any "pure academic intentions" or high accuracy metrics achieved, such work contributes to the long history of connections between racial phrenology, eugenics, and statistics by lending an air of scientific legitimacy to dangerous pseudoscience. In fact, the *New York Times* reports that the Chinese government has extended *individual* facial recognition to AI-enabled *racial profiling* in support of its campaign against the Uighur minority.

> **The facial recognition technology, which is integrated into China's rapidly expanding networks of surveillance cameras, looks exclusively for Uighurs based on their appearance and keeps records of their comings and goings for search and review. The practice makes China a pioneer in applying next-generation technology to watch its people, potentially ushering in a new era of automated racism.**
>
> *NY Times,* "One Month, 500,000 Face Scans: How China Is Using A.I. to Profile a Minority," *April 14, 2020,* www.nytimes.com/2019/04/14/technology/china-surveillance-artificial-intelligence-racial-profiling.html

If we consider only the technical aspects of how AI should be built, we ignore all of the ways that our models might worsen unjust circumstances that already exist in the real world. Even if everything is done correctly from a technical perspective, anyone, including parties outside the development team, can appropriate and weaponize a perfectly accurate model's predictions to cause harm.[4]

Despite the high likelihood of false positives, matches produced by facial recognition software have already been used as the sole evidence for making arrests in the United States. In 2020, reports broke of three arrests made based on facial recognition matches alone—the first in US history.[5] Each of the men arrested were quickly found innocent of the crimes committed due to falsely being matched with a face image. Whether the specific facial recognition software

---

[4] Readers interested in learning more about cases of data and/or models being reappropriated for harmful purposes should watch this video from Lesson 4.1 of Rachel Thomas's data ethics course: https://ethics.fast.ai/videos/?lesson=4.

[5] Two of these cases are discussed in this article from the *Detroit Free Press:* www.freep.com/story/news/local/michigan/detroit/2020/07/10/facial-recognition-detroit-michael-oliver-robert-williams/5392166002/.

used was provided by Clearview AI or some other company, the fact remains that this particular application of facial recognition would be considered wrong by most people.

Takeaways

- Technical solutions are not a panacea for social problems.
- Real-world contexts can make even accurate models harmful.
- Technology developed for an innocent purpose can later be abused in a different context.

The Data: Representation Is Everything

Far more information exists in the world than can be recorded as data, which necessitates that we carefully choose what information becomes recorded as data for modeling. If the goal is to create a model that predicts well on new data (rather than just explaining the available data), then choosing a diverse representative dataset becomes even more important. After all, a model can only generalize well to new data if the new data is similar enough to the data on which the model was trained and validated. For example, a model trained to predict the expected total career earnings of a child in Denmark over the course of their life would likely fail to accurately predict the expected career earnings of a child in Yemen. Similarly, a recurrent neural network (RNN) trained only to synthesize speech from English text (as in shown Figure 4.4) would fail miserably if it were made to synthesize speech from texts written using simplified or traditional Chinese characters.

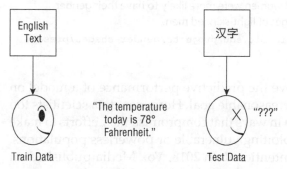

Figure 4.4: Example of how a speech synthesis model trained only on English text-to-speech examples would fail in generating speech for Chinese text examples

Real-world examples of train-test data mismatches are both more subtle and more harmful. In 2016, Joy Buolamwini, then a graduate student at MIT, found that her robot consistently failed to recognize her dark-skinned face. Wearing a white mask solved the problem and the robot began to recognize her. Her personal encounter with algorithmic bias kicked off her own research into the subject, culminating in the publishing of her master's thesis, "Gender Shades," investigating gender and racial bias within facial recognition.[6] This project revealed that facial recognition algorithms being sold by Microsoft, IBM, and Face++ were 11.8% to 19.2% more likely to misclassify the gender of a darker-skinned face than a lighter-skinned one. This error percentage doubled to anywhere between 20.8% and 34.4% when the algorithm predicted the gender of darker-skinned females. The reason? The model was trained on too little data from certain groups, specifically individuals with darker skin. After continued pressure from Joy Buolamwini, Deborah Raji, and Congress, each of the three companies identified in the study have since greatly expanded their training datasets and greatly reduced these gaps in predictive performance. Figure 4.5 shows an image from the Gender Shades project that depicts the difference in error rates between dark-skinned women and light-skinned men for the IBM facial recognition model.

Figure 4.5: Error rate difference between darker-skinned women and lighter-skinned men for the IBM model. Images of darker-skinned women were more likely to have their gender misclassified 34.4% more often than images of light-skinned men.

Source: The Gender Shades Press Kit (www.media.mit.edu/projects/gender-shades/press-kit/). License: CC BY

Acquiring more data to improve the predictive performance of a model on high-error subsets of the data is a reasonable goal. However, data scientists too often go about gathering new data in ways that compromise their efforts to make a fair and responsible model, exploiting vulnerable or powerless populations. Sometimes, this exploitation is intentional: In 2018, Vox Media published an article stating that it found that there are more than 3,000 children's game apps that track "clicks, searches, purchases, and sometimes geographic information as you move through various apps." The games themselves, however engaging,

---

[6] While "Gender Shades" encompasses a wide variety of materials, we specifically recommend that interested readers scroll through the project overview to get a quick idea of its results: gendershades.org/overview.html.

are incidental to the main purpose of the apps, which is data gathering. Other times, the ethical missteps in pursuit of data are unwitting, but nonetheless harmful. The Cambridge Analytic team that built an app to scrape Facebook ended up in the midst of a major scandal when its data was put to use in service of manipulative promotional efforts on behalf of populist political causes. One of the developers claimed that he thought he was working on a legitimate social-science survey. Other examples abound, including those from major tech companies.

- In 2019, the *New York Daily News* reported that Google contractors gathering data for Google's upcoming Pixel 4 phone targeted homeless black individuals for face scans by offering $5 gift cards as incentives.

- In 2019, Techcrunch.com reported that Facebook, via its "Facebook Research" smartphone application, had been offering younger users $20 per month to gain access to their message history, apps used, and online order histories.

If anything, Clearview AI's data collection practices are even more egregious than either of these examples, where consent was at least nominally respected. As of 2020, there is no way of knowing whether your images are on Clearview's servers, and there is no process to request that any specific images be removed. This is far from being a responsible data acquisition process, where data subjects are included only after providing informed consent and are given the opportunity to remove themselves from the dataset if desired.

Takeaways

- Ensure that training data is representative of the test data (or real world).

- When gathering data, be careful not to exploit information asymmetry.

- Be transparent with users about how and why their data are collected.

The Model: Garbage In, Danger Out

Models solve specific well-defined tasks on some small part of the real world. However, models exist separately from the real world and cannot learn directly from it. Instead, they rely on data, usually gathered at least in part by humans, to make any predictions about how the world behaves. Once data gathering is complete, data scientists are inclined to rest easy, knowing that the vast majority of their work is done and now in the hands of a capable model. After all, the algorithmic prowess of modern black-box modeling methods like random forest or XGBoost can easily reach reasonable thresholds of predictive performance with minimal tuning. Once the best performing model is deployed, can't we go ahead and say "job well done"?

Alarm bells ought to have been going off before you finished reading the previous paragraph. Nowhere in the previously outlined scenario did we consider the ethical consequences of deploying a model in a real-world context or check the dataset for representativeness. The model is now fully primed to amplify any biases that are present in the data and wreak havoc in the real-world context that we ignored. We could very well be feeding garbage into our model, endangering our clients, users, and/or data subjects with the bad results that it produces.

Not testing the datasets for bias could lead to a "Gender Shades" situation wherein the model, despite achieving high performance in the aggregate, performs notably worse for important subgroups. This is especially relevant for the Clearview AI example. With only Clearview AI's vague statements of excellent accuracy to go on, it seems likely that its algorithm would have issues identifying the gender of darker-skinned feminine faces similar to those identified in "Gender Shades." It's entirely possible that Clearview AI does not know this, as they haven't indicated that they have made any effort to interpret the inner workings of their black-box facial recognition model or test whether it unfairly targets certain demographic groups. Other data issues were likely in play as well. For example, the founder of Clearview AI complained in an interview that the sheer number of surveillance camera images in their database reduces their model's ability to properly identify images that are taken head-on. Again, even if this issue were fixed and the Clearview AI model became perfectly accurate, the circumstances where it's used in the real world would mean that it continues to cause harm.

Takeaways

- Good models depend on responsibly acquired, representative data and well-defined tasks that have a low chance of causing harm within their given real-world context.

- Aggregate predictive performance metrics are misleading—there's more at work here!

- Most commonly used models are black-boxes, which are uninterpretable by humans.

Model Interpretability: Human Understanding for Superhuman Models

In improving our ability to predict the state of the world, black-box models have traded away their ability to help us understand it. In this dangerous bargain, users of black-box models are forced to assume that the high predictive performance achieved by black boxes is enough to avoid harmful predictions. While checking the model against multiple performance metrics can be a useful means of identifying instances where the model doesn't perform well, doing so cannot get around the fact that we are still working with a model built upon mathematics that we fundamentally cannot understand.

How can we reduce the chances that a model that makes reasonable predictions upon a given dataset will not later generate harmful predictions when provided new data in the future? What if there was some way that we could check our models to see whether they produce fair outcomes, or a way to interpret the underlying machinery of our models so that we could understand how they leverage their features?

Fortunately, methods to "audit" the underlying functionality of a model to determine if it is fair exist in the form of various methods that fall under the umbrella of *fairness* and the better-defined category of *model interpretability*. The use of these methods is necessary for humans to begin to understand the models that they use and to proactively diagnose and reduce harmful factors prior to model deployment.

DEFINITION FAIRNESS In a data science context, this typically refers to the size of disparities in predictive performance between individuals or groups within a model. How these disparities ought to be measured, what constitutes an unfair disparity, and how these disparities can be mitigated (at least in part) are all topics that we will cover in greater detail in the "Fairness" section of this chapter and in Chapter 7, "Auditing a Responsible Data Science Project."

DEFINITION MODEL INTERPRETABILITY This refers to a human's ability to understand the relationships between a model's inputs and its predictions. It can be achieved using models that are intrinsically interpretable (such as linear regression and logistic regression models) or with black-box models (random forest, XGBoost, neural nets, etc.) through the application of *interpretability methods*. Model interpretability can indicate how features interrelate, whether they have equivalent impacts across a whole range of inputs, and even whether certain features ought to be brought into the dataset. Also referred to as "model explainability" and "explainability methods."

R and Python each has several available packages that can take arbitrary black-box models, including neural networks, and calculate fairness metrics or display visualizations from interpretability methods that help explain how the model makes decisions. Figure 4.6 illustrates an interpretability method example from the `NoiseTunnel()` function within Captum, an open source software package for applying interpretability methods and fairness interventions to models built using Pytorch.

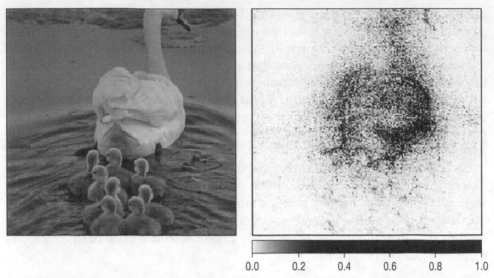

Figure 4.6: Pixel-level attributions for why an image was labeled as containing a swan. Darker pixels indicate pixels that were more important in the CNN's decision for a swan classification.

Source: `captum.ai/tutorials/Resnet_TorchVision_Interpret`. License: `github.com/pytorch/captum/blob/master/LICENSE`

We discuss interpretability methods and fairness in much greater detail in Chapter 5, "Model Interpretability: The What and the Why," Chapter 6, "Beginning a Responsible Data Science Project," Chapter 7, "Auditing a Responsible Data Science Project," and Chapter 8, "Auditing for Neural Networks," giving special attention to interpretability methods (and model interpretability more generally) in Chapter 5 on account of the wide applicability of these methods. For now, it should be enough to know that, together, considerations for fairness and the usage of interpretability methods are a critical component of any machine learning model audit and any modern data science framework more generally.

Takeaways

- We avoid understanding our models at our own peril.
- By auditing models, we catch issues that might slip through task design or dataset creation.
- Auditing models for fairness and interpretability helps humans to understand models and to diagnose possibly harmful factors.

We have illustrated the various ways that an AI model can cause harm in the real world. Armed with an understanding of how problems can occur at each level of the modeling pipeline, let's review the responsible data science frameworks that have already been proposed by researchers, corporations, and governments. Picking and choosing the best characteristics from these in combination with our takeaways can get us closer to an ideal responsible data science framework.

Efforts Toward a More Responsible Data Science[7]

Despite all the negative examples covered so far throughout this book, there is still reason to be optimistic about the future of AI and data science. Since the publishing of the 2018 "Gender Shades" study, the ongoing work and advocacy of researchers around the harms of facial recognition has compelled mainstream media outlets, corporations, and governments to pay attention. These discussions have already made a difference: all of the companies identified in the initial "Gender Shades" paper have greatly improved the fairness of their models only a year later.[8] In 2020, other tech companies like Microsoft, IBM, and Amazon all committed to freezing the sale of facial recognition technology to law enforcement until stronger regulations around the use of the technology are passed. Interest in curtailing facial recognition has also kickstarted discussions surrounding the ethical concerns of using AI within other contexts, including finance, real estate, healthcare, and law.

Beyond calling out the harms of bad models, data scientists and their stakeholders have also put forth numerous frameworks for making new AI models more transparent, fair, and accountable. Sector-leading tech companies like Google, Microsoft, IBM, and Amazon have followed suit, creating their own responsible AI principles to govern their work internally. Forward-looking governments and regulatory agencies in more than 12 countries have also issued their own guidelines for the responsible usage of AI methods in data science. Altogether, more than 90 different frameworks exist for responsible data science as of June 2020.[9]

There are many ideas discussed in these frameworks that we ought to include in our own. Rather than going through each framework individually, we summarize the main points from them as an aggregate.

NOTE While we use the phrase *responsible data science* to refer to data science done in a way that minimizes possible harms, this phrasing is not yet universally accepted. Currently, the phrases *ethical data science*, *accountable data science*, *fair and transparent data science*, *responsible data science*, *trustworthy data science*, and others are all used to describe roughly the same ideas. We refer to each of these as *responsible data science* frameworks within this book.

---

[7] This and subsequent sections in this chapter © 2021 Datastats LLC and Grant Fleming.

[8] Follow up discussed within Raji and Buolamwini (2019): https://dl.acm.org/doi/10.1145/3306618.3314244.

[9] Readers interested in comparing responsible data science frameworks should read the blog post at blog.einstein.ai/frameworks-tool-kits-principles-and-oaths-oh-my/ or either of the following comprehensive reviews: www.nature.com/articles/s42256-019-0088-2 and link.springer.com/article/10.1007/s11948-019-00165-5.

Principles Are the Focus

The responsible data science frameworks of today have converged around a set of five guiding principles. While none of these principles is present across every framework, all of them are covered in most frameworks. We do not use the names of these principles explicitly within our framework; however, they are useful to keep in mind if we want to grade the outcomes of our framework against standards that other frameworks have agreed upon as being useful. For each term, we provide a summary of its meaning (as it is used within the other frameworks), followed by brief commentary on translating these principles into practice.

Nonmaleficence

Nonmaleficence covers concepts associated with causing or avoiding harm. At a high level, following this principle requires that data scientists ensure that their models do not cause foreseeable harms, or harms of negligence. While unforeseen harms are sometimes unavoidable, they should be accounted for as much as reasonably possible. Harms that ought to be avoided include discrimination, risks of physical harm, legal risks, reductions in future opportunities, privacy violations, emotional distress, facilitation of illegal activities, and other results that could negatively impact individuals.

Nonmaleficence is the hardest principle to guarantee in practice; we recommend thinking of it as more of a goal to strive for (minimize) than a necessary box to check for every data science project. A model can be fair, transparent, accountable to users, and respecting of privacy, yet still make predictions giving advantage to some people while conceivably causing harm to others. For example, any medical triaging algorithm for prioritizing scarce medical resources cannot be fully nonmaleficent. After all, any patient not selected to receive a treatment could argue that they were harmed as a result.

Fairness

Fairness covers concepts associated with equal representation, antidiscrimination, dignity, and just outcomes. Fair models are models that either do not make decisions that unfairly disadvantage specific groups or make decisions that actively uplift specific groups. Dimensions of interest for fairness evaluations typically involve human-specific factors such as ethnicity, gender, sexual orientation, age, socioeconomic status, education, disability status, presence of preexisting conditions (healthcare), and history of adverse events. Model fairness is primarily a function of whether the model produces fair outcomes, with earlier factors (e.g., how the model uses certain features, how the features were created, etc.) being less relevant.

Fairness is a difficult concept to pin down. What is fair for one person or context might be unfair for another. One person might consider it fair for everyone to pay the same absolute amount in taxes. Another person might think everyone should pay the same share of their income in taxes. Another might think the wealthy should pay a higher share of their income in taxes. Yet another might think that the wealthy should pay *all* the taxes. There is no universally agreed definition, in this case, of what constitutes fairness.

Because fairness in a modeling context is primarily a function of ensuring fair predictions, or at least a fair process, it can be easier to translate into practice than the other four principles. However, bias mitigation methods are still very underused, in large part because they are still an area of active research. Fairness is almost always talked about exclusively in the context of models that make predictions for individual people; for example, whether a person should be provided a loan. In actuality, fairness is relevant for any modeling task where the goal is either to minimize differences between groups or to maximize predictive performance with respect to specific groups. In a spam email classification task, it might make sense to use fairness interventions to make the spam classification model more balanced in how well it classifies spam across different identified topics. While this isn't a use case that deals directly with people, it can still be beneficial to consider fairness as a way to ensure that the predictive performance of the model is maximized.

Transparency

Transparency covers the concepts associated with user consent, model interpretability, and explanations for other modeling choices made by the creators of a model. Typically, this communication is conveyed via clear documentation about the data or model.

As a concept, transparency is as simple as it appears: where possible, record and convey decisions about the modeling process. However, transparency quickly becomes complex when trying to move it from a principle to a practice. For example, data scientists within the modeling team, regulators, and users or clients all might require mutually exclusive forms of transparency due to their different needs and technical abilities. Documentation about the datasets used, explanations for choices made within the modeling process, and interpretations for individual predictions made for one group might need to be completely revamped for another. We recommend practices in Chapters 6 through 8 for handling situations like these.

Accountability

Accountability covers concepts associated with legal compliance, acting with integrity, responding to the users' concerns, and allowing for user recourse for harmful modeling decisions. For example, people who receive a loan denial ought to be entitled to not just an explanation for why that decision was made, but also the ability to appeal the decision and to receive an indication of the minimum set of differences that would have resulted in a change in the decision.

In practice, accountability typically does not go beyond ensuring that a model achieves legal compliance (which itself has become more difficult due to regulations like General Data Protection Regulation [GDPR]). In fact, at the time of writing we were not able to identify any real-world examples of platforms that provide capabilities for users to directly appeal adverse algorithmically derived decisions (other than via sending an email or a letter).

Privacy

Privacy covers the concepts associated with only gathering necessary information, storing data securely, ensuring that identifying information is removed once it's used in a model, and ensuring that other aspects of user data cannot be inferred from the model results.

Fortunately, there are already several well-understood approaches for maintaining the privacy of systems (via preventing hacks, unintentional disclosures, physical attacks, etc.). Making data available for analysis in models circumvents some of these protections, necessitating the use of differential privacy methods that add randomization to the underlying data. Unfortunately, differential privacy methods are not yet built into many popular modeling packages.

Bridging the Gap Between Principles and Practice with the Responsible Data Science (RDS) Framework

The next logical step after establishing an agreed-upon set of responsible data science principles is providing recommendations for putting these principles into practice. Unfortunately, this is where responsible data science frameworks tend to break down (and probably why they are not more widely used). Though most of the more than 90 existing responsible data science frameworks suggest that there are technical solutions to making their principles actionable, almost none of them provide any specific recommendations for doing so. When recommendations are offered, they typically go no further than proposing documentation or policy changes. For example, frameworks often require that users be provided explanations for individual predictions. However, they generally stop short of describing what actually constitutes a *good* explanation or how a model can be made to produce one.

NOTE   The Scoping, Mapping, Artifact Collection, Testing, Reflection, Post-Audit (SMACTR) framework developed in the 2020 academic paper "Closing the AI Accountability Gap: Defining an End-to-End Framework for Internal Algorithmic Auditing" by Deborah Raji and her collaborators is perhaps the closest to a practical framework for responsible data science released so far. However, this framework focuses primarily on the auditing phase of data science projects and generally doesn't provide recommendations for practices outside of that scope.

While principles are undoubtedly a crucial part of any responsible data science framework, neglecting to recommend steps for actually implementing them in code makes these responsible data science frameworks theoretical aspirations at best and holier-than-thou moral grandstanding at worst.

Data science is ultimately about practice. If we want to go about practicing data science ethically, then we need a responsible data science framework oriented toward practice instead of principles. The RDS framework described in this chapter accounts for all of the takeaways discussed in the earlier sections of this chapter and making the aforementioned principles actionable. By doing so, we can structure real-world data science projects with an eye to minimizing unintended harms to data subjects and clients, improving understanding of the underlying task, maximizing reproducibility, and ultimately performing data science more responsibly. Though this framework is especially useful for modeling tasks that deal directly with people or otherwise have a high potential to cause harm, it serves just as well as a guide for best practices in more innocuous, less ethically charged modeling tasks. Figure 4.7 shows how the different stages of the framework connect.

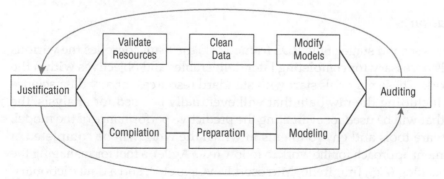

Figure 4.7: The RDS framework can be thought of as a general "best practices" framework for end-to-end data science.

We briefly describe each stage of the framework in the following sections, and explore each of them in detail in Chapters 6 through 8.

Justification

The first stage of the RDS framework is Justification. At this point, data scientists and project managers ought to be coordinating with users and other relevant stakeholders to define the real-world interest problem as well as deciding upon a proper modeling approach to solve it. As part of their conversations, the team must expand their scope of consideration to the nontechnical. Broadly, the team ought to consider the various ways in which their model or findings might cause harm. We recommend accomplishing this via writing an *impact statement*.

> **DEFINITION IMPACT STATEMENT**   A narrative document produced by a team for a model that explains the possible ethical concerns of the work and the design of the project. This document should be relatively short (i.e., two pages or less) and serve primarily as a summary of the concerns that the team has considered.

By the end of this stage, the team ought to be able to affirmatively answer the following questions:

- Have we studied other similar projects and come to understand what ethical concerns there are relevant to our project?

- Do we have the elements necessary (e.g., diversity on the team, ability to solicit feedback from others, etc.) to assess potential harms to individuals or groups relevant to our models?

- Have we anticipated and accounted for future uses of the technology that we are developing beyond what the current users seek?

Compilation

Within this second stage of the RDS framework, the team compiles the various materials necessary for completing later deliverables and objectives within the framework. These materials start with standard resources for any data science project, including the raw data that will eventually be used for analysis, the metrics that will be used for evaluating the predictive performance of the model, the software tools and environments in which the work will be completed, a development approach for the work to follow (e.g., Agile), a tool for managing the project backlog (e.g., Jira, Trello, Microsoft DevOps, etc.), and a data dictionary.

However, advances in research and industry have clarified the need for two additional documents ensuring that the final product of the project is minimally harmful and reproducible.

- **Datasheets:** Narrative documents that augment a data dictionary by explaining considerations for how the data was gathered, preprocessed, and intended to be used. Datasheets are intended to be less technical and speak more to ethical or "nontechnical" considerations for the data, rather than factors relating to more technical aspects of the data, like its distribution. We will discuss datasheets in greater detail in Chapter 6.

- **Audit reports:** Technical documents that present figures and metrics showing the results of the deployed model's final audit. These reports should be as long as necessary to include the results relevant to the auditing criteria in the impact statement. They should also include the work completed during the Compilation stage, as the reports are intended to be a deep dive into how the team identified and addressed the model's possibly dangerous facets. We will discuss audit reports in greater detail in Chapter 7.

While the team ought to be prepared to create a datasheet at this stage of the process, the primary work around audit reports should be centered for now on deciding which fairness metrics and fairness criteria the team expects prior to modeling to be relevant for their particular modeling task. As we will discuss in Chapter 7, choosing the appropriate fairness metrics and fairness criteria requires careful consideration.

By the end of this stage, the team ought to be able to affirmatively answer the following questions:

- Have we acquired all the relevant data for our project?
- Was the data acquired in a manner that was nonexploitive and respected consent?
- Have we provided our current and future stakeholders with sufficient information about our data?
- Have we developed appropriate auditing criteria to allow us to sufficiently ensure that our model functions appropriately and is unlikely to cause harms?

Preparation

Within this stage, the team prepares for modeling by performing any additional data cleaning, feature engineering (not necessary in the case of neural networks), and feature selection (not necessary for black-box models and neural networks) necessary for modeling. While no new documents need to be produced at this stage, the team should augment its datasheet with information about whether additional data cleaning was undertaken and whether any new features were created from the raw data.

By the end of this stage, the team ought to be able to affirmatively answer the following questions:

- Have we changed the raw data in a way that doesn't unnecessarily distort it?

- Have we ensured that any data cleaning or feature engineering on the training datasets have been applied to the holdout sets as well?

- Have we solicited and accounted for subject-matter-expert feedback during the cleaning, feature engineering, and feature selection processes as needed?

Modeling

Finally, we arrive at the Modeling stage of the RDS framework. Here, we recommend that the team begin by establishing performance baselines with which to compare their later models. These performance baselines should represent performance metrics achieved by past approaches and/or basic untuned and unaugmented models on the low end, and optimistic best-case scenario metrics on the high end. Any models that the team produces should be sandwiched between these two performance metrics, though ideally they end up closer to the higher one (optimistic best-case scenario), rather than the lower (baseline model or past-performance benchmark).

We also recommend at this point that the team choose whether it wants to use an intrinsically interpretable or black-box model moving forward. Moreover, we recommend that the team maximize the final model's predictive importance via tuning (searching for the highest-performing combination of hyperparameters), log experiments with different hyperparameter combinations in external files, and ensure that the final model chosen for deployment is the best model according to multiple performance metrics.

By the end of this stage, the team must be able to affirmatively answer the following questions:

- Does our model perform sufficiently better across multiple metrics than pessimistic measures of baseline performance to justify continuing the project?

- Have we provided our current and future stakeholders with sufficient information about how to use and understand our model?

- Is the increased difficulty of interpretability justified by the increased predictive performance of choosing to build a black-box model, rather than an intrinsically interpretable one?

Auditing

The final and perhaps most important stage of the RDS framework is Auditing. Auditing our models gives us an opportunity to catch any "wolves in our code" that might have slipped by unnoticed until now, minimizing the chance that our model could cause unexpected harms when it's deployed or otherwise finished.

Though the audit is performed with respect to the model itself, the findings of the audit might indicate issues with procedures related to model tuning, feature selection, feature engineering, raw data acquisition, or even the specification of the modeling task itself.

As such, it makes sense to see the audit as moving in reverse: going back through each stage of the framework so far, while diagnosing and mitigating issues if possible within each. In this way, auditing becomes a cycle. Each time this cycle is done, we should again move forward through the framework (culminating in another audit) to ensure that any issues discovered are appropriately addressed.

Specific procedures for auditing models are covered in Chapters 7 and 8.

By the end of this stage, the team must be able to affirmatively answer the following questions:

- Have we provided useful explanations for the model's predictions to stakeholders?

- Have we checked to ensure that our model is not unfairly biased against certain groups?

- Have our mitigation procedures addressed the issues discovered during previous audits?

Summary

Prior to this chapter, we covered a broad history of modeling harms stretching from the beginning of statistics to the modern day. Within this chapter, we have come to understand more about why those problems continue to occur and where current modeling approaches and responsible data science frameworks fall short in addressing them. Moreover, we now have developed a framework for performing data science more responsibly ourselves.

The next chapter covers an in-depth introduction to model interpretability and interpretability methods, concepts that we have alluded to a few times so far within our discussions of intrinsically interpretable and black-box models in previous chapters. Used correctly, interpretability methods can enable people to come much closer to model interpretability (i.e., human understanding) of the otherwise incomprehensible and highly powerful black-box models, a crucial aspect of any ethical data science framework.

After covering model interpretability in the upcoming chapter, we will finally have all the knowledge necessary to utilize the RDS framework in practice within the remaining chapters of the book.

Model Interpretability: The What and the Why

In this chapter, we will establish why understanding model interpretability and how to achieve or approximate it is a key step in discovering the circumstances in which a model might unexpectedly generate harmful predictions. We begin this chapter by presenting a real-world example that motivates the need for humans to better understand the operation of complex black-box models. We then follow that example by presenting model interpretability as a way to diagnose issues of fairness in models that may have otherwise produced harmful predictions in the future had they not been addressed. Over the remainder of the chapter, we will discuss the reasons why model interpretability (or the lack of it) is necessary for responsible data science as well as how black-box models, which are otherwise uninterpretable to humans, can be made to generate meaningful explanations via interpretability methods.

The Sexist Résumé Screener

Issues in models are often discovered after deployment by the very users or clients they are intended to serve. The history of harms caused by statistical methods, both unintentionally and intentionally, ought to have provided data scientists ample guidance on avoiding them. However, even multinational corporations on the forefront of data science progress continue to embroil themselves in controversies caused by their harmful models. Why does this cycle keep repeating itself? And what can be done now and, in the future, to mitigate the challenges presented by the growing adoption of algorithmic decision-making?

Perhaps one of the most informative examples of harmful modeling practices is Amazon's experience with developing a model that could evaluate candidate résumés. In 2014, Amazon undertook efforts to automate its hiring process by training a natural language processing (NLP) model on a set of résumés from applicants over the previous 10 years. These résumés were rated by Amazon employees on a scale from one to five, with five representing an ideal applicant and one representing a definite reject. The model's job was to learn from this training data how to predict ratings for new résumés based solely on the résumé text. The model was successful, ultimately identifying several terms associated with highly rated résumés and, presumably, with individuals who would have successful careers at Amazon. The resulting terms, however, proved shockingly biased. With a colder, more honest eye than any human could offer, the model concluded that the prime differentiating factor between "good" and "bad" applicants was not a relevant skill, experience, or personality trait.

It was their gender.

Specifically, the model adapted to the overwhelmingly large number of highly rated male applicants in the data that it was trained on by penalizing résumés containing terms associated with women, such as "women's chess club captain" or the names of women's colleges. No bug in the software or malicious action on the part of an Amazon employee caused the model to become sexist. Rather, the model accurately picked up on the unconscious biases encoded into the training data by the (primarily male) employees who served as human raters for the training data. Based on the labels that humans had placed on the training data, simply being male was the most powerful predictor of success. In a very real sense, the model did exactly as it was designed to do.

More than a year passed before Amazon became aware of the discriminatory, unfair predictions made by its model. By this point, the model had already been in use in recruitment efforts across the company. While, in hindsight, discrimination against women might seem an obvious issue to check for, the model creators carefully avoided including gender as a predictor and, therefore, thought they had protected themselves. The ways in which the model was able to guess gender were not obvious as it was being built; the inner workings of the model were not visible—only the result. As with Optum, the well-meaning healthcare company discussed in Chapter 1, "Responsible Data Science," whose algorithm unintentionally discriminated against African Americans, Amazon likely did not intend to discriminate against women. However, the damage was done. What could these companies have done differently to identify these issues in their model prior to its release, and how do these recommendations fit into a larger definition of responsible data science?

The Necessity of Model Interpretability

As we first mentioned in the previous chapter, *model interpretability* refers to the ability to explain the relationships that a model generates between its input features and its outputs. Whether because of growing public ire surrounding misapplied models, swelling demands from public officials for increased regulation, legal exposure to laws and regulations already on the books, or because people simply want greater transparency for the algorithms that affect their lives, model interpretability has risen to the status of an ethical issue in data science. In cases where an incorrect model prediction can cause harm to an individual or group of people, maintaining model interpretability becomes a critical part of responsible data science.

Model interpretability is easy to achieve in the case of linear models like linear or logistic regression. By default, these models transform input feature values into outputs in a linear fashion that can be easily understood by both humans and software. For example, consider the following output in Figure 5.1 from the R coding language of a binary logistic regression run on the German Credit Data dataset from the University of California Irvine (UCI) Machine Learning Repository:

term	estimate	std.error	statistic	p.value
<chr>	<dbl>	<dbl>	<dbl>	<dbl>
1 Duration	0.968	0.00832	-3.91	0.0000930
2 Age	1.02	0.00781	2.31	0.0210
3 CheckingAccountStatus.lt.0	0.343	0.348	-3.07	0.00212
4 CheckingAccountStatus.0.to.200	0.511	0.353	-1.90	0.0576
5 CheckingAccountStatus.none	1.92	0.363	1.79	0.0731
6 CreditHistory.NoCredit.AllPaid	0.476	0.377	-1.97	0.0490
7 CreditHistory.ThisBank.AllPaid	0.516	0.362	-1.83	0.0673
8 CreditHistory.Critical	1.96	0.200	3.36	0.000771
9 Purpose.NewCar	0.539	0.189	-3.27	0.00109
10 Purpose.UsedCar	2.54	0.331	2.82	0.00485
11 SavingsAccountBonds.lt.100	0.577	0.218	-2.53	0.0114
12 OtherDebtorsGuarantors.Guarantor	4.05	0.544	2.57	0.0101
13 Property.Unknown	0.648	0.238	-1.82	0.0681

Figure 5.1: Output from R of a logistic regression run on the German Credit dataset. Coefficients in the "estimate" column have already been exponentiated.

The goal of this modeling task in Figure 5.1 is to determine whether individual borrowers have good or bad credit. Rows within the German Credit dataset represent individual customers, whereas the columns (the variables listed in the term column of the table) represent attributes, such as age or credit history. A logistic regression for these data is *intrinsically* interpretable. All that an interested party must do to generate an explanation of the model's inner workings is exponentiate the model's coefficients and generate an odds ratio, which can then be interpreted directly. For example, the exponentiated coefficient for "Purpose. NewCar" tells you that the odds of a person having bad credit decrease by a factor of 0.539 when the purchase is buying a new car, all other factors being held equal. We can interpret the coefficient of each feature in similar fashion to learn how it contributes to the overall functioning of the model.

We have already discussed in earlier chapters cases where unintentionally misapplied models caused harm and public controversy. When model interpretability is present, this harm becomes much easier to detect and negate prior to the model's deployment. Unfortunately, model interpretability for black-box models is more difficult to achieve than for interpretable models like logistic regression. This difficulty stems from the mathematical complexity of black-box models. Black-box models rely on various ensemble approaches to make complicated transformations of input features that are not directly interpretable by humans or software. Recall, in Chapter 2, "Modeling: Black-Box," how we first developed a simple decision tree with easily interpretable rules. Ensemble approaches for tree methods improve predictive performance; however, we lose the model interpretability that a single decision tree allows for. For example, a random forest model fit on the same German Credit data in R produces the output shown in Figure 5.2.

```
Type:                              Probability estimation
Number of trees:                   500
Sample size:                       1000
Number of independent variables:   19
Mtry:                              4
Target node size:                  10
Variable importance mode:          none
Splitrule:                         gini
OOB prediction error (Brier s.):   0.1583695
```

Figure 5.2: Output of the `rand_forest()` command from R's parsnip package, which produces a model object with the above output

Nothing in the output of Figure 5.2 can tell us how the underlying random forest model was able to leverage individual features to produce its predictions. The model produces no coefficients, standard errors, or hypothesis test results that data scientists could use to interpret and justify their findings. Because of the complex mathematics underlying them, these black-box models assume the role of oracle, producing predictions without providing human-interpretable explanations for their outputs. These predictions are often more accurate than linear models because of their ability to model complex relationships between predictor features and the outcome of interest. However, moving away from the built-in interpretability of intrinsically interpretable models clearly poses challenges. For example, the inability to interpret the decision rules of the model can make it harder to gain the trust of users, clients, and regulators, even for models that are otherwise well designed and effective. We all are familiar with these fears. After all, science-fiction films and other forms of popular media have long relied upon using the actions of incomprehensible, devilishly intelligent AI agents or evil algorithms as key plot elements.

Connections Between Predictive Performance and Interpretability

Life is complex—this truism lies at the heart of AI's rapid growth and its improvement over simpler methods like regression. AI methods like tree ensembles and neural networks offer the flexibility and complexity, coupled with an iterative tuning process, that are needed to help "decode" life. Consider the relatively simple modeling task of predicting home prices across the whole of the United States. Generally speaking, the bigger the house, the more expensive it is. But homes in central Manhattan, where space is extremely scarce, tend to be smaller and more expensive than homes in the United States on average, so it is not a simple linear relationship between space and price. Likewise, houses with more rooms tend to be more expensive than homes with few rooms, but this relationship depends on another factor—home size. For smaller homes, lots of rooms can indicate chopped-up layouts with poor livability (perhaps many residents), so they may be less valuable than well-laid-out homes of a similar size.

As the home prediction example demonstrates, the relationships between complex phenomena in the real world are often nonlinear in nature. In these cases, forcing linear modeling approaches can result in oversimplification, causing the loss of useful information about the world. Perhaps this was the motivation behind the following statement by renowned twentieth-century British statistician George Box:

"All models are wrong, but some are useful."

So, why use simpler models at all? Now that they are available, why not choose more flexible black-box models that can better capture these hidden patterns? There are three separate considerations at work here.

- Black-box models are prone to overfitting (see "The Return of Bias-Variance Trade-Off" on the next page).

- Black-box models do not yield good (or any) explanations for their predictions, which makes it more difficult to understand why they might generate harmful and unfair predictions.

- Black-box models have been shown to perform roughly as well as or slightly worse than simpler, intrinsically interpretable models in risk modeling tasks like recidivism prediction or healthcare triaging.[1]

---

[1] See hdsr.mitpress.mit.edu/pub/7z10o269/release/3#discussion by Rudin et al. (2020) for a deeper discussion on this. The paper by Hand (2006) (projecteuclid.org/ euclid.ss/1149600839) is also useful for a more fundamental understanding of the relation ships between model complexity and predictive performance.

THE RETURN OF THE BIAS-VARIANCE TRADE-OFF

There is a trade-off between the two ways a model can err. A model can be too flexible and complex, capturing so much information that it is overfitting the data and modeling noise as well as real information. By analogy, a custom-made form-fitting suit might capture transitory features of the body (a swollen elbow, temporary hunched over posture on the day of fitting) and overfit, not serving well in the long run. Alternatively, the model can be too simple, underfitting the data and failing to capture some useful information. The analogy to this is an off-the-rack suit that is baggy enough to accommodate moderate changes in the body, not capturing the form fully but providing some longevity. Models that provide coefficients (like regression) and rules (like simple decision trees) tend to fall on the "underfitting" (high bias) side of the scale, simplifying or ignoring many of the underlying relationships in the data to produce coefficients or decision rules. At the same time, these simple coefficients and decision rules allow for ready interpretation and understanding. Black-box models like neural nets, as well as decision tree ensembles, fall on the "overfitting" (high variance) side of the scale and are not easily interpretable due to how precisely they fit the subtle nonlinear relationships within the data. At the same time, if their overfitting can be corrected with ensembling, holdout datasets, or other cross-validation approaches, and if the relevant relationships in the underlying data are nonlinear, then they usually achieve better performance than the simpler intrinsically interpretable models. We are again referring to *bias* in the statistical sense here (model errors tending in a specific direction). Elsewhere, unless otherwise noted, we will use it in its lay meaning to refer to unfairness (differences in a model's predictive performance across groups in the data).

How is this discussion of underfitting and overfitting relevant to model interpretability? Because model interpretability illuminates the underlying reasoning of a model, the explanations generated by a model are limited by how well the model fits the data. This means that regardless of how accurate the explanations are for an intrinsically interpretable model (like the coefficients for a logistic regression), our understanding of the true relationships within the data is limited to the "underfitted" explanations that the model is capable of producing. Limited model explanations confine our understanding of the underlying data, which in turn limits our understanding of the world and our ability to know how our model understands it. This brings us back to considering the compound telescope diagram (see Figure 5.3), which was first shown in Chapter 4, "The Responsible Data Science (RDS) Framework."

By better approximating the underlying relationships within the data, black-box models retain more useful information about the data than intrinsically interpretable models do across the many instances when relationships in the data are nonlinear. The explanations that could be generated by a model are therefore inextricably bound by the predictive performance that the model can achieve. Generally, the higher performing the model, the more likely that the explanations we gather from it are clear reflections of the underlying data.

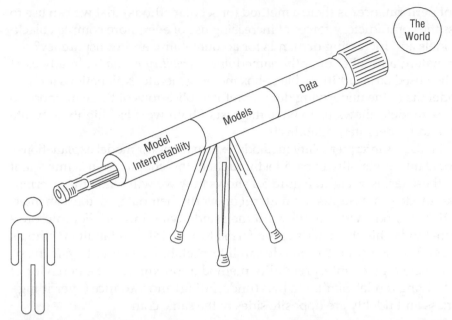

Figure 5.3: Diagramming how information about the world is translated by the modeling process into human understanding

NOTE This relationship between better predictive performance and more useful explanations holds only if we are considering the model's out-of-sample performance *and* only if we are choosing an appropriate set of performance metrics. We should *not* base our trust in the predictive performance of a model only on the performance it achieves on the training data, or on a high score on just one performance metric.

Unfortunately, black-box models typically do not include built-in mechanisms for providing human interpretable explanations for their predictions or structure. The information within them is locked away as a consequence of our goal of higher predictive performance. Are we always doomed to choose to optimize for one characteristic (interpretability or predictive performance) over the other? What if there were some way that we could strike a bargain, achieving or approximating model interpretability while maintaining the high predictive performance of black-box models?

Uniting (High) Model Performance and Model Interpretability

Wouldn't we want to know how black-box models, which often perform better than their linear alternatives, better fit features in the data and reach higher levels of performance? Is there a method (or set of methods) that we can use to address the contradictory forces of increasing use of ever more complex black-box models and increasing demands for accountability and transparency?

Fortunately, a number of aptly named *interpretability methods* already exist that, when used on an arbitrary black-box model, generate explanations for how the model fits to the underlying data. Careful applications of these methods to black-box models allows us to have the best of both worlds—highly accurate models and model interpretability!

We will discuss interpretability methods, explanations (or model explanations), and model interpretability in parallel throughout this chapter, so it is important to keep these terms straight. Figure 5.4 shows how we will relate these terms.

Just as models themselves can underfit or overfit their data, so, too, can interpretability methods underfit or overfit their underlying models. For interpretability methods, this characteristic is referred to as an interpretability method's *robustness*. We also want to consider an interpretability method's *fidelity*, or how precisely a given interpretability method approximates the behavior of the underlying model. Similar to bias (underfitting) and variance (overfitting), robustness and fidelity are opposite sides of the same coin.

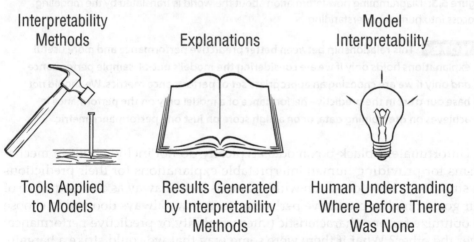

Interpretability Methods	Explanations	Model Interpretability
Tools Applied to Models	Results Generated by Interpretability Methods	Human Understanding Where Before There Was None

Figure 5.4: Diagram showing how to relate interpretability methods, explanations, and model interpretability

DEFINITION ROBUSTNESS   This is the sensitivity of explanations generated by an interpretability method to varying characteristics of the underlying model. Highly robust explanations are explanations that are not sensitive to minor changes in model characteristics—they do not change easily as a model is tweaked. We can think of robustness as the "bias" of interpretability methods.

DEFINITION FIDELITY This is how well an explanation approximates the behavior of the underlying model. High-fidelity explanations often differ after the underlying model changes due to how closely they approximate it. We can think of fidelity as the "variance" of interpretability methods.

We can see that there is a trade-off between robustness and fidelity—the higher fidelity an explanation for a model is, the less robust it is likely to be. How this trade-off is managed determines the reliability of an interpretability method. After all, we wouldn't want to use an interpretability method that produces different results every time it was run or one that could not do a good job approximating the underlying model. Finding the ideal trade-off between robustness and fidelity is complicated by the fact that it is influenced not just by the interpretability method selected but also by the bias and/or variance of the underlying model. To account for this, we need to make sure we have a wide range of interpretability methods at our disposal.

Categories of Interpretability Methods

Individual interpretability methods can measure and approximate many different types of underlying information relevant to the model. However, interpretability methods can be broken into the following two general categories:

- **Global methods:** Global interpretability methods measure how individual features impact predictions globally (on average) across the model. These methods tend to have lower fidelity and higher robustness.

- **Local methods:** Local interpretability methods measure how individual model predictions are locally influenced by their individual feature values. They produce explanations with respect to individual predictions, which can vary across the model. For example, we might learn that the prediction of a high value for a particular home was due primarily to its view in a particular direction (a feature that might operate similarly for certain other homes but not generally all homes). These methods tend to have higher fidelity and lower robustness.

Global Methods

Global methods are the closest analog to the coefficients and decision rules provided by intrinsically interpretable models. They can be used to improve interpretability for black-box models (our main focus here), though they are also relevant for intrinsically interpretable methods like logistic regression (where they can provide diagnostics information about interactions between features).

The most widely used global methods produce diagnostic plots showing how a range of feature values impact the model's predictions. To best understand how they work, we will explore the three most commonly used global interpretability methods—permutation feature importance, partial dependence plots (PDP), and individual conditional expectation (ICE) plots—in the context of a home price prediction task.

Permutation Feature Importance

When modeling packages include capabilities for calculating feature importance, the default method is almost always a variant of *permutation feature importance*.

> **DEFINITION PERMUTATION FEATURE IMPORTANCE**   This calculates how important a feature is by comparing how much the model error increases when all the values of a feature are randomized. Features are ranked in descending importance by the increase in error.

Feature importance measures like permutation importance are extremely helpful for informing us about which features are most useful to our model. Besides helping to inform our decisions of which features to keep or discard during feature selection, identifying important features via these methods also shines light on possible learning or debugging opportunities. If an unexpected feature is highlighted as important, we could check to see whether there is a bug in the model or in the underlying data. If an expected feature is highlighted as important, then we can have more confidence that our assumptions about the model were correct. Figure 5.5 shows an example feature performance calculation for a random forest model fit on the Ames Housing Dataset. We can see that the most important features are main living area square footage (gr_liv_area), basement square footage (total_bsmt_sf), and garage square footage (garage_area).

ICE and PDP Plots

Individual conditional expectation plots and *partial dependence plots* depict how changes in a feature of interest are related to changes in the values of the target variable. For example, both ICE and PDP plots can show how changing values of the square footage of a home are related to its sale price. Where an intrinsically interpretable model might produce a linear coefficient plot to describe this relationship, ICE and PDP plots are each built piecewise, allowing them to show a higher-fidelity polynomial relationship between square footage and sale price. After all, we would expect that the marginal cost of each additional square foot decreases past a certain point as other home amenities become comparably more valuable.

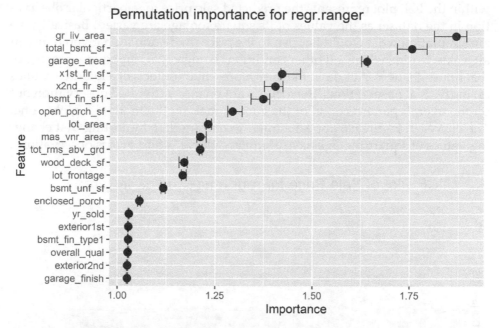

Figure 5.5: Feature importance plot of the top 20 most important features in a random forest model fit on the Ames Housing Dataset

DEFINITION ICE PLOT   This is a global interpretability method that depicts what happens to individual predictions when you change the values of a feature for a specific observation, holding other feature values constant. Each ICE plot has multiple curves, with each curve representing how the predicted value produced by the model (the y-axis) for a particular observation changes when you change the values of the feature of interest (x-axis).

DEFINITION PDP PLOT   This is a global interpretability method derived from ICE plots that depicts the average impact that the values of a particular feature have on all of the model's predictions (i.e., the average across ICE plots). The PDP plot can be thought of as a visual approximation for a coefficient within a linear model.

Where the ICE and PDP plots differ from each other is in how many lines are drawn. For example, consider the combined ICE plot in Figure 5.6, derived from a random forest model to predict home sale prices. Each of the curves within the ICE plot represents the predicted sale price for a particular observation in the dataset as the values of its square footage are varied. Basically, we are simulating what would happen to the price prediction for a given house in alternate worlds where, all other conditions being equal, the square footage of that house changes. Although the lines represent the effects of a feature's values on individual observations, the focus is not on any individual observation but on the overall patterns of all of the curves, making the method a global one. The curves in Figure 5.6 appear similar to one another, indicating that changing values of square footage have a similar "global" effect across observations.

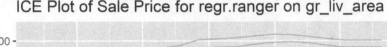

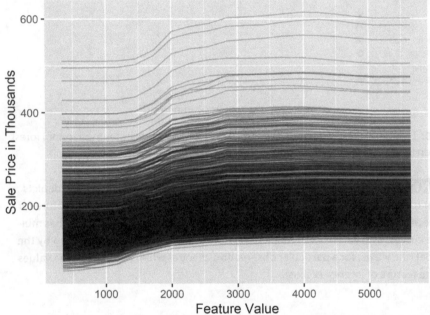

Figure 5.6: ICE plot showing the relationship between changes in the square footage of a home (x-axis) and its sale price (y-axis). We can see clear evidence of a curvilinear relationship between square footage and home price.

The ICE plot in Figure 5.7 for a linear regression fit on the same data would have us believe that there is a linear relationship between square footage and sale price. As we just showed with the general trends of the ICE plot from our random forest model, this is obviously not the case.

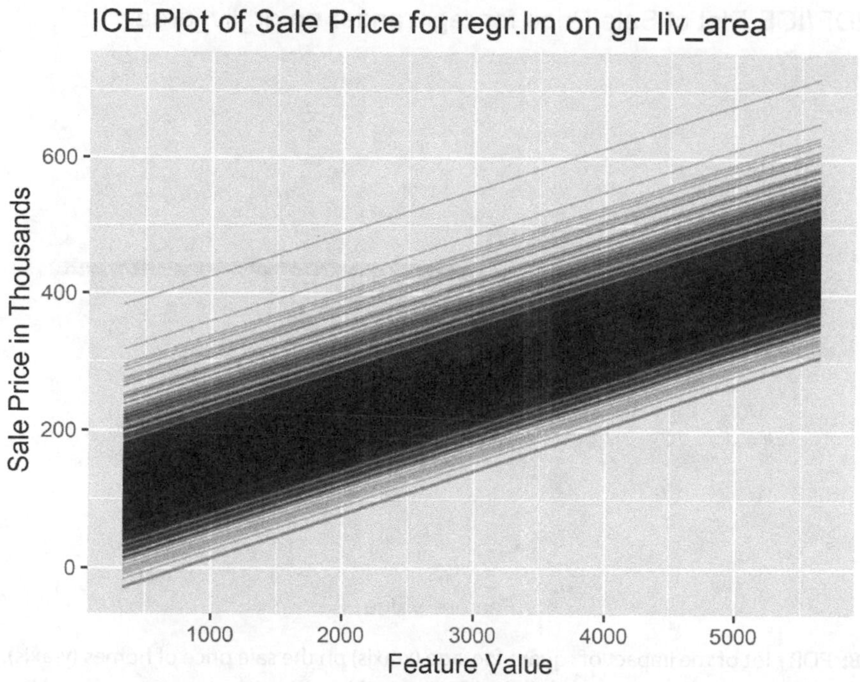

Figure 5.7: ICE plot showing the relationship between changes in the square footage of a home (x-axis) and its sale price (y-axis). Even though they were built from the same data, the ICE plots from this linear regression indicate an incorrect linear relationship.

> **NOTE**   A set of observations within an ICE plot all following a similar curvature is evidence of minimal interaction between the feature of interest and other features. Conversely, a widely varying set of of observations within an ICE plot indicates a differing effect of feature values among observations, probably due to differing values of other features (indicating likely interaction between features).

PDP plots are useful for getting a cleaner, more easily understandable approximation of ICE plots. The PDP plot is generated as the point-by-point averaging of all the points along all of the other ICE curves. This produces a plot that shows the average change in the values of the target variable across all observations, as we vary the values of the feature of interest. We can see in Figure 5.8 from overlaying the PDP plot over a 95% confidence band of the ICE plot curves that square footage has a nonlinear impact on the sale price.

Again, the PDP and ICE plot in Figure 5.9 show that the nonlinear nature of this relationship would have gone entirely undetected had we used a linear model.

PDP/ICE Plot of Sale Price for regr.ranger on gr_liv_area

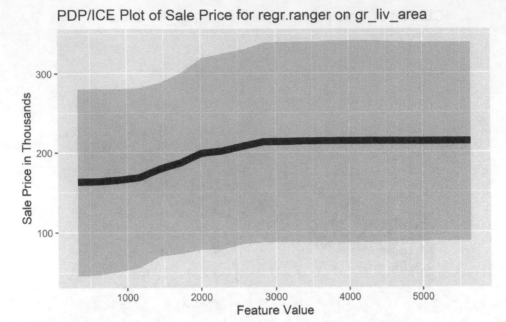

Figure 5.8: PDP plot of the impact of square footage (x-axis) on the sale price of homes (y-axis). The PDP plot (bold line) is the average of all the ICE plots, which themselves are represented by the 95% confidence band. The nonlinear relationship between the square footage and sale price is clearly shown by both plots.

PDP/ICE Plot of Sale Price for regr.lm on gr_liv_area

Figure 5.9: PDP plots for a linear model of the impact of square footage (x-axis) on the sale price of homes (y-axis)

Local Methods

Local interpretability methods describe how each individual feature contributes (positively, negatively, or negligibly) to the predicted value for an observation of interest. Local interpretability methods are relevant primarily for black-box methods. For intrinsically interpretable methods like linear regression and single trees, all the model information for an observation is already provided in the coefficients (for regression) or rules (for trees). No further local information from the model is uncovered, although residuals (error not explained by the model) are useful to examine.

Local interpretability methods like Shapley values can produce these explanations, increasing user trust by showing how each unique prediction was generated by the underlying black-box model.

> **DEFINITION SHAPLEY VALUES**   A local interpretability method that calculates how much individual feature values contribute to a prediction. They are calculated for each observation as the average marginal contribution of each feature over all combinations of features. Shapley values can be interpreted with explanations akin to "75% of the decision to grant you a loan was based on your credit score," or "15% of your home's final predicted sale cost comes as a result of your home having a garage."

In the context of the home price prediction task discussed in the "Global Methods" section, the plot of Shapley values in Figure 5.10 shows how much each feature value contributed to the final predicted price. We can see that the high-feature values for gr_liv_area and open_porch_sf contributed most positively to the final sale price for that observation, while the small garage_area and lot_area (at least for this dataset) contributed most negatively.

Many open source software packages provide simple implementations of interpretability methods for users of both R and Python to leverage in their current modeling workflows. In fact, the plots in this section were generated in R simply by inputting fitted model objects into the iml package's ICE, PDP, and Shapley functions.

Real-World Successes of Interpretability Methods

Besides providing human explanations for the inner workings of a model, interpretability methods yield insight into the quality of a model—insight beyond the model's achieved performance metric. By "opening the hood" of our model, we can see whether it is operating in a fashion that we would approve of and trust or understand as inherently flawed and in need of repair. Once we know how it is using the data, we could even go back and collect more or different data to fix fairness issues in its predictions or, in the case of a model that already appears effective and fair, improve the performance of the model even further.

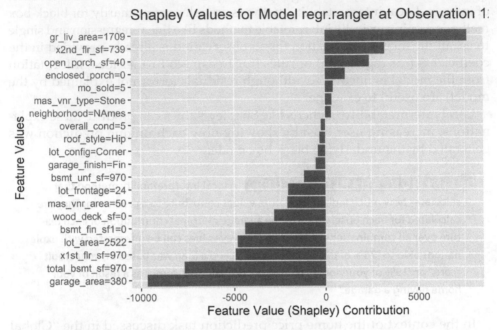

Shapley Values for Model regr.ranger at Observation 1:

Figure 5.10: Plot of Shapley values (feature contributions) for observation 122 of a home price prediction dataset. The square footage of the first floor (gr_liv_area) and second floor (x2nd_flr_sf) contribute most positively to the home's final predicted sale price.

Interpretability methods and their potential are not merely a theoretical construct. Throughout this section, we consider how data scientists, researchers, and corporations that are building black-box models have *already* benefited from using interpretability methods.[2]

Facilitating Debugging and Audit

Of the 30 organizations interviewed in the Bhatt et al. article, all integrated at least one interpretability method into a part of their pipeline. Most organizations utilized the explanations generated by these methods to reconcile differences with the opinion of a subject matter expert or stakeholder. Many organizations

---

[2] Most of the examples discussed in this section were first described in "Explainable Machine Learning in Deployment" Bhatt et al. (2020), published in the 2020 proceedings for the Fairness, Accountability, and Transparency [in AI] Conferences.

found that they could use interpretability methods to identify spurious corre-lations within models, make changes to improve their model's performance, and minimize the risk of unfair predictions. For example, one organization that used two different facial-expression identification models, one to detect smiles and one to detect raised cheeks, was having trouble with the latter. They found that both models were heavily correlated in their output due to each placing a very high importance on pixels around the mouths of individuals in the images. This finding was helpful in their efforts to diagnose what was going wrong with their model for detecting raised cheeks. While focusing on the mouth may have made sense for a smile-detecting model, a model designed to detect raised cheeks ought to have been deriving much of its information from elsewhere.

Financial organizations use interpretability methods for internal auditing. One used Shapley values as a final sanity check for internal stress testing after the model's outputs had been examined by company loan officers. The interpret-ability method served there as a stop light, flashing red in case of last-minute pitfalls that would have otherwise jeopardized the credibility of the deployed model. Eventually, this organization as well as others want to provide similar explanations to their users as a service feature. Outside of the realm of tabular data, researchers and companies have found that interpretability methods can prove useful in debugging issues within DNNs as well, especially for convo-lutional neural networks (CNNs) used to identify objects within images. Local interpretability methods like *locally interpretable model explanations (LIME)* can be used for vision prediction tasks to highlight, for each image, which pixels were pivotal in assigning a particular classification.

DEFINITION LOCALLY INTERPRETABLE MODEL EXPLANATIONS   This is a local interpretability method that fits interpretable models on small regions of the input data to generate approximate explanations for the predictions of the black-box model within that region.

Figure 5.11 shows an example of using LIME, which displays key pixels in image classification decisions, to diagnose why an image of a husky might have been misclassified as a wolf. We can see from the LIME output in the right-side image that the CNN picked up on the snow in the image's background to make its wolf classification, indicating an opportunity for debugging the model and improving its performance. Methods for debugging these sorts of issues in neural networks will be discussed in Chapter 9, "Conclusion."

Clients, users, and regulators trust models more when they see explanations showing that a model is functioning as expected. Conversely, they trust models less when interpretability methods reveal that a model relies on irrelevant relationships within the data, or relationships and patterns that cannot legally or responsibly be used. Data scientists ought to see value in both cases, as the interpretability methods either increase trust in a model that is worth trusting or decrease trust in a model that ought not be trusted (or should be trusted only in certain circumstances where we can be reasonably confident in its predictions).

(a) Husky classified as wolf   (b) Explanation

Figure 5.11: LIME output for an image of a husky incorrectly classified as a wolf

Source: Ribeiro et al. 2016. "'Why Should I Trust You?' Explaining the Predictions of Any Classifier," found at https://arxiv.org/abs/1602.04938

Leveraging the Improved Performance of Black-Box Models

In contexts where predictive performance is of higher importance than all other factors, like within most Kaggle model prediction competitions, black-box models are almost always the most highly performing models. The reasons for these successes are many. However, most black-box models share the following useful traits: First, most black-box models use some form of ensemble learning. This ensembling typically takes the form of bagging, wherein many models are fit independently to bootstrapped resamples of the data (as in the case of random forest models), or sequential methods like boosting, wherein many models are fit sequentially on the whole dataset, with higher weights being assigned successively to the observations that previous models had the most trouble predicting (i.e., the highest residuals). Second, black-box models can perform their own regularization to find an ideal balance between over- and underfitting. Taken together, these capabilities make a strong case for using black-box models when possible.

Acquiring New Knowledge

Interpretability methods have helped us learn more about how neural networks work. Neural network–specific interpretability methods have helped scientists discover that CNNs focus more on texture than shape; how networks can be fooled into making incorrect predictions with small changes to their inputs, where the individual components of complex natural language processing (NLP) models like BERT focus within a body of text; and even how neural networks learn to construct their own self-designated "concepts" (features) to describe individual classes. In Figure 5.12, we can see how an implementation of a global interpretability method called ConceptSHAP generates human-interpretable explanations for the features that the network looks for when making a class prediction.

Figure 5.12: Depiction of ConceptSHAP output for a CNN. The three series of thumbnails show the "concepts" most associated with certain image classes.
Source: Yeh, Chih-Kuan, et al. "On Completeness-Aware Concept-Based Explanations in Deep Neural Networks." ArXiv:1910.07969 [Cs, Stat], June 2020. arXiv.org, http://arxiv.org/abs/1910.07969.

The top concepts for each classification category (lion, tiger, or zebra) correspond to patches of images that humans can easily recognize and confirm as reasonable. Black and white stripe patterns correspond to zebras, images containing orange and black "tiger-like" patterns correspond to tigers, and images of large cats that do not contain tiger patterns correspond to lions. Concepts containing primarily landscape shots like Concepts 21 and 39 indicate evidence of overfitting in the network and opportunity for improvement, because, as in the wolf/husky example, the background landscape should not contribute to the classification prediction.

Addressing Critiques of Interpretability Methods

Unfortunately, using interpretability methods and black boxes together is not a silver bullet for all of our data science woes. Just as much of data science is actually a data art, so, too, is there an art to choosing the correct combination of interpretability methods for explaining a black-box model. If we fail to implement the correct interpretability methods or fail to understand the explanations produced by them, we may be left worse off than if we hadn't attempted to interpret our models at all. Critics point out the shortcomings in robustness and fidelity of various interpretability methods, and if we want to develop an effective art of using interpretability methods, then we need to at least consider how these critiques can be addressed.[3]

Explanations Generated by Interpretability Methods Are Not Robust

Ideally, a good interpretability method strikes a balance between being robust to unimportant changes in the underlying model, while being sensitive to meaningful changes within it. After all, we wouldn't want our explanations to change just because we switched from a random forest model to XGBoost if the models are similar in their performance. Similarly, we would hope that our explanations for individual observations would only rely on changes in the values of important features and ignore changes in unimportant ones. Most critiques of interpretability methods have centered upon their robustness, with some researchers noting that a handful of popular interpretability methods are overly sensitive to changes in the underlying characteristics of the model. This sensitivity appears tied to important characteristics of the model, including the following:

- **The model's underlying data:** At a base level, explanations generated by interpretability methods are influenced by the specific data that the model is fit on and can be unstable when the specific data points being examined are sparse or rest on a decision boundary between classes. Looking at the LIME effects in Figure 5.13 for the top five most important variables in the home price prediction task, we can see that some variables like gr_liv_area and garage_area are highly variable in how much their values contribute to the predictions for each observation on average.

- **Model form:** Interpretability methods have been shown to work differently across different forms of models. For example, LIME-based local interpretability methods were shown to produce different explanations for the impact of feature values on the same observation when the underlying model is a logistic regression versus a random forest. In Figure 5.14, we build our own comparison of the mean percent difference in LIME feature contribution (to sale price) between a random forest model and an XGBoost model for the home price prediction task. Each percentage point along the x-axis represents the mean absolute percent difference in contribution to sale price per square foot. Both sets of LIME values were calculated for the same set of 250 observations. Across the different

---

[3] See "Stop explaining black box machine learning models for high stakes decisions and use interpretable models instead" by Cynthia Rudin (2019), "How Do I Fool You?: Manipulating User Trust via Misleading Black Box Explanations" by Himabindu Lakkaraju and Osbert Bastani (2020), and "Fooling LIME and SHAP: Adversarial Attacks on Post hoc Explanation Methods" by Slack et al. (2020).

features, we see differences in the average feature contribution of over +/- 50%, indicating that, assuming the two models perform similarly, we should not trust LIME to be a robust interpretability method for this task.

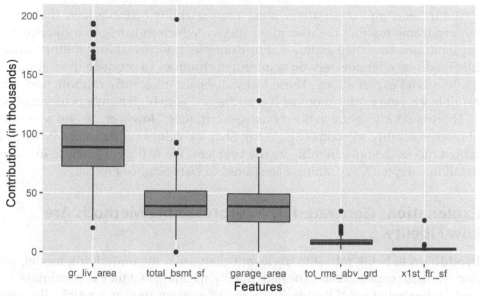

Figure 5.13: Boxplots of the top five features by mean LIME contribution. Boxplots show the total range in contributions to sale price across all observations.

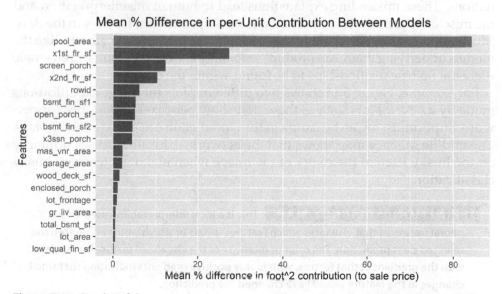

Figure 5.14: Barplot of the mean absolute percent difference in per-unit LIME feature contributions for each feature. Put more simply, for each feature, how different are the contributions of one-unit increases across the two models?

■ **Model hyperparameters:** Explanations generated by interpretability methods have been shown to be sensitive to model hyperparameters. For example, neural networks that have been explicitly modified to be more robust in their predictions showed an increase in the robustness of their explanations relative to comparable unmodified neural networks.

To further complicate matters, most interpretability methods have their own hyperparameters that the user must specify, which in turn can influence the explanations that they generate. For example, interpretability methods like LIME and its offshoots rely on sampling techniques to produce their approximate model explanations. These techniques are inherently random and can result in varying explanations unless addressed with high numbers of samples.

There is clearly justice to the robustness critiques. However, careful selection of interpretability methods (e.g., using Shapley values rather than LIME) and robust model design can mitigate the problem. We will discuss those in more detail in Chapter 7, "Auditing a Responsible Data Science Project."

Explanations Generated by Interpretability Methods Are Low Fidelity

In addition to being robust to irrelevant changes in the underlying model, we also want our explanations to be high fidelity, meaning that they approximate the underlying behavior of the black-box model as accurately as possible. Because they are only approximating the underlying behavior of the black-box model, lower-fidelity interpretability methods may produce factually incorrect explanations. These misleading explanations lead to human misinterpretation and the mischaracterization of important relationships between features in the data. Much attention has been paid to cases where interpretability methods, like the models underlying them, can produce seemingly reasonable results, even where there are no true relationships to be found within the data.

For example, Figure 5.15 shows two different plots for image classifications made by a CNN. Plots such as these that show per-pixel importance (or per-word importance for text examples) for a prediction are called *saliency maps*. The middle saliency map shows that the network, naturally, focuses primarily on the husky itself at the center of the image when making a (correct) husky classification.

> **DEFINITION SALIENCY MAP**   This is a local interpretability method for neural networks that visualizes which features (pixels or words) most influenced the selected class prediction. The color or intensity of the visualized feature is associated with the gradient at that feature, with highly positive gradients indicating that small changes in the feature would have changed the prediction.

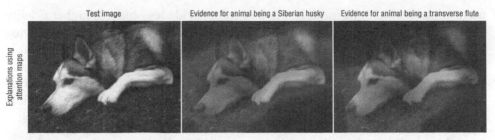

Figure 5.15: The target image (left) and saliency plots for two separate predictions for the target image class

Source: Rudin, 2019. "Stop explaining black machine learning models for high stakes decisions and use interpretable models instead" found at `https://www.nature.com/articles/s42256-019-0048-x`

On its own, this saliency map would seem very sensible, highlighting the regions of the image that most humans would focus on when trying to determine what they were looking at. However, the model produces almost the same saliency map when explaining the network's classification of the image as a transverse flute, an obviously incorrect classification!

Keep in mind, though, that using inflexible methods like regression and simple trees also produces low-fidelity explanations. While model interpretability for models like decision trees or linear/logistic regression is achieved through their intrinsic decision rules or coefficients, these rules or coefficients are not very high fidelity themselves. Regardless of the underlying structure of the data, they always assume linear relationships (or, in the case of simple trees, locally binary relationships) between the model's input features. If the features are not related in those simple ways, the actual relationships can go almost entirely undetected, hurting predictive performance relative to a more flexible (high variance) black-box model and preventing practitioners from understanding what may be important relationships in the underlying data.

NOTE   Intrinsically interpretable Generalized Additive Models (GAMs) allow for these nonlinear relationships in the data (and other elements of the underlying data that may violate the assumptions of a conventional linear regression) to be approximated with higher fidelity. However, GAMs are not widely used on account of the sheer number of options that they allow users to leverage in expanding upon conventional linear models.

The Forking Paths of Model Interpretability

How can we best maximize model interpretability in modeling tasks where incorrect predictions can cause harm? On the one hand, using interpretability methods and black-box models together can provide less-biased, higher fidelity explanations than intrinsically interpretable models do. At the same time, applying interpretability methods can be finicky. Moreover, intrinsically interpretable models reach a guaranteed degree of model interpretability from the outset, providing estimates of global feature impact and basic explanations for individual observations. We have seemingly reached a fork on the road of our responsible data science journey. The two paths forward can be summarized as follows:

- **Minimizing risk:** Stick with using intrinsically interpretable models to minimize the overall risk of a project, as well as the time spent learning new interpretability methods and layering them over the original model.

- **Maximizing performance:** Spend time developing expertise and toolchains that will allow for using black-box models and interpretability methods together to achieve higher performance and better explanations for predictions.

External pressures might dictate choosing one option over the other. Companies or teams that operate in more tightly regulated or risky industries, like health insurance or consumer credit, may have no choice but to minimize risk and stick with the first path. However, teams in tech, finance, and retail may opt for the second path, using black-box models to maximize performance and maintain a competitive advantage over peer companies. Regardless of whether the option to choose is available, practitioners ought to explore the change in predictive performance obtained by moving from intrinsically interpretable models to black-box models within their specific project. After all, an intrinsically interpretable model might achieve the best predictive performance in some cases!

The Four-Measure Baseline

The full spectrum of a predictive model's performance can be approximated with a *four-measure baseline*.

- **The featureless predictor:** The lower bound of performance in a modeling task should be a measure representing the performance of a *featureless predictor*. This "model" shows the hypothetical performance achieved by predicting every observation as belonging to the most common class (classification) or by always predicting the mean value of all observations (regression).

> **DEFINITION FEATURELESS PREDICTOR** This is a "model" that naively predicts the most common value as the outcome of every observation. For classification models, this value is usually the most common class, whereas for regression models this value is usually the average of value of the all of the inputs.

- **The optimal performance measure:** The upper bound of performance in a modeling task should be a measure representing the best guess for the highest performance that human experts, other groups, or already existing automated systems achieve within a particular modeling task. Ideally, the final production model for a particular task approaches the performance of this measure, or at least is closer to it than to the featureless predictor. Note that the inclusion of this measure does not make sense for all modeling tasks. For example, a task that is relatively new, specific to a niche domain, or deals with sensitive material might not have any past performance measures available.

- **The interpretable baseline:** The performance of a simple interpretable model is the most important measure to consider when benchmarking. It shows the average "realistic" performance measure for a model within a given modeling task, establishing a "baseline" performance for the specially tuned interpretable and black-box models to beat. Every percentage point increase in performance over this baseline serves to justify the additional, more involved work completed by a modeling team.

- **The black-box baseline:** This measure represents the performance of an untuned black-box model, such as a random forest, with its baseline parameter settings. Ideally, a tuned black-box model would approach the performance of the optimal performance line more closely than this untuned baseline model. We would expect that the black-box baseline measure would indicate higher performance than the interpretable baseline performance measure.

By comparing the predictive performance of these four measures, we acquire an understanding of the trade-offs involved in whichever modeling path we choose to go down. If we choose to minimize risk by deploying only an intrinsically interpretable model, we will be able to make that choice knowing the difference in predictive performance (large or small) that we would forgo. Similarly, comparing a black-box model with our baseline interpretable model will give us the confidence that the increased difficulty of achieving model interpretability is outweighed by the increase in performance and possible resulting improvements to the fidelity of the explanations generated.

Building Our Own Credit Scoring Model

We will be using a variant of the German Credit Data dataset from the UCI Machine Learning Repository to show how to establish a four-measure performance baseline for classification models. The German Credit Dataset contains loan application information across 62 variables for 1,000 separate people, all of which are used to make a binary classification of whether each person is a "Good" (low) or "Bad" (high) credit risk for the bank.

> **NOTE**   The code for this exercise can be found within the repositories at www.wiley.com/go/responsibledatascience or www.github.com/Gflemin/responsibledatascience. This variant of the dataset is sourced directly from the *caret* package within R and has already undergone some feature engineering. We will build up the coding practices used within this exercise as we work through it and later exercises later in the chapter. We will only be looking at abbreviated segments of the code in this exercise, with the fully reproducible code and related exploratory data analysis available on the GitHub repository.

For setup, we include here the code for loading our packages, helper functions, and the raw data:

```
library(here)

source(here("ch5_packages.R"))
source(here("ch5_helpers.R"))

data(GermanCredit)

df_raw = GermanCredit %>%
    as_tibble()
```

Following that, we can take a quick a look at a print view of the data. Just want to know what we are working with here!

```
## # A tibble: 1,000 x 62
##    Duration Amount InstallmentRate~ ResidenceDurati~   Age
##       <int>  <int>            <int>            <int> <int>
##          6   1169                4                4    67
##         48   5951                2                2    22
##         12   2096                2                3    49
##         42   7882                2                4    45
##         24   4870                3                4    53
##         36   9055                2                4    35
```

```
##       24    2835              3              4   53
##       36    6948              2              2   35
##       12    3059              2              4   61
##       30    5234              4              2   28
## # ... with 990 more rows, and 57 more variables
```

Using Train-Test Splits

After loading in the data, we need to next consider how we want to handle dividing our data groups for model validation. For large datasets and for a model meant for deployment, we would likely want to consider a cross-validation approach like *k*-folds cross-validation. However, because our data is relatively small and because we are only attempting to establish a performance baseline for later modeling attempts, we will simply split our data into train and test sets.

We will use the `initial_split()` function from the rsample package to split our data into train and test splits. Using the rsample package rather than base R functions like `sample()` or `sample.int()` allows us to easily pipeline our workflow through tidymodels, a relatively new but already robust set of modeling packages. We will use more functions from these packages as we progress through this example.

For now, let's set the prop argument within `initial_split()` to 0.7 so that we get a 70% train and 30% test split.

```
data_split = df_raw %>%
   initial_split(prop = 0.7)

 training_data = training(data_split)
 testing_data = testing(data_split)
```

Great, we have split the data into train and test sets. However, printing either of our splits shows that we have 62 features in our dataset. Many of these features are likely not important, are highly correlated, or are otherwise "dirty" enough that they ought to be dropped.

Feature Selection and Feature Engineering

We need to perform feature selection and feature engineering when modeling to ensure that we are using only the relevant features. Using irrelevant predictors, or sets of highly correlated predictors, can introduce noise, impair predictive performance, and heighten the chances of getting spurious results. Many books on data science cover feature engineering and selection in depth, and we encourage readers of this book to explore them if they want a detailed treatment of that subject.[4] For our purposes, we will stick with recommending a few general feature engineering steps that are most relevant to our current credit scoring task.

■ **Checking feature importance:** We have already discussed feature importance earlier in this chapter as an example of a global interpretability method. To reiterate, feature importance refers to any number of methods used to rank features within a model by how much each feature positively contributes to that model's predictions on average. In this example, we will use an R implementation of the Boruta algorithm. Boruta works by iterating through multiple models, each time randomly permuting the values of one feature. It uses a random forest model to classify the features as important, tentative, or unimportant by how much the error of the model increases after their values are randomly permuted. For our benchmarking, we will only keep the features that are classified as "Confirmed" (which means important in this case).

```
imp_feats = Boruta(training_data, training_data$Class)
```

The previous code ran Boruta and confirmed 14 features as important, 8 as tentative, and 40 as unimportant when considering "Class" as the target feature. Readers curious to see the plotted Boruta feature importance values can see them by running the *ch5_walkthrough.Rmd* script within the chapter repository.

To pull out only the important features from our original data, we "pull" the important variable names from the Boruta object and filter our dataframe down to those variables.

```
imp_confirmed = enframe(imp_feats$finalDecision) %>%
    filter(value == "Confirmed") %>%
    mutate(name = str_remove(name, "train_data\\.")) %>%
    pull(name)

df_imps = training_data %>%
    select(all_of(imp_confirmed))
```

All the way from 62 features to 14 features in only 7 lines of code. Not bad!

■ **Ensuring that numeric variables are on similar scales:** Predictive models will pay much more attention to features with values ranging from 1 to 100,000 than to features with values ranging between 1 and 5. Usually, such a difference does not reflect a difference in variable importance.

---

[4] Readers interested in learning more about best practices for feature selection should seek out "Feature Engineering and Selection: A Practical Approach for Predictive Models" by Max Kuhn and Kjell Johnson, as well as "Hands-On Machine Learning with Scikit-Learn, Keras and Tensorflow" by Aurelien Geron.

(Consider what would happen if you switched from kilometers to meters in measuring a distance.) To avoid this issue, we recommend standardizing or normalizing numeric variables.

For our final preprocessing step, we will standardize our numeric variables, Duration and Amount.

```
df_processed = df_subsetted %>%
  mutate(Duration = (Duration - min(Duration))/(max(Duration) -
min(Duration)),
        Amount = (Amount - min(Amount))/(max(Amount) - min(Amount)))
```

Now, both variables are bound between 0 and 1 and have the same range as the dummy variables within the dataset. Again, readers can confirm these results for themselves by either running these scripts locally on their machines or by running them in the code linked in our GitHub.

Baseline Models

Next, we will move on to creating our baseline interpretable and black-box models. Rather than relying on loading individual modeling packages and being forced to use their distinct syntax to create our models, we will use parsnip, a modeling package from the tidymodels metapackage, which allows for writing multiple different types of models with the same code syntax.

First, we build our interpretable baseline model (in this case, a logistic regression) and an example black-box model (in this case, a random forest).

```
mod_log = logistic_reg() %>%
   set_mode("classification") %>%
   set_engine("glm")
mod_rf = rand_forest() %>%
   set_mode("classification") %>%
   set_engine("ranger")
```

Fitting the models is just as easy.

```
mod_log_fit = mod_log %>%
  fit(Class ~., data = data[["train"]])
mod_rf_fit = mod_rf %>%
  fit(Class ~., data = data[["train"]])
```

Generating predictions for our models is slightly more complicated, requiring us to bind multiple dataframes together.

```
preds_mod_log = mod_log_fit %>%
   predict(data[["test"]], type = "prob") %>%
   bind_cols(data[["test"]]) %>%
   mutate(pred_class = factor(if_else(.[, 1] > .[, 2], "Bad", "Good")))

preds_mod_rf = mod_rf_fit %>%
   predict(data[["test"]], type = "prob") %>%
   bind_cols(data[["test"]]) %>%
   mutate(pred_class = factor(if_else(.[, 1] > .[, 2], "Bad", "Good")))
```

There is now a results dataframe for both models that contains the test data, the predicted probabilities, and the actual class for each observation. We will now use the `roc_auc()` and `roc_curve()` functions from another tidymodels package, yardstick, to easily generate area under the curve (AUC), sensitivity, and specificity metrics to allow us to approximate the performance of our models via a plotted ROC curve (shown in Figure 5.16).

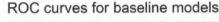

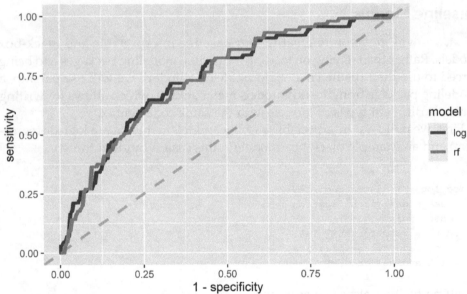

Figure 5.16: ROC curve comparing the relative performance of a logistic regression and random forest

```
log_auc = preds_mod_log %>%
   roc_auc(truth = Class, .pred_Bad)
rf_auc = preds_mod_rf %>%
   roc_auc(truth = Class, .pred_Bad)
```

```
aucs = bind_rows(log_auc, rf_auc)

log_rocs = preds_mod_log %>%
  roc_curve(truth = Class, .pred_Bad) %>%
  mutate(model = "log")

rf_rocs = preds_mod_rf %>%
  roc_curve(truth = Class, .pred_Bad) %>%
  mutate(model = "rf")

rocs = bind_rows(log_rocs, rf_rocs)

rocs %>%
  ggplot(aes(x=1-specificity, y=sensitivity,
  group = model, color = model)) +
    geom_line(size = 1.2) +
    geom_abline(lty = 2, alpha = 0.5, color = "gray50", size = 1.2) +
    ggtitle("ROC curves for baseline models")
```

Interestingly, the ROC curves for each of the two baseline models show relatively similar performance. The AUC values for the curves confirm this, as they are less than 0.1% apart! Would we really be confident arguing for using a black-box model over an intrinsically interpretable model given such a small difference in performance? Plus, we only looked at the performance of each model over one split of the data. Are we confident that others who would want to run this script would be able to reproduce the same results?

The Importance of Making Your Code Work for Everyone

Unfortunately, the previous steps created many intermediate objects that could cause confusion when we or other individuals want to reproduce this code later. In fact, if you ran the script multiple times, you might even notice that you end up with a different number of important variables or highly correlated variables within each iteration. These differences are caused by two main sources of variability.

Execution Variability

Formatting R code into .Rmds and Python code into Jupyter Notebooks makes code easier to follow and encourages experimentation. However, these benefits come as part of (yet another) trade-off. Jumping back and forth between code chunks often leads to situations where users re-execute code that modifies objects in place, silently changing the object. For example, if we have a code chunk that nests lists together, rerunning the code chunk after it has already been run once will create an additional nesting layer that will likely cause code chunks later in the script to fail.

The code shown so far for this credit scoring model example does not address this. We need to update our code practices to ensure that the results of our script are reproducible, generating consistent outputs and minimizing unexpected results between runs.

Addressing Execution Variability with Functionalized Code

Functionalizing our code takes care of execution variability and is a generally good practice for any code that is meant to be either used multiple times or used by multiple different people. Wrapping the previous code within a function ensures that we always generate the appropriate result every time it is run, giving us an opportunity to control for stochastic and execution variability, should users decide to rerun code chunks. Given the same raw data, our functionalized code ought to always generate the same results regardless of how many times it is run.

```
data = preprocessor(df_raw)
```

Plus, writing and understanding one line of code is much simpler than trying to write and understand tens of lines.

Stochastic Variability

Regardless of the programming language used, most data science workflows rely on functions that are based on stochastic (random) operations. For example, functions like `initial_split()` sample the data for each split randomly. Of course, randomness when creating splits is a useful characteristic, as it eliminates nonrandom sources of difference between the splits. Fortunately, this randomness can be made reproducible. Each random operation within R or Python is associated with a discrete "seed" that can be specified by the user. Ensuring that these seed values are consistently set is critical for producing reproducible results.

Addressing Stochastic Variability via Resampling

Fitting our two models over multiple resamples of the original data ought to give us a better idea of whether the miniscule observed performance difference between them is real. To accomplish this resampling, we will build another wrapper function that allows for comparing the average performance of our two baseline models over a user-specified number of bootstrap resamples. For maximum flexibility, we also have included options for the user to specify the inclusion of a featureless classifier and an estimated distribution of metrics for expected optimal performance. Again, this optimal performance metric is a guess made on the part of the user, but ideally it is informed by some past performance standard or expert knowledge about the modeling task.

The scores produced by each of these values ought to serve as the lower and upper bounds for the performance of our final model within this task.

```
benchmarks = benchmarker(df_raw, num = 30)
```

The output of the `benchmarker()` function is a list comprised of the mean bootstrapped performance estimates, the bootstrapped dataframes, a plot comparing the performance of the logistic regression and random forest models, and a plot comparing the two models with the performance of a featureless predictor and an estimate of the optimal predictive performance within this modeling task.

The first element of the `benchmarker()` function output is formatted as a table in Figure 5.17. Moving from left to right, the table columns contain the name of the model used, the performance metric (in this case, accuracy), the mean estimate for that performance metric over all bootstrap resamples, the p-value for a two-sample t-test of differences in means between the interpretable model and the others (0 indicating extremely low p-values, and NA indicating that we are testing a mean against itself), and the p-value for a two-sample t-test between the black-box model and the others.

Benchmarker() Metrics Output				
model	metric	estimate	pval_intep	pval_bbox
featureless	accuracy	0.430	0	0.00
logistic_reg	accuracy	0.745	NA	0.00
rand_forest	accuracy	0.759	0	NA
optimal	accuracy	0.904	0	0.02

Figure 5.17: Table of outputs of metrics object from `benchmarker()`. The final two columns represent the rounded p-values from two-sample t-tests of differences of means between models.

NOTE   The `benchmarker()` function generates a distribution of the performance metric of choice for the featureless predictor and optimal performance measure. Creating a distribution of these values allows us to present them as distributions, which we can then t-test for significant differences. The distributional parameters can be changed by the user to suit their specific needs.

After bootstrapping, the magnitude of the accuracy difference between the interpretable and black-box models has increased. Moreover, the t-test results in columns four and five of the dataframe confirm that the two accuracy estimates for the models are significantly different from each other. Good thing we tried bootstrap resampling!

The second element of the `benchmarker()` function output shown in Figure 5.18 visually compares the performance of the interpretable and black-box models using boxplots of all of their estimated bootstrap performance metrics.

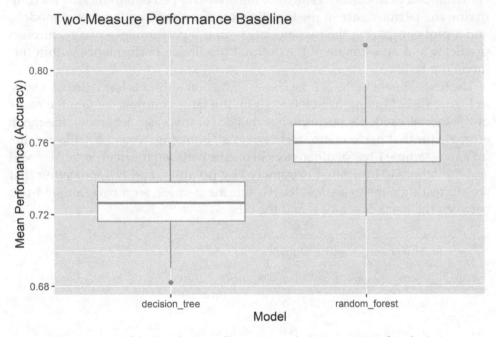

Figure 5.18: Boxplots of the distribution of bootstrapped accuracy metrics for a logistic regression and random forest model. Each boxplot was generated from 30 different bootstrap resamples.

Generating boxplots of the performance profiles of the two bootstrapped models best communicates the difference in performance between baseline interpretable and black-box models. Here, we can clearly see that the interpretable and black-box model baselines have significantly differing performance.

The third and final element of the `benchmarker()` function output (shown in Figure 5.19) is a barplot comparing the performance of the two baseline models with the performance of the featureless predictor and the theorized optimal performance measure.

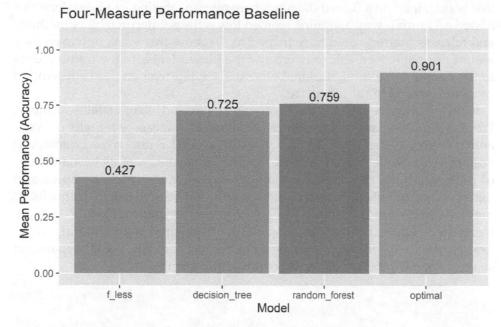

Figure 5.19: The four-measure performance baseline, showing one barplot for each of the four "models" representing their mean performance (accuracy) over 30 bootstrap resamples

The plot clearly shows that both baseline models beat the performance of the featureless predictor by a large margin. Moreover, we can see that the black-box model performs slightly better than the interpretable model, while itself being well below the theorized optimal performance measure. Tuning the hyperparameters of the black-box model will help close this gap. Eventually, it will even help us achieve better model interpretability!

Summary

Knowing what we know now, is there anything that Amazon could have done to avoid the issues of fairness within their résumé prediction model? To begin with, Amazon ought to have been tracking the predictive performance of their model with respect to fairness metrics, especially for gender. This would have allowed Amazon to recognize early on that their model was generating unfair predictions. Clearly, the application of interpretability methods would also have been helpful. If properly applied, interpretability methods would have helped Amazon to understand *why* their model was generating these unfair predictions. In an alternate world, these changes ought to have enabled Amazon to identify and begin to address the issues in their model much earlier. Still, this was a model that was trained on a flawed dataset where human labeling had been done in a biased and unfair way, assigning women low ratings. Interpretability methods and fairness metrics could have helped to diagnose this issue; however, they would not have been able to overcome the biased labels in the training data or the deeper, systemic issues that were dissuading women from applying to work at Amazon in the first place.

In this chapter, we explored model interpretability and interpretability methods. We also discussed many of the ethical and procedural reasons for why data scientists or society need model interpretability, as well as how it can be achieved or approximated for even the most complex of black-box models, via the use of interpretability methods. As companies deploy ever more complex and high-performing black-box models, they will also need to use interpretability methods to go beyond simply recognizing whether harmful predictions are being made and get at the reasoning behind those predictions. Starting in the next chapter, we will begin working through the compilation and preparation steps of the RDS framework using real-world examples.

Part

III

EDS in Practice

In This Part

Chapter 6: Beginning a Responsible Data Science Project
Chapter 7: Auditing a Responsible Data Science Project
Chapter 8: Auditing for Neural Networks
Chapter 9: Conclusion

CHAPTER

6

Beginning a Responsible Data Science Project

Armed with the historical, social, and technical knowledge that we have acquired over the past five chapters, we are finally ready to work through our own example data science projects. Arriving at this point may have been an unexpectedly long journey; however, each of the cases that we have discussed so far ought to have impressed upon us the need for deeper consideration of every aspect of our data science projects. We must go beyond our roles as technical experts and engage with broader questions beyond those that we can answer with code and mathematics alone. Data science is difficult to do well; doing it well *and* responsibly raises that bar even further.

If we want to learn to use the Responsible Data Science framework to identify potential modeling harms, then we need to become more familiar with the harms themselves. Rather than shying away from ethically charged modeling tasks (e.g., crime prediction or recidivism prediction), we will work through these tasks ourselves to learn firsthand the challenges that they present.

Over the course of this chapter, we will work through the Justification, Compilation, and Preparation stages of the Responsible Data Science framework introduced in Chapter 4, "The Responsible Data Science Framework." In completing these stages, we accomplish the following:

JUSTIFY:

➤   The tractability of the modeling task, the relevance of the dataset to the modeling task, and the efficacy of the specific modeling approach chosen

➤ The modeling task, by indicating consideration of relevant ethical issues and past successes or failures from similar modeling tasks

COMPILE:

➤ The datasets, software environments, and project management tools that will be used throughout the project to ensure reproducibility and collaboration

➤ Ideas and artifacts for documentation, including datasheets, model cards, and audit reports, that we will flesh out and refer to in subsequent stages of our work (especially in Chapters 7, "Auditing a Responsible Data Science Project," and 8, "Auditing for Neural Networks.")

PREPARE:

➤ The raw data for modeling, by cleaning it, performing feature engineering, and selecting features for modeling

➤ The cleaned data for modeling, by splitting the dataset into appropriate training, validation, and test sets as well as deciding upon a cross-validation approach

Prior to beginning our work in earnest, we want to make sure to provide a caveat to the Responsible Data Science framework.

How the Responsible Data Science Framework Addresses the Common Cause

In Chapter 4, we discussed the common reason why otherwise well-meaning groups continue to build harmful AI. To summarize, we discussed how most of the cases of publicly known modeling harms occurred, in large part, as a result of an overbearing focus on achieving technical excellence within the project, such as leveraging impressive new modeling approaches to eke out the best possible performance.[1] This single-minded focus on achieving better predictive performance serves the same purpose as blinders that keep a horse focused singularly on what's in front of them, in the hopes that this will help them stay ahead of the adjacent horses. However, data science is not horse racing. It requires awareness of the context that our blinders obscure. Standard best

---

[1] Readers interested in a deeper dive into this idea should seek out Birhane et al.'s paper "The Underlying Values of Machine Learning Research" (2020).

practices in data science teach us to understand what the business problem is, how it translates into an analytics problem, and how organizational dynamics relate to success or failure. Best practices for responsible data science go further in this direction, requiring that we broaden our understanding of the context surrounding the data we gathered, the parties that will need to deeply understand our models, and the groups that will be affected by our model's predictions. For example, we need to grapple with how our model's predictions might unfairly impact different groups of people, especially those that are protected by law. We need to understand the potential range of uses to which our AI models might be put and whether they might result in people being denied recourse to human decision-makers.

As part of the Responsible Data Science framework, data science teams should consider model performance across multiple metrics, as well as broader social, legal, and institutional factors that are relevant to their specific modeling context. Handling these broader considerations is just as important as achieving high performance. Quantifying them, however, is trickier than measuring model accuracy, making it harder to provide specific one-size-fits-all guidance. The diversity of the modeling team, the project's goal, the population affected by the deployed model, the organization's structure facilitating the project, the results of similar past projects run by other groups, the sentiment of the public toward AI, and numerous other factors *all* have varying importance across projects.

Regardless of the specific project's context, we recommend that teams do the following:

- Solicit as much feedback from other groups as possible, *especially* from any populations or stakeholders who might be affected by the model's predictions. Centering their experiences within the model design process greatly reduces the chance of missing some factor in the model that might have otherwise caused them harm.

- Understand your training data and the population well in order to foresee possibly devastating failure scenarios.

- Set procedures in place for addressing failure scenarios.

- Acquire more data. Among our recommended "technical" interventions for improving model performance and reducing issues of fairness, acquiring more training data (especially for groups underrepresented in the data) is the simplest and most impactful.

We turn now to some practical case studies that will illustrate how to implement the Responsible Data Science framework. Let's start with a review of the datasets used.

Datasets Used

We will work through one classification and one regression example within this chapter to see how the Responsible Data Science framework works across differing conditions and circumstances. We have posted notes and code for both of these datasets to the repositories at `wiley.com/go/responsibledatascience` and `github.com/Gflemin/responsibledatascience`. Links to the original source of each dataset can be found in the hyperlinks section of each of the project's datasheets. Both datasets that we cover in this chapter represent real nonsimulated data.

In our examples, we will be referring to protected categories and groups (e.g., race, age, ethnicity, etc.). In the interest of clarity when discussing these groups, we use the same terms and categories used by the creators of the datasets, avoiding larger questions of how these groups ought to be best defined.

Regression Datasets—Communities and Crime

The Communities and Crime dataset comprises socioeconomic data for individual communities combined across various sources, namely, the 1990 U.S. Census, the 1990 Law Enforcement Management and Admin Stats (LEMAS) survey, and crime data from the 1995 FBI Uniform Crime Reporting program (UCR). Each of these predictor features can be used within a model to generate predictions for crime statistics per capita within each community.

The dataset itself is a CSV file comprising various crime and demographic counts in 1990 for individual communities within the United States. The 147 features in the data comprise 125 predictor features, 4 identifiers, and 18 different potential outcome features. Each of these outcome features represents counts for a unique category of crime. We use the version of the data posted to Kaggle, rather than the data from UCI, because the Kaggle data is unnormalized.[2]

Rather than attempting to create an ethically fraught pre-crime model ourselves, our goal for using the Communities and Crime dataset is to explore fairness and interpretability in a regression context via tracking the relationships between demographic characteristics and the overall percentage of people in poverty within that community. The analysis for this data that would otherwise go in Chapter 7 is instead available on the book's GitHub repository.

Classification Datasets—COMPAS

The Correctional Offender Management Profiling for Alternative Sanctions (COMPAS) dataset comprises the records of 11,757 individuals arrested in Broward County, Florida, between 2013 and 2014 who were scored by the pretrial

---

[2] `www.kaggle.com/kkanda/analyzing-uci-crime-and-communities-dataset`

risk assessment tool, COMPAS, developed by Equivant (formerly known as Northpointe). The data was made available online in 2016 by ProPublica, a public interest investigative news group, after they received the data in fulfillment of a public records request issued to the Broward County, Florida, Sheriff's Department. ProPublica used the outcomes present in the dataset to show that, in addition to being only 61 percent accurate, the original COMPAS algorithm was unfairly biased against African American defendants and consistently rated them as more likely to re-offend than white defendants with similar histories. The COMPAS dataset has since become the go-to dataset to work through for anyone looking to teach or understand issues of fairness in modeling.

The main dataset for COMPAS is a SQLite3 database containing information for each individual about their criminal history, past jail and prison time, demographics, and COMPAS risk scores. However, ProPublica also provides two separate CSV files for predicting whether an individual will recidivate violently or nonviolently in the upcoming two years. We use the nonviolent recidivism CSV file (`compas-scores-two-years.csv`) as the basis for our analysis in this chapter and in Chapter 7.

Our goal for using COMPAS is to understand the racial and age-related biases in both types of recidivism prediction outcomes, create explanations for these biases that would be useful to lay users, and attempt to implement approaches that help to reduce these biases.

Common Elements Across Our Analyses[3]

We will complete our analyses of these datasets in a systematic fashion. We will discuss the static elements of our analyses that would otherwise be duplicated across each example. Maintaining consistency across projects (e.g., with unified software tools and project file structures) is a general "best practice" that we want to integrate in our work here.

As we did with the code in Chapter 5, "Model Interpretability: The What and the Why," we will work through the examples using ad hoc coding practices before switching to a more robust functionalized workflow. This mirrors how code is often written in practice, where more exploratory, less reproducible code is written initially prior to being refactored later in the project timeline as the team's approach is solidified.

Project Structure and Documentation

All data scientists have experienced the pain of attempting to replicate another person's work on their own machine. Beyond the issues of execution variability

---

[3]This and subsequent sections in this chapter © 2021 Datastats LLC and Grant Fleming.

(e.g., nonfunctionalized code) and stochastic variability (e.g., differences in random seeds) that we discussed in Chapter 5, collaboration with other data scientists forces us to contend with how a responsible data science project ought to be structured. There's no shortage of views on this subject and no single perfect structure to follow. Adjusting to these interproject differences can be difficult, with different requirements for documentation, filenaming schemes, folder structures, and collaboration practices increasing the overhead required to onboard new team members. Moreover, rigorous documentation practices and convoluted directory structures can greatly add to the overall workload for each team member.

Still, most experienced data scientists and software engineers would argue that the benefits of maintaining comprehensive documentation and a clean, consistent project structure is worth the short-term increase in work. Unified project structure and good documentation reduce the time it takes to get new team members oriented, minimize the time spent combing through files and folders, improve project robustness by codifying knowledge that may otherwise be unique to certain team members, highlight instances where decision points occurred, and, more generally, provide a form of insurance if any decisions need to be justified in the future. These benefits hold true even if we consider the standard practice of providing only a README, license, data dictionary, and commented scripts or notebook files of the actual analysis.

Project Structure for the Responsible Data Science Framework: Everything in Its Place

No data science project proceeds from start to finish without iteration over the intervening steps. Complicated tuning procedures might need to be tweaked or added to as different models are trialed. Additions to the raw data might necessitate rerunning the entire modeling pipeline. Throughout the modeling pipeline, steps like these often must be repeated, delaying the project's completion. The complex structure of large data science projects contributes to these issues, as it's often unclear how objects and functions scattered across scripts relate to each other.

Targets and the Joy of Workflow

Workflow automation tools like GNU Make help software engineers and data scientists solve the problems of creating a workflow for a modeling pipeline by defining the various disparate objects within a modeling pipeline as a set of interconnected *targets*, which can represent a script, data file, function, output, or any other object that can be stored in memory within a coding environment. Workflow automation tools greatly improve the ease of iterating within modeling pipelines by only rerunning the changed targets. These changes are detected automatically, saving time and reducing opportunities for unintended changes relative to relying on users to manually alter and rerun downstream targets.

We will use the *drake* package as our workflow automation tool for our examples in R. Not only will this make our modeling pipelines more robust to user error, but the visualizations that we can produce from it will enable our modeling pipelines to be more easily understood as well.

> **NOTE**   drake is an R package that facilitates improved debugging, reproducibility, and transparency for modeling pipelines. Because of its complexity, we recommend that readers who seek to adapt the RDS framework to their own projects spend more time learning drake outside of what we cover in this book. Good places to start include *The drake R Package User Manual*, especially the "Why drake" chapter (`books.ropensci .org/drake/index.html#why-drake`), as well as any of the example projects in the drake-examples page on William Landau's GitHub (`wlandau.github.io/ drake-examples/`).

Figure 6.1 shows an example of these visualizations for a completed modeling pipeline. Note that the first split in the graph shows the preprocessed data branching into train and test sets, which themselves are then fed into one of three different modeling branches before being reunited again, where their performance metrics are next bound together and compared.

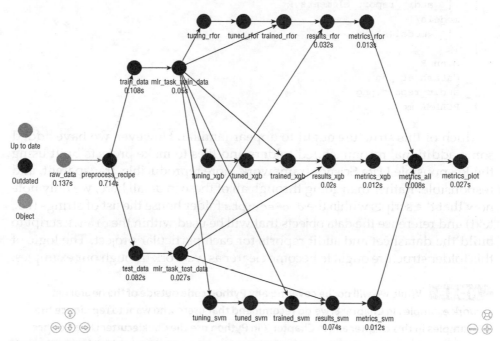

Figure 6.1: A plot of the directed acyclic graph (DAG) generated via the drake package for a modeling project comparing the performance of three different models. Each of the circles represents an individual target within the workflow.

Folder Structure

For any projects built using the Responsible Data Science framework within R, we recommend using a project structure similar to the following (where files in brackets represent placeholders for multiple files). Note that this is a structure to build on, and not necessarily inclusive of every file or folder relevant for some types of projects.

```
./
|_ analyses/
|    |_ <script(s).R>
|
|_ data/
|    |_ <datafile(s)>
|
|_ setup/
|    |_ functions.R
|    |_ packages.R
|
|_ doc_scripts/
|    |_ datasheet_elements.R
|    |_ datasheet_template.Rmd
|    |_ audit_report_elements.R
|_ models/
|    |_ <model(s).rda>
|
|_ plan.R
|_ datasheet.png
|_ audit_report.png
|_ README.md
```

Much of this structure ought to appear familiar. However, we have added some additional recommended folders and files to make projects built using the Responsible Data Science framework more reproducible, transparent, and responsible. Rather than going through all of these in detail here, we only note now that the scripts within the doc_scripts folder house the list of strings (i.e., text) and reference the data objects that will be used within the plan.R script to build the datasheet and audit reports for each particular project. The logic of this folder structure ought to become clearer as we work through our examples.

> **NOTE** While we will not be covering any Python code outside of the neural network examples in Chapter 8, we do recommend that users who want to reproduce the examples in this chapter and in Chapter 7 in Python use the Cookiecutter Data Science project structure, modified to use the Snakemake package rather than GNU Make (as Snakemake is built specifically for Python). You can find more information at drivendata.github.io/cookiecutter-data-science/.

Documentation: The Responsible Thing to Do

Building more comprehensive documentation can be a tedious and thankless affair. Nevertheless, it's the responsible thing to do and a necessary step for teams looking at following the Responsible Data Science framework. We will now explore in more detail the three critical forms of documentation that were introduced in Chapter 4: impact statements, datasheets, and audit reports.

Impact Statements: For Credibility

Impact statements for data science became popular, or, more accurately, infamous, on account of the prestigious Neural Information Processing Systems (NeurIPS) Conference requiring the inclusion of a "Broader Impact Statement" for submissions to the 2020 conference. NeurIPS provided the following guidance for the statement:

> **In order to provide a balanced perspective, authors are required to include a statement of the potential broader impact of their work, including its ethical aspects and future societal consequences. Authors should take care to discuss both positive and negative outcomes.**

Reactions to the guidance were mixed, with some researchers questioning whether data scientists were well equipped to make such judgments. Unified standards and requirements for AI impact statements had not then (and still have not) been broadly established, but by requiring an impact statement for all submissions to the conference, NeurIPS dramatically raised the profile of ethical considerations in AI research. For their work to be deemed credible, researchers now had to contend with the ethical implications of their work. This perspective spread to the large tech companies and the academic institutions that employed them. Leading AI companies like OpenAI, Google, Microsoft, and IBM have since begun leveraging variants of impact statements to make their own models and software products more transparent.

Regardless of whether someone agrees with the moral necessity of issuing impact statements, they ought to recognize that the practices set by these firms and research firms determine the direction of the entire field. In this case, it would be foolish not to follow where they go. Moreover, considering the possible impacts of our model's predictions and other ethical challenges within any project that has the potential to generate harmful predictions is, again, the responsible thing to do.

For our projects within this book, we use the impact statement to address the following five questions:

- What is the goal of our project?
- What are the expected benefits of our project?

- What ethical concerns do we consider relevant to our project?

- Have other groups attempted similar projects in the past, and, if so, what were the outcomes of those projects?

- How have we anticipated and accounted for future uses of our project beyond its current use?

These questions can be answered in an impact statement that is either included directly in the README.md file or included as another .md, .doc, or .pdf file within the project directory.

> **NOTE** Rather than show fully fleshed out impact statements as we work through our illustrations, we will show the content that would otherwise go into impact statements as responses to individual questions. Readers interested in examples of impact statements can look at this article written by members of the Centre for the Governance of AI: medium.com/@GovAI/a-guide-to-writing-the-neurips-impact-statement-4293b723f832.

Datasheets: For Reproducibility

Data dictionaries are almost ubiquitous across data science projects. However, they are not uniform in their formatting or in the information that they contain. Where one team might use a simple .txt file including information on the names and types of columns within a dataset, other teams may rely on an unwieldy Excel file containing multiple sheets of information about every data aspect of their data. Knowing that the data dictionaries would contain a predictable set of information about the data and present it all in a predictable manner would make life easier for all data scientists. Creating a unified format for data dictionaries would go far in making this situation easier for anyone who works with these datasets in the future.

In 2018, Dr. Timnit Gebru, a research scientist at Google, led a team of other researchers across industry and academia in proposing a standardized process for documenting datasets called "Datasheets for Datasets" (see Figure 6.2).[4] Her proposal for datasheets justified the need for recording not only the technical characteristics of the data, but also relevant nontechnical information like the data's collection process, intended uses, sensitive features, and other information relevant to users of the dataset that might otherwise have gone uncaptured.

In this chapter, we will work through an abbreviated process of building our own datasheets. Full code and explanations for building these and other datasheets can be found in the GitHub folder for this chapter.

---

[4]Gebru, Timnit, et al. "Datasheets for Datasets." ArXiv:1803.09010 [Cs], Mar. 2020. arXiv.org, http://arxiv.org/abs/1803.09010.

Figure 6.2: A portion of the data card (datasheet) that Google Research added to its Open Images Extended

Source: `research.google/static/documents/datasets/open-images-extended-crowdsourced.pdf`. Used with permission.

Model Cards and Audit Reports: For Safety

Complementary work to Dr. Gebru's soon followed. Later in 2018, Dr. Margaret Mitchell and other researchers at Google proposed a standardized process for documenting the performance and nontechnical characteristics of models in their paper "Model Cards for Model Reporting" (see Figure 6.3).[5] Just as datasheets served as nutrition labels for datasets, so, too, did model cards for models.

Also, note that datasheets and model cards are different documents that are not necessarily integrated with one another. Consider the "purpose" section of each document—the purpose for the creation of the data and for the model may well be different. Indeed, the field of predictive modeling is built upon the idea that

---

[5]Mitchell, Margaret, et al. "Model Cards for Model Reporting." Proceedings of the Conference on Fairness, Accountability, and Transparency, Jan. 2019, pp. 220–29. `arxiv.org/abs/1810.03993`, doi:10.1145/3287560.3287596.

data captured for one purpose (e.g., transaction recording) may be repurposed for another (e.g., marketing). While this is a testament to the wide-ranging applicability of these methods, it is nonetheless something that we as data science practitioners must keep in mind as a possible risk in our work.

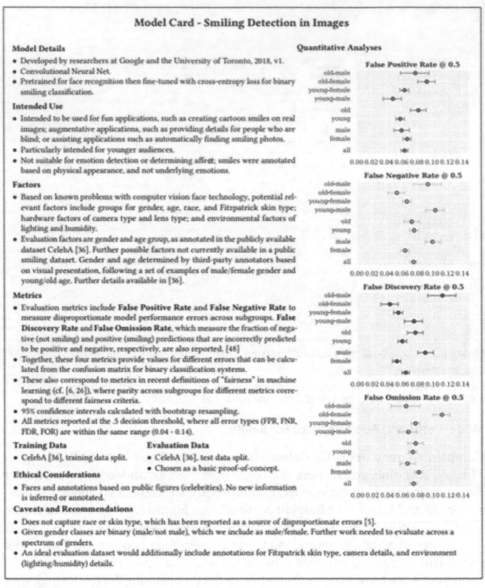

Figure 6.3: An example of a manually designed model card for a smile detector trained and evaluated on the CelebA dataset. The summary page of an audit report in the Responsible Data Science framework looks like this.

Source: Mitchell, Margaret, et al. "Model Cards for Model Reporting." Proceedings of the Conference on Fairness, Accountability, and Transparency, Jan. 2019, pp. 220–29. arxiv.org/abs/1810.03993, doi:10.1145/3287560.3287596. Used with permission.

Perhaps because so much of the attention of data scientists is focused on models rather than the data they are fit upon, the idea of model cards has caught on quickly across the industry. Companies like IBM (through its FactSheet Project), Microsoft (through its Azure Transparency Notes), and OpenAI (through its Model Cards) have adapted model cards to provide a consistent format for salient information about their models. Their adoption by these companies seems likely to grow in the future, as some of them have already invested significant resources into expanding their use. For example, in 2020, Google released the Model Card Toolkit (MCT), an official package for automating the generation of model cards for models fit using TensorFlow. Figure 6.4 shows an excerpt of a model card that was automatically generated via this package.

Providing these "nutrition labels" for datasets and models greatly increases their transparency. However, each form of documentation depicts a snapshot of the data and model(s) at a particular point in time, specifically, at the conclusion of the project (or some otherwise near-final point). The *process* that the team undertook to verify that the data and model are functioning as expected *is not* captured by these documents. This leaves little room to discuss special considerations for protected groups, comparisons of predictive performance between the final model and other candidate models, differences in predictive performance across groups, and, in the case of black-box models, interpretability method outputs.

Other researchers have noted the need to capture these elements in more detail. Most recently, proposals to address this need have coalesced around the idea of audit reports. Recent work on the subject, like the work of Deborah Raji and her collaborators on the SMACTR auditing framework (which we touched upon in Chapter 4) or the Partnership on AI's work on ABOUT ML, represent great examples of how models and the modeling process itself can be evaluated for fairness.

For work within the Responsible Data Science framework, audit reports supersede model cards, as we are able to integrate much of the information that would otherwise go into a model card into an audit report. Here are the main elements:

- A summary page for general model performance information
- Detailed model performance pages for each protected group within the data, showing the following:

  - Comparisons of final model and candidate model performance across groups within the data
  - Visualizations of interpretability method outputs for the final model to show how the model is using its features when creating predictions
  - Descriptive text for findings from the plots/metrics and other relevant considerations

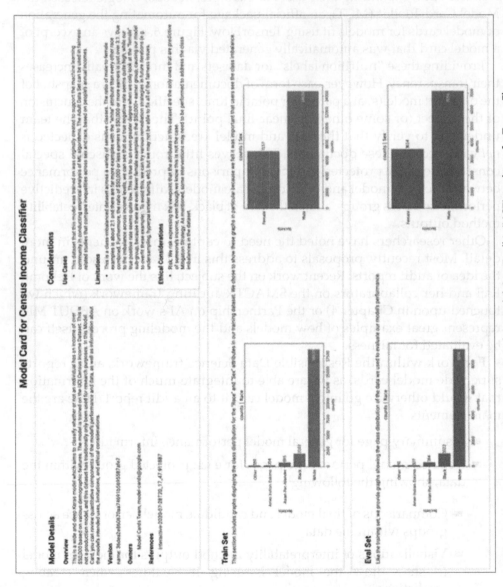

Figure 6.4: A model card generated via Google's Model Cart Toolkit (MCT) package for TensorFlow

Source: `github.com/tensorflow/model-card-toolkit`. Used with permission.

Though we will discuss the final components that ought to go into an audit report in Chapter 7, the final audit reports themselves will be posted in the code repositories for Chapter 7 rather than in Chapter 7. This is due to the longer format of an audit report being better suited to reading on a computer screen or as a separate document rather than as one reprinted in a book.

Beginning a Responsible Data Science Project

Let's transition now to working through our practical examples of using the Responsible Data Science framework. We begin with the Communities and Crime dataset.

Communities and Crime (Regression)

To begin this example, we will work through providing the information necessary to fill out an impact statement. We will accomplish this by answering a series of questions as if we were actually completing this project in the real world.[6]

Justification

What is the goal of our project?
Policing cannot be disconnected from social issues, such as homelessness, drug addiction, and compromised mental health. Most police officers would concur that a small set of individuals suffering from these problems are responsible for most of the crime in a community. So, a relevant goal (for our project) can be stated as follows:

> **The goal of this project is to leverage demographic and economic data within individual communities for predicting crime rates to better inform the provision of necessary mental health and social services.**

Crime prediction models are fraught with ethical challenges: Unencoded differences in who gets policed and why, inflation of crime data in certain communities due to racist practices in policing, and the actual policy responses enacted as result of the predictions of these models all present grave challenges. These factors, and the influence that AI models have in the criminal justice system, all make the use of AI in crime prediction justifiably controversial. That said, if we truly want to understand how to identify issues of bias and at least attempt to

---

[6]The authors do not endorse crime prediction as a modeling task. Rather, we include crime prediction tasks here to exemplify modeling tasks that are almost certain to be unfair in ways that are identifiable within an audit.

rectify them, modeling a dataset like this is perhaps one of the best examples for us to learn from.

What are the expected benefits of our project?

First, our project would better enable government and charitable organizations to allocate their scarce resources to the communities that most need them, increasing social welfare and the relative impact of each dollar spent. Second, a better understanding of the connection between crime and social circumstances could yield better support in police departments (a key factor) for policy initiatives to address the problems. Furthermore, a successful audit of this project ought to clarify the economic and social circumstances that are associated with crime increases, which would be useful for future researchers or organizations seeking to proactively identify communities most in need of public assistance.

What ethical concerns do we consider as relevant to our project, and how do we plan on addressing them?

We have considered several ethical concerns for this project and propose the following to address them:

- **Misuse**—This model could be repurposed to justify increased policing in areas with high crime predictions, which could contribute to over-policing and increased tensions within the community. Again, if we were attempting to implement this project in the real world, we could justifiably face objections that the model may be used in the future to inform police crackdowns on high crime areas.[7]

- **Alternatives**—We may have chosen the wrong target to model. Our logic in developing the goal was that crime reduction is a worthwhile goal and that the provision of social and mental health services will help reduce crime. Thus, we could simply focus on crime prediction for the purpose of this modeling task. Objections might be raised that, if our goal were truly to develop a modeling approach for determining which communities are most likely to require increased public assistance, we would be better off choosing socioeconomic metrics that are more closely associated with community well-being than crime statistics. Anticipating different perspectives in this way can help assure that we aren't blindsided by issues that we did not consider. In this case, to keep the scope of our project manageable, we will proceed on the basis that crime reduction is a good thing in itself, so it is not wrong to focus our study on that, as opposed to other social goals.

- **Efficacy**—Predictions generated by this model are not guaranteed to change or affect policy. Public institutions are comprised of a complex web of stakeholders who often have distinct competing interests. Many

---

[7]Note that this data was already used for a real-world crime prediction software tool in 2002. Readers interested in learning more can check out this article: www.sciencedirect.com/science/article/abs/pii/S0377221701002648.

of these interested parties are not necessarily motivated by "what is best for the overall community," but rather are motivated primarily to achieve short-term political goals. Our project, even if it makes successful predictions (and if it were implemented), may not be seen as relevant to many of these interests. We ought to not let that be a reason to give up at the outset. After all, a well designed and easily interpretable project has a better chance to foster change than a poorly designed project.

Have other groups attempted similar projects in the past, and, if so, what were the outcomes?

Schools of social work have conducted studies to guide the use of social workers to augment or supplant policing for some types of emergencies. Efforts like the Crisis Assistance Helping Out on the Streets (CAHOOTS) program, which sends crisis responders rather than armed police officers to nonviolent situations, have proven effective and been welcomed by police management in almost 20 cities. Other programs that have had social workers accompany police on patrol (e.g., in New York, New York, and Alexandria, Kentucky) have been similarly effective. Police forces have been largely receptive to it because they already bear the burden of social work in many cases, as police, rather than social workers, are often tasked with de-escalating individuals who are experiencing violent opioid withdrawals in public. Often these efforts to put social workers "on the beat" founder when funds become scarce or when the cultures of the altruistic social worker and the tough beat cop clash.[8] The lesson we can take from this is that it's important to involve the police as stakeholders in the overall project, because they stand to benefit.

For a related but somewhat different goal involving the same data, refer to the UCI web page where the Communities and Crime dataset was first uploaded (`archive.ics.uci.edu/ml/datasets/communities+and+crime`). The relevant papers section at the bottom of the page indicates that a similar version of the dataset was used by the original dataset author and a collaborator in 2001 for developing a piece of software called the Crime Similarity System (CSS). The stated goals of this software were to serve as a "proactive management" tool for police departments that "utilizes socioeconomic, crime, and enforcement profiles of cities to generate a list of communities that are best candidates to cooperate and share experiences."

Have we anticipated and accounted for future uses of our project beyond its current use?

We have noted the potential for our study to be repurposed as simply a crime prediction tool, ignoring the primary purpose of informing the direction of social and mental health resources. How can the data scientist anticipate and, more importantly, deal with this? Our project goal is to predict on the basis of

---

[8]The following piece explains this tension in greater detail: `socialwork.tulane.edu/blog/why-police-officers-are-taking-on-social-worker-responsibilities`).

demographic and economic factors, not on the basis of social issues. As we delve deeper into the project, we must be fully alert to the possible need for further study in the future (which we will not get into within the context of this book) of the connection between those factors and the factors we are studying.

> **NOTE**   After answering the previous five questions, we integrate them into a single document, forming our impact statement. We aren't showing it here, as we are making the impact statement using nothing more than markdown-formatted text. Interested users can, nevertheless, see examples of these documents within the GitHub repository for this chapter. The same applies to the COMPAS classification example later in this chapter, though we will not include this note again there.

Compilation

Finally, we have arrived at the code! We won't linger on the environment setup aspect of the project, except to mention that we are following the first R project structure outlined in the previous "Common Elements Across Our Analyses" section.

First, we load in our necessary packages as well as the raw data from a CSV file.

```
# load our packages
library(here)

# source packages
source(here("setup/packages.R"))

# source helper functions
source(here("setup/helpers.R"))

# get raw crimes data
crime_raw = read_csv(here("data/crimedata.csv"))

# set a seed
set.seed(10)
```

Then we take a look at the data.

```
print(crime_raw)
## # A tibble: 2,215 x 147
##     communityname state countyCode communityCode  fold population
##     <chr>         <chr> <chr>      <chr>         <dbl>      <dbl>
## 1 BerkeleyHeig~ NJ    39         5320              1      11980
## 2 Marpletownsh~ PA    45         47616             1      23123
## 3 Tigardcity    OR    ?          ?                 1      29344
```

```
##  4 Gloversville~ NY    35          29443          1        16656
##  5 Bemidjicity   MN    7           5068           1        11245
##  6 Springfieldc~ MO    ?           ?              1        140494
##  7 Norwoodtown   MA    21          50250          1        28700
##  8 Andersoncity  IN    ?           ?              1        59459
##  9 Fargocity     ND    17          25700          1        74111
## 10 Wacocity      TX    ?           ?              1        103590
## # ... with 2,205 more rows, and 141 more variables: racepctblack <dbl>,
```

We want to predict crime at the level of the community, which means predicting crime rates for each row. While we can't see much of the dataframe itself
due to the space limitations of a book page (which isn't well suited to showing
100+ lines of code output at once), examining the output of the previous print
command shows a number of issues.

- There are five identifier columns present (`communityname`, `state`,
  `countyCode`, `communityCode`, and `fold`, an identifier used for the initial
  analysis that the dataset was created for), when we only need and
  want one.

- `?` appears to be used throughout this data to represent missing values
  rather than an NA or NULL value.

- Name formatting for columns is inconsistent (e.g., `racepctblack` versus
  `racePctWhite`).

- Our chosen outcome (assaults) is being treated as a character feature rather
  than a numeric feature.

- According to the documentation for the dataset (`archive.ics.uci.edu/ml/
  datasets/Communities+and+Crime+Unnormalized`), there are 18 outcome fea-
  tures total in the dataset. We only want to include one outcome feature;
  otherwise, our results would be invalidated.

Let's go ahead and write code to address these issues. The next code chunk
does the following, by line:

- Relocates assaults (our target) to make it the first column
- Drops columns 131 through 147 because they are all outcome features
  that we don't want to use
- Drops columns 2 through 6 because they are all identifiers
- Changes assaults from a character vector to a numeric vector
- Unifies naming conventions by making all columns lowercase

```
crime_data = crime_raw %>%
  relocate(assaults) %>%
  select(-c(131:ncol(.))) %>%
```

```
select(-c(2:6)) %>%
mutate(assaults = as.numeric(assaults)) %>%
rename_with(tolower)
```

Now, let's go about addressing the rows with ? entries. Again, it seems like these values ought to represent a missing value; however, there is nothing in the documentation that clarifies this.[9] We ought to do our due diligence, however, to make sure we're correct.

Let's see if we can rule out the presence of actual NA values by using an anti-join to filter down to only those rows containing NA values.

```
no_na_rows = crime_data %>%
  drop_na()

na_rows = crime_data %>%
  anti_join(no_na_rows)

print(na_rows)
```

```
## # A tibble: 14 x 125
##     assaults   population householdsize racepctblack racepctwhite
##       <dbl>        <dbl>         <dbl>        <dbl>        <dbl>
## 1        NA        18827          2.59         48.1         51.6
## 2        NA        34507          2.47         0.51         98.8
## 3        NA        13057          2.67         5.81         85.9
## 4        NA        12871          2.88         0.65         76.9
## 5        NA        18309          3.11         3.25         93.2
## 6        NA       169759          2.66         4.52         87.1
## 7        NA      1630553          2.64         28.1         52.7
## 8        NA        53418          2.76         0.82         97.6
## 9        NA       180650          2.86         8.87         79.7
## 10       NA       223019          2.48         24.5         73.8
## 11       NA       156983          2.72         19.2         68.6
## 12       NA       266406          3.04         2.54         71.4
## 13       54        19460          2.54         50.3         49.3
## 14       NA        60640          2.53         2.08         96.0
## # ... with 119 more variables: racepcthisp <dbl>, ...
```

Interesting. There are 14 rows with NA values in addition to the ? values; however, all but one of the NA values are in our target feature, assaults. If these missing values were instead in our feature columns, we might consider imputing them (especially because there are so few).

---

[9]Documentation for this dataset is available at: archive.ics.uci.edu/ml/datasets/communities+and+crime.

That said, if the proportion of them is low enough, how about imputing the ? values? We'll assume that any column with 20 percent or fewer ? values is safe to impute on. Let's find the proportion of missing values across our columns.

```
map(crime_data, function(x) sum(x == "?")/length(x)) %>%
  enframe() %>%
  rename(proportion_missing = value) %>%
  unnest(proportion_missing) %>%
  filter(proportion_missing >= 0.10) %>%
  arrange(-proportion_missing)
## # A tibble: 22 x 2
##    name                 proportion_missing
##    <chr>                             <dbl>
##  1 lemasswornft                      0.845
##  2 lemasswftperpop                   0.845
##  3 lemasswftfieldops                 0.845
##  4 lemasswftfieldperpop              0.845
##  5 lemastotalreq                     0.845
##  6 lemastotreqperpop                 0.845
##  7 policreqperoffic                  0.845
##  8 policperpop                       0.845
##  9 racialmatchcommpol                0.845
## 10 pctpolicwhite                     0.845
## # ... with 12 more rows
```

We can see that there are 24 columns where more than 50 percent of the values are ?s, meaning imputation is definitely out of the question. Let's drop these columns.

```
drop_cols = map(crime_data, function(x) sum(x == "?")/length(x)) %>%
    enframe() %>%
    unnest(value) %>%
    filter(value >= 0.10) %>%
    pull(name)

crime_subsetted = crime_data %>%
  select(-all_of(drop_cols))
```

Now that we have our final subset of usable variables, let's identify our protected classes.

Identifying Protected Classes

Looking at the data. we see that there several features dealing with ethnicity (racepctasian, hisppercap, etc.), country of origin (numimmig, pctimmigrecent, etc.), and lack of housing (numinshelters, numstreet, etc.). Contained within each of these features are demographic groups who have been disadvantaged historically (Black Americans, immigrants, homeless individuals, etc.). Each of these groups consists of people we must ensure that our model treats fairly. Still, forcing a model to ensure fairness for one group often comes with a trade-off in the treatment of other groups.

For this example, we will only treat as protected groups the features that pertain to race. Additionally, we will later fit our model on the data with and without the features for the protected groups included so that we can see the impact (or lack thereof) that they have on the model predictions. After all, high correlation between these removed features and the nonprotected features that remain in the model will result in it effectively fitting on those protected features anyway!

Before we do that, let's do a sanity check to ensure that all the separate `racepct` variables add up to 100 percent.

```
crime_subsetted %>%
  select(contains("racepct")) %>%
  rowwise() %>%
  mutate(total = sum(c_across(everything()))) %>%
  arrange(-total)
## # A tibble: 2,215 x 5
## # Rowwise:
##    racepctblack racepctwhite racepctasian racepcthisp total
##           <dbl>        <dbl>        <dbl>       <dbl> <dbl>
## 1           0.2         84.8          0.3        90.1   175
## 2          2.78         96.3         0.26        72.7   172
## 3          0.16         80.4         0.06        90.9   172
## 4          0.07         78.4         0.09        90.8   169
## 5          0.16         80.6         0.15        88.2   169
## 6          0.12         70.8         0.38        93.9   165
## 7          0.21         75.8         0.11        87.6   164
## 8          0.39           70         0.36        92.0   163
## 9          0.47         74.2         0.44        85.9   161
## 10         0.17         79.4         0.48        79.7   160
## # ... with 2,205 more rows
```

Wow, good thing we checked that! The sums of the different `racepct` categories range anywhere from 175.41 percent at the top (shown in the previous code excerpt) down to 72.95 percent. Multiple factors could be contributing to this issue.

- Despite the presence of an `otherpercap` feature, there is no corresponding `racepctother` feature within the dataset. Having that feature would help to fix a number of the under 100 percent sums.

- The racial category information for the 1990 Census contained 15 race categories in total.[10] How these 15 categories were collapsed into the five categories used within this dataset is unclear.

---

[10]www.census.gov/data/datasets/1990/dec/mars-data.html)

- Reports issued by the U.S. government and nongovernmental research groups in the late 1990s mention that some multiracial people marked multiple individual racial categories rather than following the Census's guidelines (at the time) of choosing only one response.

- Confusingly, the guidance to mark only one race applied for all racial categorizations *except* for "Hispanic," which could be selected with any other race.

The bottom line is that since people were allowed to select more than one race category, the category percentages are not constrained to add up to 100 percent. We will keep the racepct features in our dataset despite these issues. However, we need to keep in mind how they might influence the findings that we uncover in the modeling process moving forward.

For now, let's go ahead and indicate features for protected groups by adding the phrase _protected to each of the relevant column headers. We will also drop the per-capita racial features, as these would otherwise be duplicated by the pctrace features. Finally, we will add a rowid column to help us keep track of individual rows after we split our data.

```
crime_protected = crime_subsetted %>%
  rowid_to_column() %>%
  relocate(rowid) %>%
  select(-matches("percap")) %>%
  rename_with(., function(x) paste0(x, "_protected"), matches("racepct"))
```

We can see the newly protected features here:

```
protected_features = crime_protected %>%
  select(matches("_protected")) %>%
  colnames()

print(protected_features)
## [1] "racepctblack_protected" "racepctwhite_protected"
## [3] "racepctasian_protected" "racepcthisp_protected"
```

At this point, our data is clean and ready to be processed into features.

Preparation—Data Splitting and Feature Engineering

We will use the same feature engineering and selection process here that was used in Chapter 5.

We start by splitting our data into training and test (holdout) sets.

```
crime_split = crime_protected %>%
  initial_split(0.7) # check rules for splitting
```

```
crime_training = training(crime_split)
crime_testing = testing(crime_split)
```

Splitting our data into separate groups, and leaving one of them untouched, enables us to avoid data leakage, should we seek to more deeply explore the distributions of our features.

We lingered on feature engineering and selection in Chapter 5, but we will be briefer here. Suffice it to say, feature engineering and feature selection are an art, however, and deserve more space and attention than we can allot within this book.

For this analysis, we will use the *recipes* package from the *tidymodels* family of packages to engineer our features. This requires us to provide a modeling formula that relates our predictor features to the outcome. We can do this like so:

```
target = "assaults"

form = paste(paste(target, "~"),
             str_c(colnames(crime_training %>%
                       select(-all_of(target))),
                         collapse = "+"))
```

We then can take this formula object and place it into a recipe function call, which enables us to then apply the following feature engineering steps (not necessarily in order):

- Drop any feature that has near-zero variance (NZV) because these features are unlikely to be useful when modeling and could be actively harmful to the model's predictive performance.

- Remove features that have a greater than +/-0.7 correlation with other features, barring our protected features (which we want to keep regardless).

- Impute any remaining missing values with the median value for that particular feature. (No imputation is being done here for factors because all of our features are numerics.)

- Standardize our features so that all of their values are between 0 and 1. This ought to be helpful because our features have large differences in the variability and range of their distributions (e.g., percentage features have a range of 0–100, while features like medincome range throughout the tens of thousands).

NOTE   Standardizing our features makes our interpretation of any model fit upon the data more difficult because the data no longer is in its original form. For example, explanations generated by local interpretability methods (e.g., Shapley values) remain faithful relative to each other; however, they no longer are provided in terms of the original data. If explanations for the original data are required, the data must be unstandardized prior to generating explanations.

```
rec = recipe(crime_training, form) %>%
  update_role(matches("_protected"), new_role = "protected") %>%
  step_nzv(all_predictors(), -has_role("protected")) %>%
  step_corr(all_predictors(), threshold = 0.7, -has_role("protected")) %>%
  step_medianimpute(all_numeric(), -all_outcomes()) %>%
  step_range(all_numeric()) %>%
  prep()
```

This recipe object specifies a "recipe" for engineering the features put into
it, in this case, the features from the `crime_training` data object. We apply this
recipe to our data by running the `juice()` function on the recipe object to extract
the transformed training data and the `bake()` function on the test data to create
the transformed test data.

```
train_data = juice(rec)
test_data = bake(rec, testing(crime_split))
```

Now we can see that we have a greatly reduced subset of features and that
all the values of our features are bound between 0 and 1, just as we wanted.

```
print(train_data)
## # A tibble: 1,551 x 39
##       rowid householdsize racepctblack_pr~ racepctwhite_pr~
##       <dbl>         <dbl>            <dbl>            <dbl>
##  1 0.               0.408           0.0142            0.920
##  2 4.52e-4          0.332           0.00828           0.959
##  3 9.03e-4          0.226           0.00765           0.946
##  4 1.36e-3          0.217           0.0176            0.978
##  5 1.81e-3          0.315           0.00548           0.893
##  6 2.26e-3          0.231           0.0260            0.960
##  7 2.71e-3          0.272           0.0166            0.970
##  8 3.61e-3          0.234           0.00362           0.975
##  9 4.07e-3          0.277           0.239             0.670
## 10 4.52e-3          0.255           0.131             0.832
## # ... with 1,541 more rows, and 34 more variables: racepcthisp_protected
```

Datasheets

Now our data is ready for modeling, and we should generate our datasheet.
It should be simple enough, right? Remember when we said that doing data
science responsibly is hard? This is one of the hard parts.

At the time of publication, there are no existing functions or packages within
R or Python that can help us programmatically generate our datasheet. This
means we must shoulder the work of developing a programmatic approach for
generating datasheets ourselves.

Unfortunately, creating datasheets is another instance where it doesn't make sense to put into print all of the text and code that goes into making it. We can, however, use our workflow tool of choice, *drake*, to create a DAG of the objects that go into making the report. See Figure 6.5.

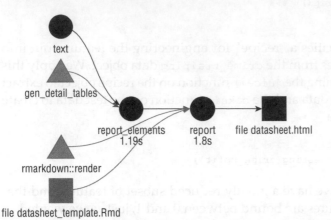

Figure 6.5: Plot showing the overall flow of targets (steps) in creating a datasheet. Note that the targets for the data that would go into `report_elements` are omitted.

The named targets in Figure 6.5 correspond to the following steps in the workflow of making a datasheet:

1. `text`: Type out all of the text that will be included in the datasheet (e.g., what the rows in the data represent, cleaning steps for the data, and other considerations) and save them to the objects in the environment. Save this text to a script named `datasheet_elements.R` located within the `doc_scripts/` folder of the project.

2. `gen_detail_tables()`: Functions that extract or produce information about the dataset (e.g., its dimensions, feature engineering steps from the recipe function call, the names of the protected features, etc.) and save these to objects in the environment. Save these functions as part of the `functions.R` script within the `setup/` folder of the project.

3. `report_elements`: A named list where each element of the list is one of the objects from step 1 or 2. Save this list as part of `datasheet_elements.R` located within the `doc_scripts/` folder of the project.

4. `file datasheet_template.Rmd`: A specialized Rmarkdown notebook that takes the list from step 3 as an input, renders all the elements, and saves the final output to a file (HTML, PNG, or PDF). Save this Rmarkdown notebook within the `doc_scripts/` folder as `datasheet_template.Rmd`.

5. `rmarkdown::render()` and `datasheet.html`: Run Rmarkdown's render function, passing `data_sheet_template.Rmd` and `report_elements` as arguments, to render and save the output, `datasheet.html`, to the root level of the project folder.

After all of the previous steps have been completed, the actual `render()` call in the final step is relatively uninvolved.

```
rmarkdown::render(
    output_file = file_out("datasheet.html"),
    params = report_elements)
)
```

Figure 6.6 shows the first page of the `datasheet.html` file.

Figure 6.6: The first page of the Communities and Crime datasheet. Subsequent pages have information on all the column names, types, and number of missing values for both the raw and the cleaned data.

We are now prepared to model this data in Chapter 7. Before we do that, though, let's go through one more example of setting up our project. This time we will use cleaner and more easily reproducible code (e.g., by using our own custom functions) to avoid repeating the narrative parts of our code and the datasheets that were covered within this example.

COMPAS (Classification)

Our next example is also centered around criminal justice: predicting *recidivism*, or the propensity for a convicted criminal to commit another crime. Propensity to commit further crimes is an important factor in the criminal justice system, particularly post-conviction at sentencing time and during incarceration (to inform treatment options). This issue gained attention when ProPublica used data on defendants in Florida (the same data that we will be looking at) to evaluate the proprietary Correctional Offender Management Profiling for Alternative Sanctions (COMPAS) algorithm, which scores each defendant according to their predicted probability to recidivate. That system, and recidivism prediction algorithms in general, are used widely in the criminal justice system.

Justification

What is the goal of our project?

The project's goal is to predict whether criminal offenders will recidivate (i.e., commit another crime) within two years.

We will be comparing the predictive performance of our model against the "COMPAS score," which is used in the criminal justice system as a proxy for propensity to recidivate. We will not be seeking to predict the COMPAS score itself. Rather, we will seek to predict recidivism directly—specifically, recidivism within two years of screening.

We use recidivism within two years (the is_recid feature) as the outcome rather than recidivism at any point in time because we will be comparing the predictive performance of our model across different ethnic and gender groups with the predictive performance that the COMPAS model achieves in the same categories. We must match the same period for which those predictions were generated.

What are the expected benefits of our project?

- Provide judges and other groups that leverage recidivism prediction algorithms with accurate predictions and a greater understanding of the biases inherent in recidivism prediction models.

- Provide judges and other groups that leverage recidivism prediction algorithms with greater control over the specific biases that manifest within the model. For example, by enabling them to minimize the model's chance of being racially biased against certain groups that are highly represented in criminal proceedings.

What ethical concerns do we consider relevant to our project, and how do we plan on addressing them?

Our primary concern, based largely on the public controversy that arose around the COMPAS system, is whether the predictions of recidivism are biased against and unfair to African Americans.

We plan to address these concerns by identifying whether prediction error differs for African Americans, in comparison to other ethnic groups.

Have other groups attempted similar projects in the past, and, if so, what were the outcomes of those?

ProPublica, a public interest lobby group, conducted an analysis of the results of the COMPAS method in Broward County, Florida. They did not develop their own model but rather found through their work that the COMPAS model was biased against African Americans. While the COMPAS model made predictions that were reasonably accurate overall, this overall accuracy concealed a fatal flaw: errors in predicting the rate of recidivism among African Americans overpredicted recidivism, while errors in predicting white offenders' recidivism were underpredicting. This led to ProPublica identifying several cases where a white person accused of a violent crime received lower risk scores than an African American accused of a nonviolent crime.

In making the relevant data for COMPAS available for public analysis, ProPublica spurred researcher interest in comparing results of the COMPAS model with their own competing models. One study by Dressel and Felarid (*Science Advances*, 2018) purported to find that the complex black-box model underlying COMPAS, composed of more than 173 features, was no more accurate than a logistic regression model that leveraged only two distinct features. You can read ProPublica's summary of other research on recidivist algorithms here: www.propublica.org/article/how-we-analyzed-the-compas-recidivism-algorithm.

Have we anticipated and accounted for future uses of our project beyond its current use?

Because of the nature of the data (limited to criminal offenders in Florida), we might expect this project to remain within the confines of the U.S. criminal justice system. For those who mistrust algorithmic decision-making applied to law, this might be a fact that is uncomfortable in and of itself. It is possible, though, to imagine other uses we might not be comfortable with, such as the following:

- The system could "migrate down" in the justice system, and be used prior to conviction, so that "who you are" (i.e., the essence of the model) might affect whether you are determined to be a criminal in the first place.

- The system could be used in other, more authoritarian countries to predict a much broader range of "criminality" (e.g., political dissent or opposition, "anti-social" behavior, etc.).

Compilation

As usual, we load our necessary packages as well as the raw data from a CSV file.

```
# load our packages
library(here)

# source packages
source(here("setup/packages.R"))

# source helper functions
source(here("setup/helpers.R"))

# get raw COMPAS data
compas_raw = read_csv(here("data/compas-scores-two-years.csv"))

# set a seed
set.seed(10)
```

Then we take a look at the data.

```
print(compas_raw)
## # A tibble: 7,214 x 53
##       id name   first  last  compas_screenin~ sex   dob         age
##    <dbl> <chr>  <chr>  <chr> <date>           <chr> <date>    <dbl>
## 1      1 migu~  migu~  hern~ 2013-08-14       Male  1947-04-18   69
## 2      3 kevo~  kevon  dixon 2013-01-27       Male  1982-01-22   34
## 3      4 ed p~  ed     philo 2013-04-14       Male  1991-05-14   24
## 4      5 marc~  marcu  brown 2013-01-13       Male  1993-01-21   23
## 5      6 bout~  bout~  pier~ 2013-03-26       Male  1973-01-22   43
## 6      7 mars~  mars~  miles 2013-11-30       Male  1971-08-22   44
## 7      8 edwa~  edwa~  ridd~ 2014-02-19       Male  1974-07-23   41
## 8      9 stev~  stev~  stew~ 2013-08-30       Male  1973-02-25   43
## 9     10 eliz~  eliz~  thie~ 2014-03-16       Fema~ 1976-06-03   39
## 10    13 bo b~  bo     brad~ 2013-11-04       Male  1994-06-10   21
## # ... with 7,204 more rows, and 43 more variables: juv_fel_count <dbl>,
```

However, not all of the rows are usable for the first round of analysis. For more information on why, we reprinted the following cleaning steps from ProPublica's analysis.[11]

1. If the charge date of a defendant's COMPAS scored crime was not within 30 days from when the person was arrested, we assume that because of data quality reasons, we do not have the right offense.

---

[11]github.com/propublica/compas-analysis/blob/master/Compas%20Analysis.ipynb

2. We coded the recidivist flag—is_recid—to be -1 if we could not find a COMPAS case at all.

3. In a similar vein, ordinary traffic offenses—those with a c_charge_degree of "O"—that will not result in jail time are removed (only two of them).

4. We filtered the underlying data from Broward County to include only those rows representing people who had either recidivated in two years (recidivists) or had spent at least two years outside of a correctional facility (nonrecidivists).

5. We followed suit with the findings of Matias Barenstein (2019) and dropped 868 rows representing records of recidivists erroneously counted in the two_year_recid field despite being outside of the two-year window for recidivating (prior to 2014-04-01).

```
compas_propublica = compas_raw %>%
  filter(days_b_screening_arrest <= 30) %>%
  filter(days_b_screening_arrest >= -30) %>%
  filter(is_recid != -1) %>%
  filter(c_charge_degree != "O") %>%
  filter(score_text != 'N/A') %>%
  filter(compas_screening_date <= as.Date("2014-04-01"))
```

Let's select the variables that we know we'll need (and drop those that we know we won't) to reduce clutter.

```
compas = compas_propublica %>%
  select(age_cat, c_charge_degree, race,
         sex, priors_count, two_year_recid) %>%
  mutate(two_year_recid = as.factor(two_year_recid))
```

Next, we should probably check for NAs.

```
compas %>%
  drop_na()
## # A tibble: 5,304 x 7
##    age_cat       c_charge_degree race        sex
##    <chr>         <chr>           <chr>       <chr>
##  1 Greater than~ F               Other       Male
##  2 25 - 45       F               African-Amer~ Male
##  3 Less than 25  F               African-Amer~ Male
##  4 25 - 45       M               Other       Male
##  5 25 - 45       F               Caucasian   Male
##  6 25 - 45       F               Other       Male
##  7 25 - 45       M               Caucasian   Fema~
##  8 25 - 45       F               Caucasian   Male
##  9 Less than 25  M               African-Amer~ Male
## 10 25 - 45       M               Caucasian   Fema~
## # ... with 5,294 more rows
```

Fortunately, we end up with the same number of rows as before, indicating that there are not any NAs in our dataframe.

Identifying Protected Classes

We know that the COMPAS data contains information on age, race, and sex. Of those, we probably want to treat race and sex as protected. Let's check to see which features contain that information.

```
compas %>%
  select(matches("age|race|sex"))
## # A tibble: 5,304 x 3
##    age_cat           race             sex
##    <chr>             <chr>            <chr>
##  1 Greater than 45   Other            Male
##  2 25 - 45           African-American Male
##  3 Less than 25      African-American Male
##  4 25 - 45           Other            Male
##  5 25 - 45           Caucasian        Male
##  6 25 - 45           Other            Male
##  7 25 - 45           Caucasian        Female
##  8 25 - 45           Caucasian        Male
##  9 Less than 25      African-American Male
## 10 25 - 45           Caucasian        Female
## # ... with 5,294 more rows
```

We can write another pair of functions to make it easier for us to demarcate protected features.

```
protected = function(x) {
    paste0(x, "_protected")
}

make_protected = function(df, string) {
  df %>%
    rename_with(protected, matches(string))
}
```

We then run the primary `make_protected()` function to "protect" our features.

```
compas_protected = compas %>%
  make_protected(c("age", "race", "sex"))
```

And then we print them to check.

```
protected_features = compas_protected %>%
  select(matches("_protected")) %>%
  colnames()

print(protected_features)
```

[1] "age_cat_protected" "race_protected" "sex_protected"

Looks like it worked. At this point, our data is clean and ready to be processed into features.

Preparation

Just like with the Communities and Crime example, we split our data into training and test sets.

```
compas_split = compas_protected %>%
  initial_split(0.7) # check rules for splitting

compas_training = training(split_compas)
compas_testing = testing(split_compas)
```

Of course, we should do feature engineering prior to modeling. We can accomplish that by adapting the `preprocesser()` function that we wrote in Chapter 5, which we will refer to here as gen_preprocessed_data(). To summarize, this function takes an rsplit object (i.e., set of train and test data), builds a recipe object from the training data, and applies the appropriate feature engineering steps to both sets of data.

NOTE   We are leaving code comments in this code snippet because the length of the function makes the process harder to follow otherwise.

```
gen_preprocessed_data = function(data_split, target = NA, corr_threshold
= 1) {

  # get column types
  col_types = data_split %>%
    training() %>%
    summarise(across(everything(), class)) %>%
    pivot_longer(cols = everything(),
                 names_to = "variables",
                 values_to = "type")

  # get training data
  df_protected = data_split %>%
    training()

  # get a formula for creating our recipe
  form = paste(paste(target, "~"),
               str_c(colnames(df_protected %>%
                      select(-all_of(target))),
                            collapse = "+"))

  # create a recipe
  rec = recipe(df_protected, form) %>%
    update_role(matches("_protected"), new_role = "protected") %>%
```

```
       step_nzv(all_predictors(), -has_role("protected"), -all_outcomes()) %>%
       step_corr(all_numeric(), threshold = corr_threshold,
               -has_role("protected"), -all_outcomes())

  # formalize our pre-processing steps
  rec_prep = rec %>%
    prep()

  # preprocess our train data by "baking" it with our prepped recipe
  train_data = bake(rec_prep, training(data_split))

  # preprocess our test data by "baking" it with our prepped recipe
  test_data = bake(rec_prep, testing(data_split))

  # get original data for output
  input_data = df_protected

  # get features
  data_feats = train_data %>%
    colnames()

  # get a formula for creating our recipe
  final_form = paste(paste(target, "~"),
               str_c(colnames(train_data %>%
                              select(-all_of(target))),
                              collapse = "+"))

  # return a list containing our two pre-processed datasets
  list("input_data" = input_data,
     "train_raw" = training(data_split),
     "test_raw" = testing(data_split),
     "train" = train_data,
     "test" = test_data,
     "features" = data_feats,
     "recipe" = rec,
     "recipe_prepped" = rec_prep,
     "formula" = final_form)

}
```

We execute the preprocessor function on our split data.

```
compas_preprocessed = gen_preprocessed_data(compas_split, "two_year_
recid")
```

Take a look at the newly processed training data:

```
print(compas_preprocessed[["train"]])

## # A tibble: 3,713 x 7
##      age_cat_protect~ c_charge_degree race_protected sex_protected
```

```
##    <fct>              <fct>         <fct>            <fct>
## 1 Greater than 45 F                 Other            Male
## 2 25 - 45            F              African-Ameri~   Male
## 3 Less than 25       F              African-Ameri~   Male
## 4 25 - 45            M              Other            Male
## 5 25 - 45            F              Other            Male
## 6 25 - 45            M              Caucasian        Female
## 7 25 - 45            M              Caucasian        Female
## 8 25 - 45            F              African-Ameri~   Male
## 9 25 - 45            F              African-Ameri~   Male
## 10 25 - 45           F              Caucasian        Male
## # ... with 3,703 more rows, and 3 more variables: priors_count
```

This looks great, and our datasheet for the COMPAS data looks as expected as well (see Figure 6.7).

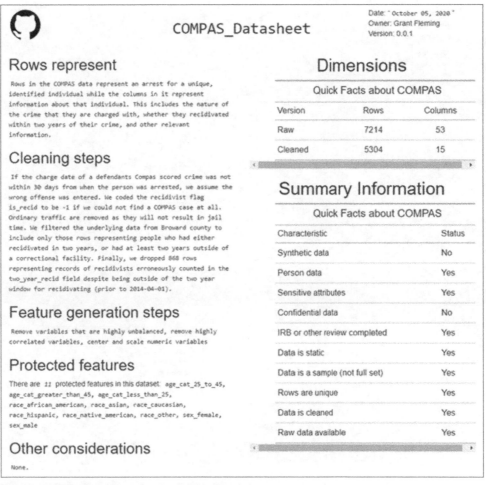

Figure 6.7: The first page of the COMPAS datasheet

Summary

Having completed our setup, we are now ready to fit models and audit them for fairness. We will accomplish that via the Modeling and Auditing steps of the Responsible Data Science framework in the next chapter.

CHAPTER

7

Auditing a Responsible Data Science Project

In the previous chapter, we worked through the Justification, Compilation, and Preparation steps of the Responsible Data Science (RDS) framework using two examples: a classification task (recidivism prediction) and a regression task (prediction of crime rates). Beyond working through the traditional technical and logistical data science project steps such as data gathering, data cleaning, and feature engineering for each of these tasks, we also considered the broader societal context that often goes ignored within projects like these. Now, we transition to creating and auditing our own models for the classification example, keeping a careful eye out for any issues of unfairness that might manifest themselves throughout.

We begin this chapter with a deeper discussion of the tricky issue of fairness: how it's commonly defined, how it can be quantified, and the limitations of the present-day data science toolkit for addressing issues of fairness. Afterward, we work through the Modeling and Auditing steps of the RDS framework across the COMPAS classification example developed in the previous chapter as follows:

MODELING the data:

➤ First, achieve predictive performance that is useful for the modeling task and sufficiently better than a baseline featureless model.

➤ Then compare black-box and intrinsically interpretable models to quantify the "cost" of interpretability in predictive performance.

➤ Ensure that the final candidate model performs well over multiple metrics of predictive performance.

AUDITING the models:

➤ Diagnose issues of predictive fairness, especially in cases where the models are biased toward or against certain groups.

➤ Explore the potential of bias mitigation techniques to improve fairness in outcomes, or otherwise provide model usage guidelines, should these issues not be remediated.

➤ Interpret candidate models to provide useful explanations for the model's predictions and inner functioning to stakeholders and users (if relevant).

The audit process proceeds as follows (see Figure 7.1):

➤ Calculate **per-group metrics** of model performance for each of the relevant groups within the model.

➤ Examine **per-group error metrics** to determine whether disparities in predictive performance between groups are due to over- or under-prediction.

➤ Visualize **fairness metrics** to more clearly compare differences in metrics of error or performance between groups.

➤ Use **interpretability methods** to better understand what factors the model deems important when making its predictions.

➤ Apply **bias mitigation** techniques to reduce issues of unfairness that have been identified.

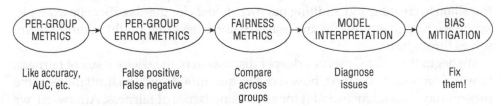

Figure 7.1: The general structure of the audit step

Prior to delving into the code for these audit steps, we begin with a deeper discussion of how fairness is tracked and operationalized for classification tasks. We provide an example of auditing for a regression task using the communities and crime dataset in the book's code repositories at www.wiley.com/go/ responsibledatascience and github.com/Gflemin/responsibledatascience. Note, however, that regression tasks are less amenable to auditing for fairness than classification approaches.

Fairness and Data Science in Practice[1]

As with societal conceptions of fairness, fairness in data science is a multifaceted and sometimes ambiguous concept. In this section, we will develop a taxonomy for thinking about fairness within a data science context, discuss how these types of fairness can work as trade-offs with one another, and introduce metrics for quantifying fairness in your own data science projects.

The Many Different Conceptions of Fairness

In a data science context, practitioners commonly define *fairness* as the absence of large differences in a model's predictive performance across individuals or demographic groups. Through this lens, fairness is a technical concept, something that a model can be tweaked and tuned toward within code. This is certainly the most popular way of viewing fairness in the context of data science at present, as evidenced by the increasing volume of resources for learning how to employ machine learning fairness; resources such as FairML, Trustworthy Machine Learning, or some other protocol for fairness as a technical element within data science projects. And why shouldn't this technical view of fairness be popular? Tracking whether a model performs worse for some groups compared to others is certainly better than simply assuming no bias, just as trying to rectify harmful disparities in predictive performance across groups is certainly better than assuming that these disparities cannot be reduced and making no effort to try.

However, we know by now that there is more to fairness in data science than ensuring equal predictive performance across groups, especially in cases where equal predictions across groups may not result in equitable consequences. After all, denying a housing subsidy to a person living on a minimum wage is likely to have a greater impact on their overall welfare than denying a similar housing subsidy for an individual in the top 10 percent of income within their community. Considerations for fairness in data science also must include the possibility that the overall purpose of a particular application of AI may be unfair. Most data science practitioners, at least in North America and Europe, would probably agree that the use of AI to identify and suppress political dissidents or cultural expressions by ethnic minorities would be unfair and morally untenable. Good predictive performance (i.e., correctly identifying dissenters and nondissenters equally across relevant demographic groups) only renders these applications of AI more harmful, turning the tools of AI fairness into tools of AI oppression.

There is clearly much more to fairness and whether a particular data science project is fair than the actual code that goes into making a model. Placing all

---

[1]This and subsequent sections in this chapter, copyright (c) 2021, Datastats, LLC and Grant Fleming. Used by permission.

our focus on the technical conception of fairness as code blinds us to broader considerations of fairness surrounding the real-world deployment context of the model: who is helped or hurt by successful completion of the modeling task, what data were encoded or ignored, how the data were gathered, who was included as a stakeholder for the project, and other relevant factors.

Even *if* we had the tools available to account for all of those factors, it would be arrogant to assume that it should be our sole responsibility as data scientists to leverage them. As data scientists, we should use our skill sets to support rather than supersede policymakers or other stakeholders who have the professional and lived experience relevant to the task at hand. Instead of seeing data science as a hammer for diagnosing and "fixing" all possible issues of fairness, we ought to think of it as a scalpel for helping other stakeholders precisely identify and address specific issues of fairness within the context of a model.

To use this metaphorical scalpel, we first need to know what we can affect through its use. To clarify this, we propose thinking about the overlap between fairness and data science as three separate but intersecting considerations. Research in the overlap between fairness and data science has converged around the following three dimensions of fairness: *procedural fairness*, *predictive fairness*, and *outcome fairness*.

DEFINITION PROCEDURAL FAIRNESS/FAIRNESS IN PROCEDURE   Refers to fairness in a broad sense for considerations of nontechnical factors in the design of a data science project. This includes whether a modeling task itself is fair, whether the real-world model deployment context is being appropriately considered, and whether the project's work is being conducted with the input of a sufficiently diverse group of stakeholders and users. Rather than being tracked through metrics, procedural fairness is tracked through soliciting feedback, addressing questions or concerns, and creating useful documentation.

DEFINITION PREDICTIVE FAIRNESS/FAIRNESS IN PREDICTIONS   Refers to technical fairness in the context of a model and code, such as whether predictive performance differs greatly across groups within the data. This fairness type is quantified per feature and helps to inform other measures of fairness. However, ensuring predictive fairness does not guarantee fair outcomes once the model is deployed, as equal predictions across groups may not lead to equitable outcomes.

DEFINITION OUTCOME FAIRNESS/FAIRNESS IN OUTCOMES   Refers to how the predictions from a model or from other project deliverables impact outcomes within the real world. This consideration of fairness is most relevant to models that make decisions about individuals or

decisions that affect individuals. This is often the most difficult conception of fairness to deal with because it involves nontechnical value judgments.

Or, to rephrase each consideration of fairness into straightforward yes or no questions:

1. **Procedural fairness:** Have we designed and conducted the creation of the project in such a way as to minimize possible harms and include input from all relevant groups?

2. **Predictive fairness:** Does our model achieve equal or near-equal predictive performance across groups?

3. **Outcome fairness:** Have we determined and accounted for how the predictions, decisions, or policy changes resulting from the completion of our project are likely to impact relevant individuals and/or groups?

Cutting across these ideas of fairness are legal requirements that may be highly specific. In some scenarios, we may be prohibited from using certain factors (e.g., age, sex, race) or their proxies as predictors, which could negatively impact our ability to ensure each consideration of fairness is met. On the other hand, we may be legally compelled to include data in our model that make the results of the model manifestly more unfair. More on this later.

The work that we completed over the previous chapters has provided us with an intuitive understanding of each of these considerations of fairness. By going through each of the stages of the RDS framework and addressing the points within them, we build in a minimum level of procedural fairness within our projects by default. By developing an understanding of the unanticipated harms of data science projects over the years, we gain a greater appreciation for how both correct and incorrect predictions from models can affect people's lived outcomes. With respect to predictive fairness, we have seen how models fit on nonrepresentative unbalanced training datasets fail to generalize to more diverse datasets.

Each project requires its own calculus for balancing these three considerations of fairness, which may work at odds with one another, in addition to incorporating specific legal requirements. Oftentimes, classification decisions confer benefits like loan approvals, lower bail bonds, or job promotion opportunities. Improving predictive fairness by eliminating performance disparities across groups could very well lead to a reduction in outcome fairness within these circumstances (observations that initially "deserved" to have certain outcomes according to the original unadjusted model instead receive the unfavorable prediction).

Different Forms of Fairness Are Trade-Offs with Each Other

To individuals who are the subjects of predictions and decisions made by models, outcome fairness is perhaps the most important form of fairness. But just as models are complex, the uses to which they are put, and the outcomes being considered, are complex as well. A predictive model might be used by the IRS to triage tax returns for taxpayer audit. The same model might also be used by researchers on the tax code to select returns for a study to determine whether lack of compliance is intentional or unintentional. The Optum healthcare model discussed earlier could be used by a variety of parties: insurance companies to set rates, hospital business administrators to forecast revenue, or medical teams to plan care. For the first two uses, the outcome being predicted—future health spending—was appropriate. The model predicted this well. For the third use, planning medical care, using future health spending as a model outcome was manifestly unfair. In effect, the model was basing predictions not just on the need for medical care, but also on the ability to pay for and access medical care in the first place. The model's outcomes were systematically biased against people with fewer resources to pay for healthcare as a result. Optum would not have been able to diagnose this issue just by measuring predictive fairness for the outcome of "future health spending." Detecting the problem would have required that the modeling team understand the different uses to which the model might be put and be able to assess model fairness for those circumstances.

Sometimes, laws and regulations directly dictate the considerations that go into fairness. In consumer lending, for example, it is illegal to use age as a factor to determine loan decisions. Does this requirement mean that loan approval rates must be the same for 55- to 65-year olds as for 25- to 35-year-olds? No—other legitimate reasons may exist as to why approval rates might differ between the two groups. The prohibition on the use of age as a predictor is an example of ensuring procedural fairness, as this (ostensibly) prevents the model from discriminating based upon age. The example of consumer lending and how age discrimination might be measured and the concept of *protected groups* are discussed in more detail later.

In some cases, an organization might be less worried about legal jeopardy or reputational harm and simply desire to address group imbalance as a matter of policy or as an affirmative action to rectify a historical inequity. A financial firm that uses a résumé-ranking algorithm, for example, might want to reduce the preponderance of Ivy League graduates in its ranks. In such a case, the "other things being equal" consideration might not be so important, and the firm might revert to the simple criterion of numbers, giving greater weight to non–Ivy Leaguers even if there are other legitimate reasons why Ivy Leaguers might get higher scores from the algorithm. While this may result in a drop in the overall predictive performance of the model, the increased diversity within the employee ranks could well be a worthy trade-off.

Now, consider that the financial firm in the previous example is interested not only in improving the ratio of non–Ivy League hires to Ivy League hires, but also in improving the geographic diversity of its hires from non–Ivy League schools. We assume that applicants from each of these regions are likely to end up with similarly ranked résumés on average, and that they are not otherwise disadvantaged relative to each other. At any particular point in time, the firm might assign a greater hiring priority to applicants from a specific geographic region to improve their ratio of hires from that region. Each time a region is prioritized, the applicants from that region experience an improvement in their ranking within the algorithm, improving outcome fairness with respect to this group. However, the applicants from other regions become comparatively disadvantaged as a result, and predictive fairness (with respect to all groups) is either unchanged or negatively impacted. Is this a worthy trade-off?

One important lesson is this: Normative notions of fair outcomes in the real world have no universally agreed "objective function" when modeling, so any single, general approach for achieving fairness in data science is bound to leave someone or some group dissatisfied. No standard data science rubric exists that can be relied upon to unearth, measure, and optimize outcome fairness; it is fundamentally task and situation dependent, and it would be hubris for us to attempt to apply a specific prescription for ensuring it. Adjustments to achieve outcome fairness typically do not lie wholly within the realm of the data scientist, but rather in the influence of organizational management, external stakeholders, community members, and subject-matter experts involved in a data science project. In this way, ensuring that a project is well designed and inclusive (i.e., procedurally fair) is key for addressing fairness in outcomes.

Fair or unfair, a model is of no use if it cannot predict well; hence, the attention we have paid thus far in the book to the potential trade-off between performance and interpretability. A similar trade-off exists between performance and fairness. To achieve each of these three (oftentimes competing) conceptions of fairness, we need to create models that we can understand, assess and tweak for different notions of fairness, and trust will predict accurately in practice. This forces us to take a step back from outcome fairness to consider predictive fairness, or ensuring that our model predicts equally well, or near equally well, across relevant groups within the data.

Ensuring predictive fairness across groups is therefore still one of the most powerful tools a data scientist possesses to achieve overall fairness in how a model works. It allows us to study in detail, and in a more objective fashion, how our model is doing with respect to important groups within our data.

Quantifying Predictive Fairness Within a Data Science Project

To quantify predictive fairness, we first need to keep in mind that fairness is almost always defined relative to different groups of observations within the data. These groups are typically encoded as categorical features that provide information about an observation. Features for demographic characteristics like sex, age, race, or socioeconomic status are common groups across which predictive fairness is often considered. We refer to any categorical feature that identifies categories that we want to ensure fairness within as a *protected feature*; the group of observations so identified by each level of that protected feature represent individual *protected groups*.

For example, sex (a protected feature) could be divided into the protected groups of male, female, or non-binary. As we noted in Chapter 3, "The Ways AI Goes Wrong, and the Legal Implications," numerous countries regulate the usage of protected groups like these when modeling. For example, the Equal Credit Opportunity Act in the United States prohibits the use of the following features in making credit decisions:

- Age
- Color
- Marital status (single or married)
- National origin
- Race
- Recipient of public assistance
- Religion
- Sex

However, prohibiting the use of a protected feature as an explicit input to the model does not prevent it from creeping in via some proxy feature or features. How can we tell? Consider a U.S.-based car insurance company that uses a model to calculate risk scores for potential customers. These risk scores are then used to provide the customer a unique monthly quote for their insurance rate. The company considers the sex and age of the driver as relevant features to leverage when calculating this risk score; however, the company does not want to discriminate based upon the income of the driver, as this is not a relevant feature for the model. After deploying the model, the company discovers that the model is leveraging ZIP code as a highly predictive feature of risk. Knowing that U.S. ZIP codes are still highly segregated by socioeconomic status, they begin to suspect that the model is leveraging ZIP codes as a proxy feature for driver income. To see whether discrimination based upon income is taking place, the company fits a second model, this time dropping ZIP code and including a measure of income in the model as a diagnostic tool.

If income has no predictive power in this new model, our hypothesis about ZIP code was probably wrong and it is unlikely to be a proxy for income. If, however, income does have predictive power, then we need to investigate whether ZIP code and income are correlated, which would suggest that our hypothesis is true that ZIP code has predictive power because it carries with it income information.

To formalize this process, we calculate *fairness metrics* for each of the groups.

DEFINITION FAIRNESS METRICS   Metrics of the relative predictive performance of a model across protected groups. Fairness metrics are typically calculated per group as a ratio or difference of predictive performance for the group of interest and a baseline comparison group.

Fairness metrics can be calculated between any two groups. In practice, we do not necessarily make all intergroup comparisons (which would result in a very large number of comparisons and consequently high Type I error risk). Rather, where the situation calls for it, we make the comparisons to an expected *privileged group*, which is a user-identified group that the model is *a priori* expected to perform best upon, *or* the group that most benefits from the current status quo of the real-world circumstances relevant to the modeling task. This allows us to quantify unfairness between groups by calculating the difference in predictive performance between groups or between the privileged (baseline) group and each of the other groups. Note that the term *privileged* has a primarily technical meaning in this context. While it can reflect a real-world advantage that a group may have relative to other groups, it primarily refers to a group being the reference level or the group that the model is expected to best predict.

In the context of the car insurance example, we calculate fairness metrics across each of the income groups to see whether there is a large difference in the risk scores assigned to each group. If the company identifies large enough differences among the groups, then we can conclude their model is not a fair model. Figure 7.2 charts the whole process for this example.

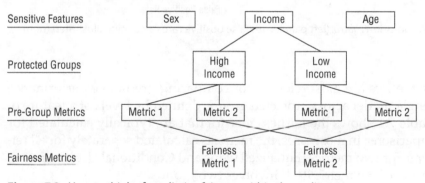

Figure 7.2: How to think of predictive fairness within the audit step

NOTE   People often think of fairness with respect to individuals. A person might think "I was denied a loan because I am over 55," but both outcome fairness and predictive fairness are judged by the treatment of the group, not the individual. However, in achieving overall predictive fairness across groups, boosting predictive performance for an underperforming group may lower predictive performance for another, which may affect some individuals adversely. Another area where individual treatment can enter the picture is procedural fairness (e.g., due process). "Do individuals have some form of recourse from the decisions of models? Can they appeal to humans?" In this book, we are concerned primarily with fairness applied to groups, rather than fairness applied to individuals.

Though the terminology associated with predictive fairness may feel new or uncomfortable, the fairness metrics that are used to quantify predictive fairness are often no different from the standard metrics of predictive performance that are regularly used. For classification tasks, fairness metrics map directly onto metrics calculated from a confusion matrix—a table that displays the counts of 1s and 0s that were correctly and incorrectly classified (see Figure 7.3). For example, the count in the upper right, false positives (FP), shows the number of false positives (actual 0s that were predicted as 1s). In the right pane of Figure 7.3, the calculation of one metric, false positive rate (FPR), is shown.

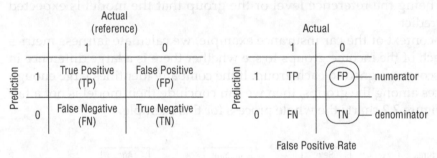

Figure 7.3: A confusion matrix (left pane), with false positive rate calculation illustrated (right pane)

Fairness metrics are most relevant for comparing predictive performance within a single model across protected groups defined by levels of a feature of interest. Table 7.1 shows the fairness metrics that are typically calculated for group comparisons. In most cases, the metric is calculated separately for all relevant groups. for two metrics (Equalized Odds and Conditional Use Accuracy), the calculation of the metric itself involves two groups.

NOTE The false positive rate is often confused with the false alarm rate (FP/FP + TP). The false alarm rate measures the probability that a predicted 1 is real; it is useful in determining next steps after medical tests and machine learning predictions but has fewer fairness applications.

Table 7.1: Popular Fairness Metrics

FAIRNESS METRIC	EQUIVALENT CLASSIFICATION METRIC	FORMULA	WHEN TO USE
Equal Opportunity	Precision (PPV)	TP/(TP+FP)	If true positives are especially important and false positives are less costly
Negative Predictive Value	Negative Predictive Value (NPV)	TN/(TN+FN)	If true negatives are especially important and false negatives are less costly
True Positive Rate (TPR)	Sensitivity (TPR)	TP/(TP+FN)	If true positives are the primary metric of interest
True Negative Rate (TNR)	Specificity (TNR)	TN/(TN+FP)	If true negatives are the primary metric of interest
False Positive Rate (FPR)	FPR	FP/(FP+TN)	If false positives are especially costly or harmful
False Negative Rate (FNR)	FNR	FN/(FN+TP)	If false negatives are especially costly or harmful
Accuracy	Accuracy	(TP+TN)/ (TP+FP+TN+FN)	If true negatives are equally as desirable as true positives
Equalized Odds (Statistical Parity)	Parity (goal) between TPR and FPR for groups 1 and 2	TPR1 − TPR2 = 0 FPR1 − FPR2 = 0	If positive outcomes are especially high stakes (true positives especially good, false positives especially bad)
Conditional Use Accuracy	Parity (goal) between PPV (precision) and NPV for groups 1 and 2	PPV1 − PPV2 = 0 NPV1 − NPV2 = 0	If we want to maximize the probability of trusting a model's predictions
Error Rate Equality	Parity (goal) between FPR and FNR for groups 1 and 2	FPR1 - FPR2 = 0 FNR1 - FNR2 = 0	If false negatives and false positives are equivalently more harmful than correct predictions
Demographic Parity	Parity (goal) between positive rates (PR) for groups 1 and 2	(PR1 - PR2)/(PR2)	If seeking to rectify a historical bias in allocation of outcomes

For notation: TP = true positives, TN = true negatives, FP = false positives, and FN = false negatives (see Figure 7.3 on the previous page). Note that parity sections are desired states, not metrics.

The predictive fairness of a model with respect to a specific feature (for example, race) is most commonly determined as the result of the following:

- **Maximum disparity**: The predictive fairness of a model with respect to a specific protected feature is equal to the greatest difference in fairness metrics between the privileged or baseline group and the other groups. Predictive fairness is now a continuous measure (e.g., "the maximum disparity in predictive fairness within this model is seen in a 5 percent disparity in performance between privileged group A and protected group B.")

- **Parity thresholds**: The predictive fairness of a model with respect to a specific protected feature is equal to the number of groups that fall within a prespecified range of deviance from the performance metric calculated for the privileged group. Predictive fairness is now a measure of the fraction of groups that score acceptably close to the privileged group (e.g., "four out of five groups are within the maximum predictive performance disparity range of ±3 percent.")

The process for calculating and comparing fairness metrics usually proceeds according to the following steps:

1. A fairness metric is chosen depending upon the specific needs of the modeling task.

2. A protected feature is selected.

3. Performance metrics are calculated for each of the protected groups within that feature.

4. Fairness metrics are calculated from the per-group performance metrics by:

   a. Subtracting or dividing each of the per-group metrics by the per-group metric calculated for the privileged group

   b. Subtracting or dividing each of the per-group metrics by the average of all of the per-group metrics

5. Fairness metrics are plotted to identify whether groups are being treated unfairly relative to each other.

Calculating these fairness metrics is useful to data scientists and nontechnical stakeholders alike when seeking to diagnose issues of predictive fairness. On the technical side, disparities in fairness metrics could indicate any number of issues: poor hyperparameters, an incorrect feature selection process, strong correlations between features that were not accounted for, issues with how the data were cleaned and processed, or important factors in the real world that were not encoded within the data and are skewing the results. On the nontechnical side, disparities in fairness metrics could inform further research into the real-world factors that are associated with these disparities and policies to reduce them.

What about fairness metrics for multiclass classification and regression? Unfortunately, no widely accepted fairness metrics for multiclass classification tasks exist as of the time of writing. In such cases, one approach is to identify a specific class of interest and consolidate the other classes into "other." The situation is somewhat clearer for regression, where error rate parity and measures for approximating fairness via feature independence have found practical use. We include reference to these methods within the regression example on the book's GitHub repository.

Mitigating Bias to Improve Fairness

Diagnosing the presence or absence of issues of predictive fairness is a useful practice in and of itself. However, discovering issues of predictive fairness within a model begs this question: What can we, as data scientists, actually change in our code to address them? As data scientists, there surely must be some sort of modification that we could make to mitigate, at least in part, the bias that we discover. In posing this question, we have stumbled upon *bias mitigation techniques*.

> **DEFINITION BIAS MITIGATION TECHNIQUES** Specific transformation techniques applied to improve either the predictive fairness or outcome fairness of a model. These methods are applied to a model's training data, the model itself, or the predictions generated by the model. At present, the trade-offs inherent in each of these methods, as well as their relative newness and lack of integration into common modeling tools, makes using these methods difficult.

Bias mitigation techniques can be divided into three main groups, each with their own benefits and trade-offs: preprocessing, in-processing, and postprocessing.

Preprocessing

Preprocessing includes the manual or algorithmic changes to the model's training data that are meant to remove biases prior to model training. These methods include suppression of sensitive features and features correlated with them, "massaging" the dataset by reweighing observations, and over- or under-sampling to make the distribution of protected groups more balanced during model training. Preprocessing techniques are typically model agnostic, as they rely only on the structure and distribution of the input data. While these methods are easy to implement, modifications to the training data can distort it and make it more difficult to interpret predictions generated by the model.

In-processing

In-processing includes the algorithmic changes to the model's objective function or other changes that are relevant during model training. It includes the addition of a penalty term to the model or fitting separate models on each protected group, which forces a model to optimize toward goals aligned with specific notions of fairness. Modifications to the model's objective function (e.g., additional fairness terms, adversarial debiasing, etc.), though they do not necessarily distort the data and compromise model interpretability, are both more complicated to implement and more situational in their use than preprocessing or postprocessing techniques on account of being specific to individual model types.

Postprocessing

Postprocessing includes the manual or algorithmic changes to the predictions generated by the model, such as techniques for changing predictions across groups to achieve parity in a prespecified fairness metric, changing the predicted class for observations in an unfairly treated group that were close to being assigned the opposite class, or modifications to the probability thresholds for classification. While these methods are easy to implement, modifications to the training data can distort it and make it more difficult to interpret predictions generated by the model.

At the time of writing, work around bias mitigation techniques is one of the most active areas of research at the intersection of fairness and machine learning. However, while we can see harbingers of tools and techniques that may become standard practice in the future, bias mitigation techniques are not widely implemented at present. The only packages for R and Python that implement bias mitigation techniques and go beyond calculating and generating visualization of fairness metrics are IBM's *AIF360* (R and Python), Microsoft's *Fairlearn* (Python only), Warsaw University of Technology's *DALEX* (R and Python), and *fair-ml* (R only).

> **NOTE** Readers interested in exploring in-depth examples of implementing bias mitigation techniques ought to view this page from the AIF360 documentation, `aif360.mybluemix.net/`, or this page from the Fairlearn documentation: `docs.microsoft.com/en-us/azure/machine-learning/concept-fairness-ml`.

Disparities revealed by particular fairness metrics can often be addressed in large part through the use of bias mitigation techniques. We emphasize "particular" here, as applying a bias mitigation technique to reduce one fairness metric, say, cross-group FPR, negatively impacts other fairness metrics like cross-group FNR or demographic parity that we may not be directly tracking. If minimizing cross-group FPR is our primary goal, then this is likely a worthy trade-off! Nevertheless, we must keep in mind that this relationship is always present.

We may not ever be able to have a perfectly accurate or perfectly fair model, but we can have a model that is fair according to at least one metric that, ideally, maps well onto the conception of fairness that we are trying to manifest within the real world.

In brief, our approach to fairness has three main aspects:

- Understanding the three main dimensions of fairness (procedural, predictive, and outcome fairness)

- Choosing an appropriate fairness metric or fairness metrics to measure model fairness for relevant groups (as we will see later, this must be done with care)

- Mitigating bias at one or more of three levels (preprocessing, in-processing, or postprocessing)

Note that there is no single approach that will optimize all metrics at once—trade-offs must be made. Judging which trade-offs are appropriate in the context of a specific project is a key component of the art of Responsible Data Science.

Classification Example: COMPAS

In Chapter 6, "Beginning a Responsible Data Science Project," we began work on the COMPAS project for predicting recidivism (i.e., the commission of another crime after being convicted of a crime). In that chapter, we generated cleaned preprocessed datasets. We are now ready for the next steps: modeling and auditing.

Prework: Code Practices, Modeling, and Auditing

Before getting to the main point of this chapter, the audit, we walk through the modeling process. We complete the audit afterward, demonstrating the final steps of the RDS framework. We use more verbose explanatory code in the chapter and provide cleaner, shorter code in the book's GitHub repository. The book's code does not use the *drake* workflowing package described in Chapter 6 for this reason.

The code that we use for our work is primarily sourced from the *tidymodels* family of packages, the interpretable machine learning (*iml*) package, or from a series of functions created by one of the authors (Fleming) to facilitate modeling within the RDS framework.[2] Many of the functions used will not be

---

[2]A future goal after the publication of this book is to create a package from these functions so that readers and other interested individuals can more easily adopt the RDS framework themselves. Updates on the progress of this will be posted to the repository at `github.com/Gflemin/responsibledatascience`.

immediately familiar to readers as a result; however, they will be noted by using the standard prefixes of `gen_` for functions that generate model or dataframe objects, or `plot_` for functions that generate plots. Source code and documentation for these functions can be found within the book's GitHub repository.

We begin the modeling process by comparing the predictive performance of multiple black-box models and intrinsically interpretable models relative to a featureless model. To get a stable measure of performance for the models, we do the following:

1. Split the preprocessed data into a model-fitting partition and a holdout partition.

2. Take 50 bootstrap resamples of the modeling partition.

3. For each resample, split it into training and test portions.

4. Fit a model to the training split and measure its performance on the test portion.

5. Average those performance metrics across all 50 resamples.

6. Repeat for additional models.

From this comparison, we quantify the relative cost of interpretability between the black-box and interpretable models, picking the model that achieves the best subjective balance between interpretability and predictive performance. Afterward, we fit our chosen model and the highest-performing intrinsically interpretable model on the original training dataset and generate predictions on the holdout data to quantify the overall predictive performance of both models, concluding the modeling step of our work.

The remainder of the work for each of the examples is spent on the audit step of the RDS framework, where we consider the model's predictive fairness in the context of our ultimate goal of improving outcome fairness. The auditing process encompasses the following steps:

1. Quantifying and visualizing the predictive performance across protected groups for each of the models.

2. Quantifying and visualizing the predictive error across protected groups for each of the models to explore failure cases for the models.

3. Deciding upon appropriate fairness metrics for the task and calculating them for each of the groups (categories) of one or more protected features.

4. Comparing fairness metrics across groups within each model to determine whether unfairness is a problem.

5. Attempting to use interpretability methods to better understand important features, global feature impacts, and possible sources of unfairness in how the model leverages the underlying features.

6. Attempting to apply preprocessing and postprocessing techniques to mitigate bias if large amounts of it are discovered. If model predictions are to be modified, model architects and organization decision-makers need to be consulted.

Let's begin.

Justification, Compilation, and Preparation Review

As usual, we load in our necessary packages as well as the raw data from a .csv file.

```
# load our packages
library(here)

# source packages
source(here("setup/packages.R"))

# source helper functions
source(here("setup/helpers.R"))

# get raw COMPAS data
compas_raw = read_csv(here("data/compas-scores-two-years.csv"))

# set a seed
set.seed(10)
```

Let's begin by reminding ourselves of what the data look like, shown here:

```
print(compas_raw)
## # A tibble: 7,214 x 53
##        id name  first last  compas_screenin~ sex   dob         age
##     <dbl> <chr> <chr> <chr> <date>           <chr> <date>    <dbl>
## 1       1 migu~ migu~ hern~ 2013-08-14       Male  1947-04-18   69
## 2       3 kevo~ kevon dixon 2013-01-27       Male  1982-01-22   34
## 3       4 ed p~ ed    philo 2013-04-14       Male  1991-05-14   24
## 4       5 marc~ marcu brown 2013-01-13       Male  1993-01-21   23
## 5       6 bout~ bout~ pier~ 2013-03-26       Male  1973-01-22   43
## 6       7 mars~ mars~ miles 2013-11-30       Male  1971-08-22   44
## 7       8 edwa~ edwa~ ridd~ 2014-02-19       Male  1974-07-23   41
## 8       9 stev~ stev~ stew~ 2013-08-30       Male  1973-02-25   43
## 9      10 eliz~ eliz~ thie~ 2014-03-16       Fema~ 1976-06-03   39
## 10     13 bo b~ bo    brad~ 2013-11-04       Male  1994-06-10   21
## # ... with 7,204 more rows, and 45 more variables
```

In Chapter 6, we introduced the COMPAS dataset for recidivism prediction and our desire to use it as a means to learn more about issues of fairness in practice. By working through the Justification, Compilation, and Preparation steps of the RDS framework in that chapter, we presented ethical concerns for the modeling task in addition to our plans for addressing them, cleaned and split the data, and produced a datasheet to document the characteristics of the cleaned data.

Given that false positives lead to more direct harms to individuals and groups than false negatives in the case of this modeling task, we want to ensure that the false positive rate across protected groups is not substantially different. We identify specificity (proportion of non-recidivators correctly classified) as our performance metric of interest given its relationship with the FPR (proportion of non-recidivators who are falsely predicted to recidivate in the future). Once it comes time to audit the model for fairness, we may need to accept an increased rate of false negatives and decreased overall model performance if we want to achieve a lower FPR. While we will not set a specific threshold for a predictive fairness parity, we aim at greatly decreasing any per-group difference in FPR relative to our competing candidate, the pre-audit model. While we are most concerned with specificity and FPR, we will begin our comparison of the various models with overall performance metrics like accuracy and AUC before delving more deeply into either of the aforementioned metrics.

Rather than going back through all the cleaning steps for the data covered in the previous chapter, we have wrapped those steps (along with a few additional transformations and tweaks) in a function, `clean_compas()`, to make our work more reproducible.

> **NOTE**   We could have been using a "clean" output file here for the COMPAS data; however, this approach ensures that the underlying data haven't changed (e.g., the cleaned data can always be regenerated). When collaborating with multiple people, this also makes it easier to avoid the possibility of having multiple similarly named but differently versioned data variants. Regardless, if the data were large enough, this approach would not be feasible.

```
compas = clean_compas(compas_raw)
```

The `clean_compas()` function does the following:

1. Completes the cleaning steps laid out in the initial ProPublica analysis
2. Collapses the levels "Native American," "Asian," into the "Other" level on account of not having enough observations for these groups within our dataset to facilitate accurate modeling
3. Drops 868 rows representing individuals outside of the two-year window of the target variable
4. Creates a binary feature, `juv_charge`, for whether an individual has a recorded misdemeanor or felony offense

We demarcate relevant columns as protected features by using `make_protected()` to append `_protected` to each column name.

```
compas_protected = compas %>%
  make_protected(c("age", "race", "sex"))
## # A tibble: 5,304 x 7
##    age_cat_protect~ c_charge_degree race_protected sex_protected
##    <chr>            <chr>           <chr>          <chr>
##  1 Greater than 45  F               Other          Male
##  2 25 - 45          F               African-Ameri~ Male
##  3 Less than 25     F               African-Ameri~ Male
##  4 25 - 45          M               Other          Male
##  5 25 - 45          F               Caucasian      Male
##  6 25 - 45          F               Other          Male
##  7 25 - 45          M               Caucasian      Female
##  8 25 - 45          F               Caucasian      Male
##  9 Less than 25     M               African-Ameri~ Male
## 10 25 - 45          M               Caucasian      Female
## # ... with 5,294 more rows, and 3 more variables
```

We then split the data into train and test sets using a 70/30 ratio.

```
compas_split = compas_protected %>%
  initial_split(prop = 0.7)
```

We run the split data into the `gen_preprocessed_data()` function to generate a named list containing our train data, test data, and other feature transformations for the data that we will leverage when modeling. This function is primarily useful for standardizing numeric features to a range between 0 and 1, dropping near-zero variance features, removing correlated features, and turning character features into factors.

```
processed_data = compas_split %>%
  gen_preprocessed_data(target = "two_year_recid")
```

Modeling

With our data ready, we can now start the process of assessing the overall predictive performance of different candidate models. First, we specify and save certain parameters that we plan to reuse throughout our analysis. These include the following:

■ The types of models. We use one intrinsically interpretable model, one model that is somewhere between intrinsically interpretable and black box (k-nearest neighbors, which is interpretable only for individual records) and two black-box models:

  ■ Logistic regression (intrinsically interpretable)

  ■ k-nearest neighbors (mostly black box)

- Random forest (black box)
- Support vector machines (SVM) (black box)
- The model "mode" (classification or regression)
- The name of our target feature. Note that we are predicting recidivism directly as our target (via `two_year_recid`) rather than predicting the COMPAS risk score itself, which may lead to different results in our analysis compared to other, similar analyses.
- The name of the event of interest
- A binary TRUE or FALSE for whether we want to tune our model
- The protected features
- The privileged groups within each protected feature; our choice of Caucasians as the privileged group for race is guided by the knowledge that, historically, other racial groups, especially African Americans, are often overpoliced and unfairly subjected to harsher legal penalties than Caucasians. Other researchers working on the COMPAS dataset have already identified this disparity as being present, most notably for African Americans.
- The performance metrics that we will track across our models. We choose multiple metrics here because they are trivial to calculate and useful for cross-model comparison.

Arguments that appear later in the code but are not included here are left in the code to improve clarity. In a production setting, we would want *all* of these parameters to be specified outside of the code (in a YAML file or separate script).

```
model_names = c("logistic_regression", "nearest_neighbor", "svm_rbf",
"random_forest")

model_mode = "classification"

target_name = "two_year_recid"

event_name = "pred_1"

tune_flag = FALSE

protected_features = c("age", "race", "sex")

privileged_groups = c("Greater than 45", "Caucasian", "Female")

my_metrics = metric_set(yardstick::accuracy, yardstick::roc_auc)
```

To facilitate fitting many different types of models, we input our vector of model names into the gen_mods() function—one of the "hand-rolled" functions that we created as a wrapper around the modeling functions in the parsnip and workflows package from tidymodels to help facilitate an RDS workflow.

The function outputs a list of model workflow objects that we can later fit and generate predictions from.

```
wflows = gen_mods(model_frame,
                 names = model_names,
                 mode = model_mode,
                 tune = tune_flag,
                 recipe = processed_data[["recipe"]])
```

To get stable assessments of model performance, we evaluate the performance of our models over multiple resamples of the data, splitting each resample into a training partition and an evaluation partition. We measure performance on the evaluation partition; 50 resamples ought to suffice for our purposes.

The gen_boots() function generates a dataframe of bootstrap resamples, where each value in the dataframe is an individual resampling of the data.

```
boots = gen_boots(processed_data[["input_data"]], num_resamples = 50)
```

Next, we iterate the gen_map_frame() function over our list of workflows to generate a list of dataframes. Each of the dataframes in the output list contains the full specification for the resampling process that we want to undertake for each model.

NOTE   Anytime the map function is used, we are iterating over the first object within the parentheses by applying the second object, a function, to it. The same applies to map2, though we are iterating over the first two objects and applying the third, a function, to each of these.

```
map_frame = map(wflows,
               gen_map_frame,
               boots,
               metrics = my_metrics,
               names = model_names)
```

We execute our resamples by mapping the gen_resample() function to our list of resample specifications in map_frame and give each of the result dataframes the proper model name identifier by simultaneously iterating over model_names. This code can take quite a long time to run, depending on the processing power of the computer used and whether parallelization is enabled. It would take even longer to run if we were tuning each of our models; however, we are using untuned models within this example for simplicity's sake.

```
resamples = map2(map_frame,
                 model_names,
                 gen_resample,
                 resample = boots,
                 metrics = my_metrics,
                 tune = tune_flag,
                 model_frame = model_frame,
                 df = processed_data[["train"]],
                 target = target_name)
```

Once the resampling is complete, we bind together the resample results from each of the models and calculate the average performance per-metric achieved by each model across all the resamples.

```
resamples %>%
  map(collect_metrics) %>%
  bind_rows() %>%
  relocate(model) %>%
  select(model, .metric, mean) %>%
  arrange(.metric, -mean)
## # A tibble: 8 x 3
##     model                .metric   mean
##     <chr>                <chr>     <dbl>
##  1 logistic_regression  accuracy  0.698
##  2 random_forest        accuracy  0.690
##  3 svm_rbf              accuracy  0.689
##  4 nearest_neighbor     accuracy  0.635
##  5 logistic_regression  roc_auc   0.718
##  6 random_forest        roc_auc   0.709
##  7 svm_rbf              roc_auc   0.696
##  8 nearest_neighbor     roc_auc   0.637
```

The results of our models appear similar to those achieved by other researchers and groups that have attempted to design recidivism prediction algorithms in the past.

Here are a few key points from the resample results:

▪ All of the models (except for k-nearest neighbors) achieved about 69 percent accuracy, which is greater than the accuracy (65.2 percent) achieved by the maker of COMPAS (Northpointe, now Equivant). In assessing classification performance, analysts typically turn first to accuracy and area under the curve (AUC). Measured by these scores, all but the nearest neighbor model were able to exceed the predictive performance of the COMPAS model that ProPublica studied.

■ Interestingly, both of the black-box models (i.e., SVM and random forest) achieve lower overall predictive performance than the intrinsically interpretable logistic regression model, which achieves the highest performance level in both accuracy and AUC.

■ For our metric of interest, specificity (proportion of 0s correctly classified), logistic regression performs best. Nearest neighbors does well, but its overall accuracy is barely better than a featureless model (more on that later).

We have now reached the "forking path" that we discussed first in Chapter 5, "Model Interpretability: The What and the Why." Is the change in overall predictive performance from using a black-box model worth the increased difficulty of interpretability over a comparable intrinsically interpretable model? Basically, what is the cost of interpretability?

The resample metrics for overall performance seem to indicate that we would be better off using an intrinsically interpretable model, specifically a logistic regression. Still, we haven't ruled out the possibility that a black-box model will have more favorable per-group performance characteristics (e.g., the errors are more evenly distributed between protected groups). We pay greater attention to this later during the audit.

Back to the task at hand. To quantify the trade-off in overall predictive performance between our best-performing black-box and intrinsically interpretable models, we use `plot_coi_comparison()` to calculate and display a plot of the percentage difference in each of the performance metrics that we calculated within our resamples. Numbers greater than zero indicate the percentage that the black-box method, in this case random forest, improves upon the logistic regression.

```
coi_plot = plot_coi_comparison(resamples,
            interp_model = "logistic_regression",
            bbox_model = "random_forest",
            metric_comparison = c("accuracy", "roc_auc", "spec"))
```

As shown in the results of the plot in Figure 7.4, from the standpoint of general accuracy, so far there seems to be no advantage to using a black box model. Pending the review of fairness metrics, we postpone the fork in the path and continue using both models.

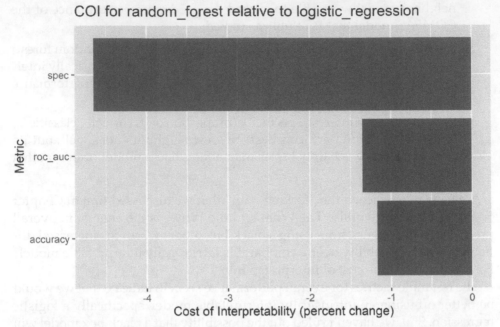

Figure 7.4: A cost of interpretability (COI expressed in percent) plot comparing a random forest and logistic regression model

At this point, we still don't know how the performance that these models achieve compares with the performance of a featureless baseline model or the hypothetical optimal performance within recidivism modeling tasks more generally. A featureless model, i.e., a model in which every case is classified as belonging to the most common class, is a useful benchmark, but not very informative on its own. To approximate optimal performance, we will use an accuracy metric of 71 percent—a figure cited in the literature as representing excellent performance for a recidivism prediction algorithm.

To get an idea of variability in model estimates, we fit the models to each of the 50 bootstrap resamples. For the featureless model, the `gen_bounding()` function estimates performance within each of the bootstrap resamples as the performance of a model that only predicts the most common class within that resample. For optimal performance, the function generates the "optimal model" as an estimate pulled from a user-supplied distribution of the optimal performance metric.

Because there is no reasonable generalization of AUC or specificity for our featureless predictor, we drop those metrics here and focus solely on accuracy.

```
bounding_models = gen_bounding(processed_data,
                    target = target_name,
                    boots = boots,
                    metrics = metric_set(yardstick::accuracy))
```

The output is a dataframe where every row is a model and performance metric for each of the bootstrap resamples. Here are the first 10 rows (accuracy for the featureless model for the first 10 resamples):

```
print(bounding_models)
## $f_less
## # A tibble: 50 x 3
##     model   metric    estimate
##     <chr>   <chr>        <dbl>
##  1 f_less accuracy      0.630
##  2 f_less accuracy      0.624
##  3 f_less accuracy      0.628
##  4 f_less accuracy      0.617
##  5 f_less accuracy      0.636
##  6 f_less accuracy      0.636
##  7 f_less accuracy      0.641
##  8 f_less accuracy      0.632
##  9 f_less accuracy      0.633
## 10 f_less accuracy      0.619
## # ... with 40 more rows
```

We can more easily interpret the performance of our models as multiple box plots rather than as multiple dataframes. To accomplish this, we use the gen_baseline_plot() function to create a plot of the distribution of performance metrics across each of the models (see Figure 7.5), ordering each of the models in descending order by performance. To improve clarity, we only display one of our metrics of interest, accuracy.

```
baseline_plot = plot_baseline_models(bounding_models,
                                     resamples,
                                     num_resamples = 50,
                                     full_plot = TRUE,
                                     display_metric = "accuracy")
```

As we would expect, none of the models is able to reach the threshold for optimal performance, and all but one of our models is able to perform consistently better than the featureless model. That's good news! Looking forward, we don't want to have to fit and audit all of the models. Let's subset down to one interpretable and one black-box model by selecting the highest-performing of each across AUC (logistic regression and random forest, respectively.)

To obtain our modeling functions for these models, we iterate over our resample results and map_frame (containing model objects) with the gen_model_struct() function. This function is most relevant for situations where we are tuning our models, as it would allow us to finalize the model equation to use the highest-scoring combination of hyperparameters seen across the resample. Here, it is being used primarily to ensure consistency and conciseness, as we are not tuning any hyperparameters.

```
model_names_small = c("logistic_regression", "random_forest")

model_structs = map2(resamples, map_frame, gen_model_struct,
                     tune = tune_flag) %>%
  set_names(model_names)
```

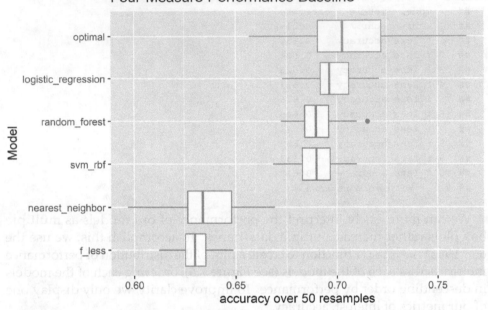

Figure 7.5: A plot comparing the performance of all models by accuracy averaged over 50 resamples

We then fit the model functions on the unprocessed input data. The workflow objects within the `model_structs` list handle the preprocessing of the raw data automatically. We use the `extract()` function to subset down the `fit_mods` list object to the two candidate models specified in `model_names_small`.

```
fit_mods = map(model_structs, fit, processed_data[["input_data"]]) %>%
  set_names(model_names) %>%
  extract(model_names_small)
```

The superior overall performance of the logistic model plus its interpretability is our reason for keeping it in consideration; Figure 7.6 shows the fitted model.

Odds of Recidivism = 0.276 + 0.585*age_catprotectedGreat_than_45 +
1.89*age_cat_protectedLess than 25 + 0.832*c_charge_degreeM +
0.853*race_protectedCaucasian + 0.776*race_protectedHispanic + 0.664*race_protectedOther
+ 1.55*sex_protectedMale + 1.16*priors_count + 1.55*juv_chargeyes

Figure 7.6: The formula for the logistic regression function fit upon the processed input data

The coefficients indicate the multiplicative change in odds associated with a unit change in the predictor. For example, if the defendant is Male (`sex_protectedMale` = 1 instead of 0), the odds of re-offending increase by 55 percent.

With the fit models in hand, we can use the `gen_pred_data()` function to generate a list of dataframes, where each dataframe contains the test dataset (with the same preprocessing parameters from the training set already applied), as well as the predicted probabilities for each class and the predicted class all bound as the final three columns.

```
pred_data = gen_pred_data(fit_mods,
                          mode = model_mode,
                          data_split = compas_split)
```

We can leverage these prediction dataframes to get multiple performance metrics for each of the models on their test datasets using the `gen_overall_metrics()` function. The code outside of the initial `map()` call binds together the performance metric dataframes for the two models and makes them more readable.

```
more_metrics = metric_set(yardstick::accuracy,
                          yardstick::roc_auc,
                          yardstick::precision,
                          yardstick::npv,
                          yardstick::sens,
                          yardstick::spec)

mod_metrics = map(pred_data,
                  gen_overall_metrics,
                  target = target_name,
                  estimate = "pred_class",
                  val_interest = "1",
                  metrics = more_metrics,
                  mode = model_mode) %>%
  map2(model_names_small, assign_names) %>%
  bind_rows()
## # A tibble: 12 x 4
##    model               metric    estimator estimate
##    <chr>               <chr>     <chr>        <dbl>
##  1 logistic_regression accuracy  binary       0.705
##  2 logistic_regression precision binary       0.646
##  3 logistic_regression npv       binary       0.721
##  4 logistic_regression sens      binary       0.395
##  5 logistic_regression spec      binary       0.878
##  6 logistic_regression roc_auc   binary       0.732
##  7 random_forest       accuracy  binary       0.696
##  8 random_forest       precision binary       0.612
##  9 random_forest       npv       binary       0.725
## 10 random_forest       sens      binary       0.427
## 11 random_forest       spec      binary       0.848
## 12 random_forest       roc_auc   binary       0.719
```

The pattern in predictive performance that we saw for each of the models fit on our resampled training sets holds for test set performance: The logistic regression exceeds the performance of the highest-performing black-box model, random forest, in four out of five of the performance metrics.

Another characteristic of the model becomes clear: it is hesitant to label individuals as recidivists. Only about 40 percent of the 1s (recidivists) are predicted as 1s (the sensitivity metric), whereas more than 85 percent of the 0s (non-recidivists) are labeled as 0s (the specificity metric).

Now, we transition to the Auditing stage to delve more deeply into why the models have different performance levels and how predictive performance differs across protected groups within each of the models.

Auditing

Having established overall performance metrics for our different models, we now begin the heart of the auditing process: calculating per-group metrics, calculating fairness metrics, and attempting various bias mitigation techniques.

Per-Group Metrics: Overall

Before calculating any proper fairness metrics, we need to understand how each of the models performs across protected groups. The `gen_protected_metrics()` function iterates over each of the test data/model prediction dataframes to calculate user-supplied performance metrics for each of the protected groups within the dataset. Each of the rows of the final dataframe represent a unique combination of the input model, protected feature, protected group, performance metric, and estimate. Obviously, this yields quite a number of rows as each of these input elements grows. In this case, we end up with 108 rows.

```
protected_metrics = map2(pred_data,
                         model_names_small,
                         gen_protected_metrics,
                         target = target_name,
                         estimate = "pred_class",
                         mode = model_mode,
                         protected = protected_features,
                         privileged = privileged_groups,
                         metrics = more_metrics) %>%
    bind_rows()
```

These 108 assessments are likely to find something suggestive, just by chance, even in the absence of systematic unfairness. We'd like to narrow our focus, if possible, by specifying a priori what we're interested in. In this case, we use our knowledge of the historical legacy of unfair treatment of African Americans in the criminal justice system of the United States to focus on race. First, we look at accuracy in Figure 7.7.

```
protected_metrics_plot_acc = plot_protected_metrics(protected_metrics,
                                        protected = "race",
                                        display_metric = "accuracy")
```

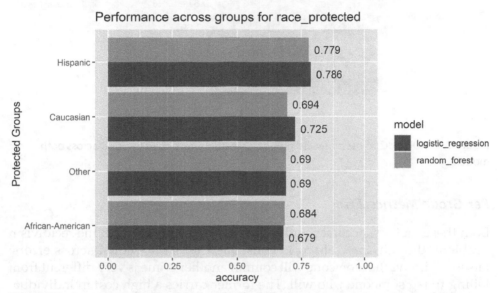

Figure 7.7: Accuracy across protected groups for feature `race_protected` across both models

```
protected_metrics_plot_auc = plot_protected_metrics(protected_metrics,
                                        protected = "race",
                                        display_metric = "roc_auc")
```

The per-group accuracy of both models is lowest for African Americans.

The picture is different for AUC, as shown in Figure 7.8, where model performance for African Americans exceeds that for Caucasians and is close to that for Hispanics. We need to delve deeper if we want to understand what is going on here. We do that by looking at per-group error metrics, specifically, the direction of the errors within each group.

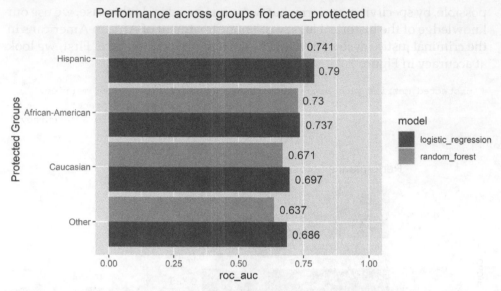

Figure 7.8: ROC AUC across protected groups for feature `race_protected` across both models

Per-Group Metrics: Error

Both these metrics, accuracy and AUC, treat all errors alike. In the recidivism problem, though, the real-world consequences are not equal across errors: falsely claiming that someone will commit another crime is very different from failing to tag someone who will. The former carries a high cost in individual rights—longer sentences, delayed probation, and higher bail, all of which are undeserved. The latter carries a cost to society (i.e., failing to protect from future crimes). In most justice systems, individual rights are favored over protecting society. In uncertain cases, the benefit of doubt lies with the individual defendant, and decisions are tilted in their favor. We ought to operate similarly here.

Let's therefore examine the rates of these different error types for the different groups. Of particular interest is the error of mistakenly classifying a non-recidivist as a recidivist—a false positive. We start with a plot of the false positive rate (FPR) across groups in Figure 7.9. FPR is the proportion of non-recidivists (0s) who are falsely classified as recidivists (1s).

```
fp_error_direction_plot = plot_error_direction(pred_data,
                                    mode = model_mode,
                                    display_feature = "race",
                                    false_positive = TRUE,
                                    model = model_names_small,
                                    target = target_name)
```

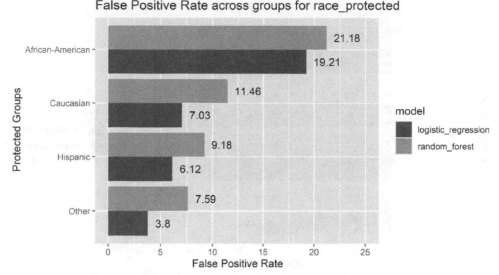

Figure 7.9: FPR across protected groups for feature `race_protected` across both models

From Figure 7.9, we can see that our model is manifestly unfair to African Americans. African American non-recidivists are about twice as likely to be falsely classified as recidivists compared to Caucasians. This is a frightening result for a model that makes such consequential decisions regarding the lives of individual people.

The flip side of the false positive story is the false negative rate (FNR)—the proportion of recidivists who are mistakenly classified as non-recidivists. The models fail to properly classify three-quarters of Caucasian recidivists, whereas the false negative rate is less than 50 percent for African Americans (see Figure 7.10). We noted earlier that the models are reluctant to classify individuals as recidivists; we see now that this caution primarily benefits the Caucasian defendants.

```
fn_error_direction_plot = plot_error_direction(pred_data,
                                mode = model_mode,
                                display_feature = "race",
                                false_positive = FALSE,
                                model = model_names_small,
                                target = target_name)
```

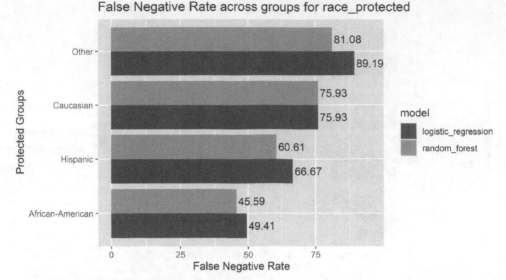

Figure 7.10: FNR across protected groups for feature `race_protected` across both models

Fairness Metrics

So far, we have calculated metrics of predictive performance by protected group. However, legal circumstances and the pressures of a rigorous analysis often require direct group-to-group comparison of performance. In the recidivism illustration, given the historical legacy of differential treatment for African Americans, comparing African Americans to Caucasians (i.e., the privileged group) is a natural comparison.

Once we have the data saved in the right format within the `pred_data` object, we calculate all comparative fairness metrics, starting with accuracy, to see how the model performs across protected groups relative to the privileged group, Caucasians.

```
fairness_metrics = gen_fairness_metrics(pred_data,
                                target = target_name,
                                model = model_names_small,
                                mode = model_mode,
                                protected = protected_features,
                                privileged = privileged_groups)
```

Drilling down into these more relevant error metrics, we see that the logistic regression seems to lose some of its advantage. We note from Figure 7.11 that the logistic model is considerably more inaccurate for African Americans relative to Caucasians than is the random forest model. (For Hispanics, both models are considerably more accurate.)

```
error_rate_fairness_plot = plot_fairness_metrics(fairness_metrics,
                        display_feature = "race_protected",
                        metric = "error_rate")
```

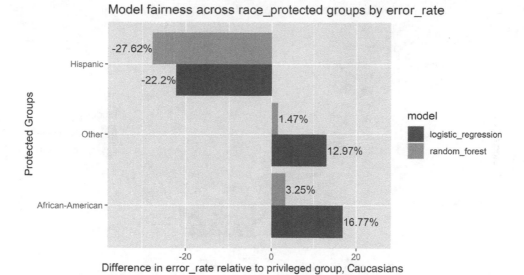

Figure 7.11: A comparison of fairness metrics as a percent difference in error rate from the privileged group, Caucasians

Most important from a predictive fairness standpoint is the relative FPR between each race group and the privileged race group, Caucasians. From Figure 7.12, we see that, for the logistic model, FPRs for African Americans are more than 170 percent greater than those for Caucasians. The random forest does better, but false positives are still 90 percent greater for African Americans than for Caucasians. This reduction in the relative disadvantage for African Americans in the random forest, however, is entirely due to a greater increase in Caucasian FP's than African American FP's. Basically, even though the FP's for both groups grew relative to the logistic regression, the gap between the two groups shrank. This illustrates that fairness metrics, involving relative comparisons, tell only part of the story.

```
fpr_fairness_plot = plot_fairness_metrics(fairness_metrics,
                    display_feature = "race_protected",
                    metric = "fpr")
```

A similar picture emerges for false negatives in Figure 7.13.

```
fnr_fairness_plot = plot_fairness_metrics(fairness_metrics,
                    display_feature = "race_protected",
                    metric = "fnr")
```

Another metric of interest here is demographic parity, as we are interested in comparing how many people *total* within each group are predicted to recidivate.

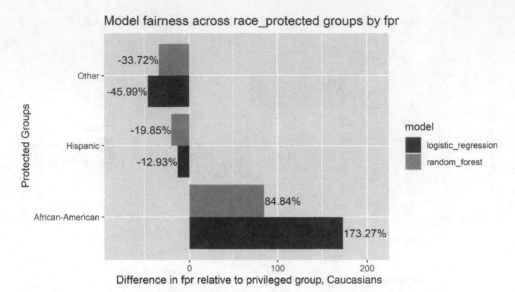

Figure 7.12: A comparison of fairness metrics as a percent difference in FPR from the privileged group, Caucasians

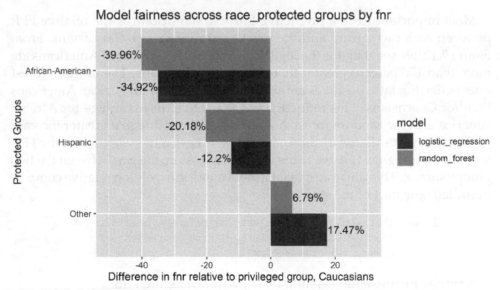

Figure 7.13: A comparison of fairness metrics as a percent difference in the FNRs from the privileged group, Caucasians

```
demographic_fairness_plot = plot_fairness_metrics(fairness_metrics,
                display_feature = "race_protected",
                metric = "demographic_parity")
```

We see in Figure 7.14 that African Americans are approximately 250–300 percent more likely to be tagged as recidivists than Caucasians, which is clearly a

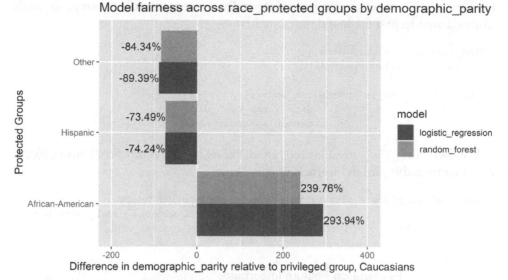

Figure 7.14: A comparison of fairness metrics as a percent difference in demographic parity from the privileged group, Caucasians

cause for concern in the context of both predictive and outcome fairness. In many popular analyses of differential treatment of groups, the story might stop here. But we know that these differences in groups arise from at least two factors: the base rate of recidivism in the data (it is highest for African Americans at 43.95 percent) and the propensity of the model to classify groups as recidivists (it, also, is higher for African Americans).

It is important for a data scientist to be able to disentangle these two phenomena and identify any other phenomena that might be working underneath the model and the data. They can do little about the first (underlying rates of recidivism), but they can address the latter in part through the use of interpretability methods.

Interpreting Our Models: Why Are They Unfair?

We've identified a serious problem with our model, one that should be corrected. It overpredicts recidivism for African Americans who don't re-offend, and it underpredicts for Caucasians. We should try to learn why and then use that knowledge to mitigate at least some of this bias.

To learn the why, let's look at interpretability method results, starting with feature importance. We do this per model and then per group. To do it, we must generate an iml prediction object first. The structure of the object produced by `get_iml_preds()` isn't particularly important; it's only a wrapper to facilitate the usage of interpretability methods via iml. Still, the *iml* package requires its own prediction function to be used internally, so we must subset our `pred_data` object down to just the test dataframe first.

```
iml_test_data = pred_data[[1]] %>%
  select(-matches("pred_"))

iml_preds = get_iml_preds(fit_mods,
                          data = iml_test_data,
                          target = target_name)
```

We then run `plot_permutation_importance()` on the iml prediction objects and produce the plot in Figure 7.15.

```
permutation_plots = plot_permutation_importance(iml_preds,
                                model_names = model_names_small,
                                mode = model_mode)
```

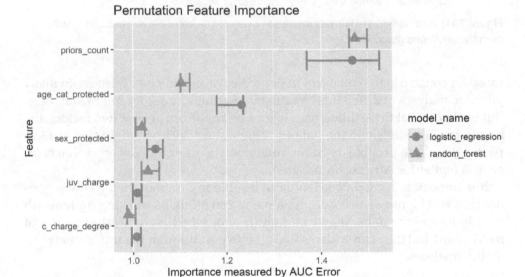

Figure 7.15: Permutation feature importance for all features in both models

Count of prior crimes and age (specifically, age < 25) are the most important features for predicting recidivism within two years. These results are in line with other analyses of the COMPAS data.

Now that we know which features are important, we must more closely examine how changing values of those features impacts the model's predictions.

A partial dependence plot (PDP) of the most important feature in both models, `priors_count`, shows us how the predicted probability of recidivating within two years changes as the value of the feature increases. We can use the `plot_global_interp()` function to generate this.

```
global_plots = plot_global_interp(iml_preds,
                                   model_names_small,
                                   display_feature = "priors_count")

print(global_plots)
```

We can see in Figure 7.16 that both models sharply penalize each additional prior crime, though the random forest model begins to level off around 10 prior crimes. Remember, the lines on this plot represent the average contribution of each value of `priors_count` across all observations. This indicates that both models are heavily relying on `priors_count`, with each model predicting a roughly 60 percent chance of recidivating based upon `priors_count` alone for defendants who have a record of 10 or more prior crimes.

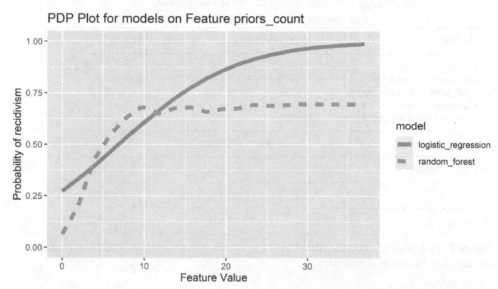

Figure 7.16: Global contributions for feature `prior_count` in both models as approximated by PDP plots

Analysis for Different Groups

What the PDP plot and the permutation plot before it in Figure 7.15 cannot disambiguate for us, though, is whether the importance of these features or their average contribution to predictions within each protected group operate differently depending on the protected group.

Let's now create separate models for each of the protected groups within the race feature, starting with logistic regression, which is more easily interpretable.

We use the gen_group_model() function to automatically fit a separate model on observations belonging only to one of each of the groups. We refer to these as the Hispanic, Caucasian, etc., models during our discussion of them. We focus our analysis on the differences between the Caucasian and African American models. We show the coefficients resulting from these two models in Figure 7.17.

```
race_groups = list("African-American", "Caucasian", "Hispanic", "Other")

per_race_logs = gen_group_model(model_structs[["logistic_regression"]],
                    df = processed_data[["input_data"]],
                    protected_group = "race_protected") %>%
    set_names(race_groups)
```

Table of Logistic Regression Coefficients (Exponentiated)

African-American and Caucasian Only Models

Model Term	Model coefficient (Afam)	Model coefficient (Cauc)
(Intercept)	0.226	0.293
age_cat_protectedGreater than 45	0.561	0.525
age_cat_protectedLess than 25	2.113	1.435
c_charge_degreeM	0.909	0.816
sex_protectedMale	1.972	1.153
priors_count	1.146	1.217
juv_chargeyes	1.534	1.620

Figure 7.17: A table of exponentiated regression coefficients for a model fit only on African American or Caucasian defendants

The role of age < 25 in the models is important, as expected. Its coefficient in the African American model is 2.113, meaning the odds of recidivism more than double if the person is 25 or younger. For the Caucasian model, the odds also increase but not by as much (43.5 percent). These results accord with the fact that the base rate of recidivism within this dataset is generally higher for African Americans (43.95 percent versus 30.09 percent, and 29.97 percent and 26.20 percent for Caucasians, Hispanics, and "Other(s)," respectively). However, the impact of *priors* (number of prior crimes) is interesting. Prior crimes is, by far, the most important predictor within each of the models. However, in the

African American model, an additional prior crime generates only a 14.6 percent increase in the odds of re-offending, while it yields a 21.7 percent increase in those odds within the Caucasian model. Given the higher prevalence of re-offending for African Americans, we would have expected the reverse.

What is happening here? Simply put, it looks like priors don't mean as much for African Americans versus Caucasians, at least within a logistic regression model. When we combine both groups in a model, we constrain prior crimes to have a single coefficient. That coefficient is inflated by the presence of other groups within the model, resulting in an artificially high coefficient for African Americans (yielding over prediction for non-re-offenders), and too low for Caucasians (yielding under-prediction). We seem to have found confirmatory evidence within these models that African Americans are over-policed compared to Caucasians—those early arrests (each unit of `priors_count`) don't reflect real "criminality," as measured by recidivism, as much for African Americans as they do for Caucasians.

Let's check to what extent these interpretations hold up with other models as well, especially more complicated black-box models. We again fit separate models to each of the protected race groups, this time using a random forest as our model.

```
race_groups = c("African-American", "Caucasian", "Hispanic", "Other")

per_race_models = gen_group_model(model_structs[["random_forest"]],
              df = processed_data[["input_data"]],
              protected_group = "race_protected") %>%
  set_names(race_groups)
```

Because we are now looking at a black-box model, we are no longer able to easily interpret our predictions using coefficients as we had been able to when using a logistic regression previously. This, of course, means that we need to apply interpretability methods to it, which requires us to use functions from the iml package to wrap our model objects.

```
iml_test_data = pred_data[[1]] %>%
  select(-matches("pred_"))

grouped_iml_preds = get_iml_preds(per_race_models,
                data = iml_test_data,
                target = target_name)

all_iml_preds = append(grouped_iml_preds, iml_preds[[2]])

all_iml_names = append(race_groups, "Original")
```

The feature importance plot in Figure 7.18 indicates that the features have roughly the same ordering of performance across each of the separate models. The most notable result here is that the age and sex features are possibly more important for the African American model, indicating that these features may also be more relevant when predicting recidivism for African Americans (within this dataset).

```
permutation_plots = plot_permutation_importance(all_iml_preds,
                                    model_names = all_iml_names,
                                    mode = model_mode)
```

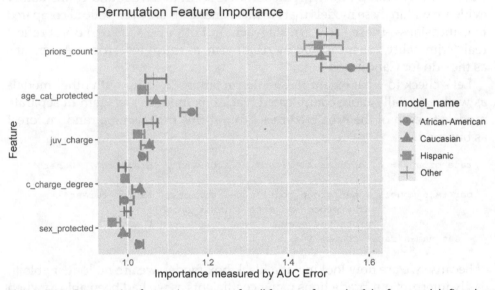

Figure 7.18: Permutation feature importance for all features for each of the four models fit only on one race group

```
global_plots = plot_global_interp(all_iml_preds,
                          all_iml_names,
                          display_feature = "priors_count")
```

Looking at the PDP plot (see Figure 7.19), we can judge to what extent more priors yield a higher recidivism probability. For Caucasians, the effect of more priors levels off at about 12 priors, where the recidivism probability has been boosted to about 60 percent (a 54 percent increase from the base rate of 39 percent). For African Americans, at 12 priors the recidivism probability has been boosted to about 74 percent (a 68 percent increase from the base rate of 44 percent).

In contrast to the case with logistic regression, the random forest seems to indicate that the number of priors is more important for African Americans than for Caucasians.

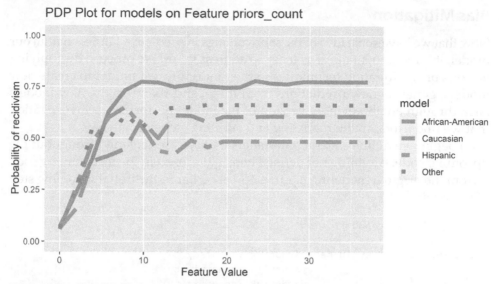

Figure 7.19: Global contributions for feature `prior_count` for each of the four models fit on one race group as approximated by the PDP plots

We've done a lot of exploration and interpretation and have made progress in understanding what is causing the excess rate of false positives for African Americans, which persists in the single random forest model, although we have not fully solved the puzzle. We have established that the interpretable logistic regression model does better than the black-box random forest model across all overall and per-group metrics, only falling short on metrics of fairness. However, we have also established that the superior performance of the random forest model on FP fairness was primarily due to its substantially worse performance for Caucasians. In effect, it appeared more "fair" by making things worse for Caucasians, at least relative to the logistic regression model: see the plot of per-group FPR in Figure 7.9.

In the end, though, neither model reached anything close to predictive fairness, approximated in this case by FPR. Our best hope for creating a fairer model now rests on bias mitigation techniques. Due to the large differences in per-group performance, we may want to try the pre-processing step of oversampling the protected groups that the model performs poorly on as well as the post-processing step of directly (manually) setting different classification cutoffs for each race group, aiming specifically for similar FP levels for African Americans and Caucasians. We could make those adjustments from either model. Switching back to the logistic model would have some advantages, since it has lower FP levels for both African Americans and Caucasians. To maintain the flow of the story, we will continue with the random forest model that we have already been working with. The adjustments that would be needed for the logistic model are available in the code online.

Bias Mitigation

Now that we have some idea of the shortcomings in predictive fairness within our model, it is incumbent upon us to try to address them. We proceed by applying various bias mitigation techniques to the random forest model to create new models, generate new predictions from these, and then run the new models back through an abbreviated version of the model performance investigation that we undertook in the modeling and auditing steps previously.

To begin, we define several parameters that we are reusing throughout the upcoming code. Anything not defined here that is used in the forthcoming code is from the original modeling parameters set earlier in the initial modeling step of our analysis.

```
bias_model = "random_forest"

bias_metrics = metric_set(yardstick::accuracy,
                          yardstick::sensitivity,
                          yardstick::specificity)

protected = "race_protected"

privileged = "Caucasian"

pred_data_orig = pred_data[[2]]
```

Preprocessing: Oversampling

Perhaps preprocessing will help mitigate a large portion of the bias found in the models against African Americans? Let's try oversampling the observations representing African Americans within the data as a way to influence the model to perform better when predicting that group, specifically as measured by FPR.

To oversample observations representing African Americans, we create two new training datasets. Each set contains 1,000 and 2,000 more observations representing African Americans, respectively.

```
oversampled_data = map(1:2, ~ training(compas_split) %>%
                       filter(race_protected == "African-American") %>%
                       sample_n(1000)) %>%
  bind_rows()

compas_train_small = oversampled_data %>%
  sample_n(1000) %>%
  bind_rows(training(compas_split))

compas_train_large = training(compas_split) %>%
  bind_rows(oversampled_data)
```

Next, we fit random forest models to each of these new datasets, generate predictions on the original test set, and bind the predictions from each of the models together to a named list.

```
fit_mods_small = model_structs[["random_forest"]] %>%
  fit(compas_train_small)

fit_mods_large = model_structs[["random_forest"]] %>%
  fit(compas_train_large)

preds_over_small = gen_pred_data(fit_mods_small,
                                 mode = "classification",
                                 data_split = compas_split)

preds_over_large = gen_pred_data(fit_mods_large,
                                 mode = "classification",
                                 data_split = compas_split)

pred_list_over = list(pred_data_orig, preds_over_small, preds_over_large)

over_model_names = c("original", "small_oversample", "large_oversample")
```

The overall performance metrics calculated for each of the three models do not show any immediately notable differences, perhaps aside from the large oversample model actually performing worse than the original and small oversample models.

```
map(pred_list_over,
    gen_overall_metrics,
    target = target_name,
    estimate = "pred_class",
    val_interest = "1",
    metrics = bias_metrics,
    mode = model_mode) %>%
  map2(over_model_names, mutate) %>%
  map(rename, model = 4) %>%
  bind_rows() %>%
  relocate(model) %>%
  arrange(metric, -estimate)
## # A tibble: 9 x 4
##   model            metric   estimator estimate
##   <chr>            <chr>    <chr>        <dbl>
## 1 original         accuracy binary       0.696
## 2 large_oversample accuracy binary       0.696
## 3 small_oversample accuracy binary       0.691
## 4 large_oversample sens     binary       0.449
## 5 original         sens     binary       0.427
## 6 small_oversample sens     binary       0.427
## 7 original         spec     binary       0.848
## 8 small_oversample spec     binary       0.840
## 9 large_oversample spec     binary       0.834
```

What about performance metrics across each protected group?

```
over_protected_metrics = map2(pred_list_over,
                              over_model_names,
                              gen_protected_metrics,
                              target = target_name,
                              estimate = "pred_class",
                              mode = model_mode,
                              protected = protected,
                              privileged = privileged,
                              metrics = bias_metrics) %>%
    bind_rows()
```

Plotting performance metrics calculated across protected groups in Figure 7.20 also does not indicate that there is meaningful improvement in the per-group spec-ificity of the oversampled models relative to the original nonoversampled model.

```
over_protected_metrics_plot = plot_protected_metrics(over_protected_metrics,
                              protected = protected,
                              display_metric = "spec")
```

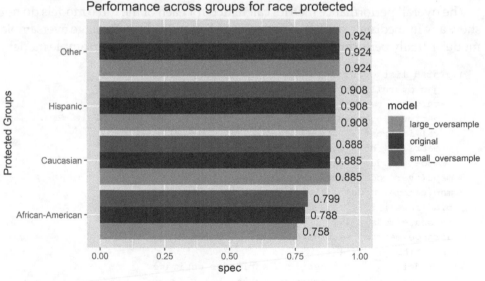

Figure 7.20: Specificity across protected groups for feature `race_protected` across the original model, the model with a small oversample (n = 1,000) of African American defendants, and the model with a large oversample (n = 2,000) of African American defendants

The plot of per-group FPR in Figure 7.21 paints a dire picture; if anything, it looks like oversampling actually increased the rate at which the models falsely predict a defendant will recidivate.

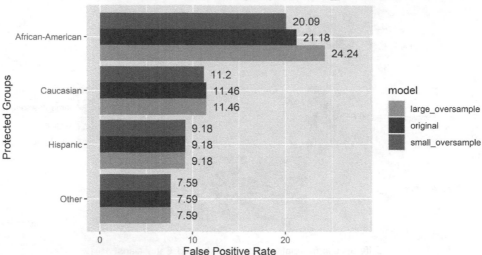

Figure 7.21: FPR across protected groups for feature `race_protected` across the original model, the model with a small oversample (n = 1,000) of African American defendants, and the model with a large oversample (n = 2,000) of African American defendants

```
oversample_error_direction_plot = plot_error_direction(pred_list_over,
                                    mode = model_mode,
                                    display_feature = protected,
                                    false_positive = TRUE,
                                    model = over_model_names,
                                    target = target_name)
```

Calculating relative fairness metrics in Figure 7.22 yields the same results as Figure 7.21, only it depicts them slightly more clearly. Oversampling observations representing African Americans to mitigate the bias against them has, at best, had no notable impact, and at worst actually made the model perform slightly worse when predicting them.

```
oversample_fairness_metrics = gen_fairness_metrics(pred_list_over,
                                target = target_name,
                                model = over_model_names,
                                mode = model_mode,
                                protected = protected,
                                privileged = privileged)
fpr_preproc_plot = plot_fairness_metrics(oversample_fairness_metrics,
                        display_feature = protected,
                        metric = "fpr")
```

We can conclude at this point that oversampling was not successful at mitigating bias in the FPR seen across protected groups within the race feature,

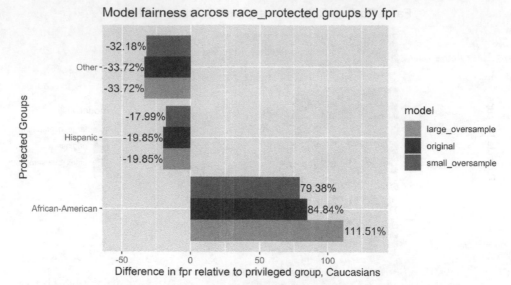

Figure 7.22: A comparison of fairness metrics as a percent difference in the FPR from the privileged group, Caucasian, across the original model, the model with a small oversample (n = 1,000) of African American defendants, and the model with a large oversample (n = 2,000) of African American defendants

especially for African Americans. Next, we try a postprocessing method to see if we can more successfully mitigate this bias.

Postprocessing: Optimizing Thresholds Automatically

It looks like the overprediction of recidivism for African Americans may reflect endemic relationships in the data that our models have not yet been able to untangle. We now turn to calibrating the classification thresholds themselves. As we are concerned with minimizing FPR across each of the protected groups within the race feature, we choose separate classification thresholds for each group. We are now joining together the realms of outcome fairness and predictive fairness. Assigning African Americans a higher threshold for a recidivism classification will give us lower per group error (ensuring predictive fairness) and leads to real-world outcomes that are fairer overall (improving outcome fairness).

We set optimal prediction thresholds for each protected group first by calibrating each prediction threshold to maximize Youden's J—a metric that should help us attain an optimal balance between sensitivity and specificity. We use the gen_optimal_thresholds() function on the predictions from our original random forest model to generate these thresholds.

```
threshold_frame = gen_optimal_thresholds(pred_data_orig,
                    protected = protected,
                    target = target_name,
                    prob_event = "pred_1")
```

```
preds_j = gen_mitigated_preds(pred_data_orig,
                              threshold_frame,
                              protected = protected,
                              prob_event = "pred_1")
```

Postprocessing: Optimizing Thresholds Manually

In setting thresholds manually, we can pay particular attention to specificity (i.e., percent of non-recidivists correctly classified) as a proxy for FPR. We want to find cutoffs that equate specificity across groups, while maintaining a good balance with sensitivity and overall accuracy. Rather than calculating these thresholds algorithmically, we plot the performance of individual thresholds calculated for a sequence of thresholds between 0 and 1 and manually choose thresholds that meet our requirements. In Figure 7.23, we can see how different classification thresholds (x-axis) affect specificity and the other performance metrics.

```
threshold_plots = plot_model_thresholds(pred_data_orig,
                target = target_name,
                prob_event = "pred_1",
                protected = protected,
                metrics = bias_metrics,
                threshold_sequence = as.list(seq(0, 1, 0.02)))
```

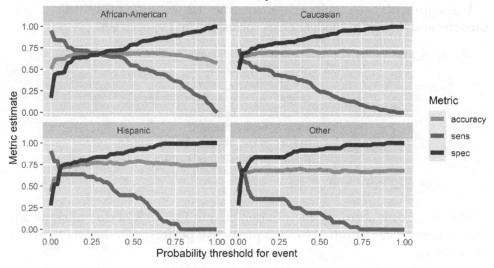

Figure 7.23: Plots of accuracy, sensitivity, and specificity metrics for each of four single-race models as the classification thresholds are varied

From Figure 7.23, looking initially at the lines in each of the plots for specificity, we can identify a threshold of 0.625 for African Americans, 0.450 for Caucasians, 0.375 for Hispanics, and 0.125 for Other as obtaining a high level of specificity that is roughly equal for all the groups, and is also well balanced against the other two metrics. Let's plug these new thresholds for each protected group into the `gen_mitigated_preds()` function predictions for each. Note that the function expects that we input the thresholds in an order that corresponds alphabetically to the protected groups.

```
preds_manual = gen_mitigated_preds(pred_data_orig,
                    threshold_list = c(0.625, 0.45, 0.375, 0.125),
                    protected = protected,
                    prob_event = "pred_1")
```

With all predictions for the newly thresholded and original models in hand, we bind these and the corresponding model names all to a list.

```
all_threshed_preds = list(pred_data_orig, preds_j, preds_manual)

post_thresh_models = c("original", "optimized_J_stat",
"optimized_manual")
```

Whereas before we were comparing various model metrics calculated from the predictions generated by the logistic regression and random forest models, we are now comparing performance across three different variants of the random forest model.

We begin with per-group performance metrics, iterating over the list of predictions and the list of model names corresponding to each set.

```
threshed_protected_metrics = map2(all_threshed_preds,
                    post_thresh_models,
                    gen_protected_metrics,
                    target = target_name,
                    estimate = "pred_class",
                    mode = model_mode,
                    protected = protected,
                    privileged = privileged,
                    metrics = bias_metrics) %>%
    bind_rows()
```

The per-group accuracy metrics depicted in Figure 7.24 do not show any immediately clear difference in the predictive performance between each of the models.

```
threshed_acc_plot = plot_protected_metrics(threshed_protected_metrics,
                    protected = protected,
                    display_metric = "accuracy")

print(threshed_acc_plot)
```

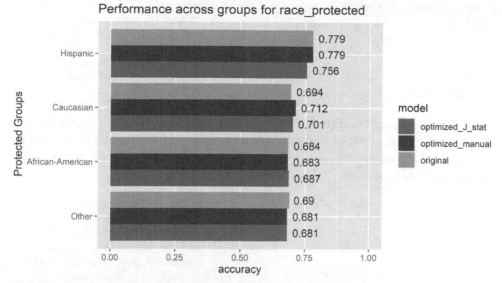

Figure 7.24: Accuracy across protected groups for feature `race_protected` across the original model, the model with classification thresholds determined by an optimal J-statistic, and the model with manually selected thresholds

Looking at FPR for these models directly in Figure 7.25, we can see that the manually selected thresholds resulted in a large decrease for African Americans relative to the original model. Somewhat confusingly, the model using thresholds based on optimal J-statistics actually results in higher FPR rates for Caucasians and African Americans.

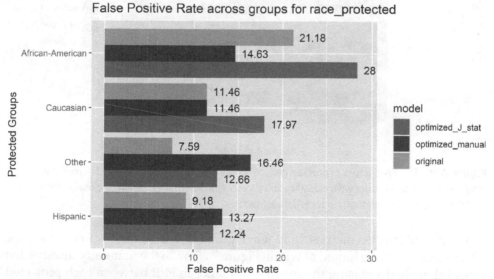

Figure 7.25: The FPR across protected groups for feature `race_protected` across the original model, the model with classification thresholds determined by an optimal J-statistic, and the model with manually selected thresholds

```
opt_fp_error_direction_plot = plot_error_direction(all_threshed_preds,
                                        mode = model_mode,
                                        display_feature = protected,
                                        false_positive = TRUE,
                                        model = post_thresh_models,
                                        target = target_name)
print(opt_fp_error_direction_plot)
```

Though we don't weigh the FNR results particularly heavily within this classification task, we show it here as a matter of interest. We can see in Figure 7.26 that both of the newly thresholded models achieve lower FNR metrics relative to the original model for African Americans.

```
opt_fn_error_direction_plot = plot_error_direction(all_threshed_preds,
                                        mode = model_mode,
                                        display_feature = protected,
                                        false_positive = FALSE,
                                        model = post_thresh_models,
                                        target = target_name)
print(opt_fn_error_direction_plot)
```

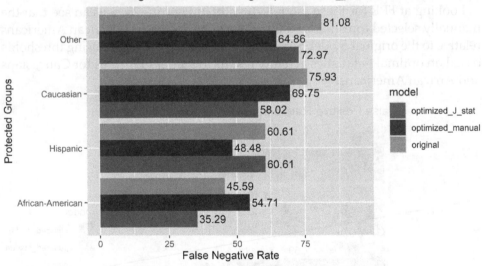

Figure 7.26: The FNR across protected groups for feature `race_protected` across the original model, the model with classification thresholds determined by an optimal J-statistic, and the model with manually selected thresholds

The plot of fairness metrics for FPR in Figure 7.27 shows much more starkly the differences that were hinted at within Figure 7.25, with the manually thresholded model sharply decreasing the relative difference in FPR between each protected group and the privileged group, Caucasians, relative to the original model. This is no surprise: this is exactly why we dramatically changed the classification thresholds. While we clearly have not achieved perfect parity yet, we are much closer, and more finely tuning the manually selected thresholds would likely yield a small enough disparity in performance for us to be satisfied that we have mitigated bias across groups, at least for the protected feature race (and as measured by FPR).

```
opt_fairness_metrics = gen_fairness_metrics(all_threshed_preds,
                                    target = target_name,
                                    model = post_thresh_models,
                                    mode = model_mode,
                                    protected = protected,
                                    privileged = privileged)

opt_fpr_plot = plot_fairness_metrics(opt_fairness_metrics,
                             display_feature = "race",
                             metric = "fpr")
```

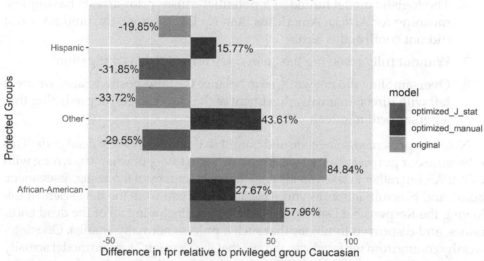

Figure 7.27: The comparison of fairness metrics as a percent difference in the FPR from the privileged group, Caucasians, across the original model, the model with classification thresholds determined by an optimal J-statistic, and the model with manually selected thresholds

Summary

We have covered a lot in this chapter. After our initial discussion of fairness and the metrics we use to measure it, we stepped through the COMPAS recidivism example in great detail.

1. In our initial assessment, the logistic regression model performed best, and, because it was intrinsically interpretable, it *seemed* to be the optimal choice.

2. For the various models we developed, we then reviewed the following per group:

   a. Performance metrics

   b. Error metrics

   c. Fairness metrics

3. We found that the models were manifestly unfair to African Americans: nonrecidivists were predicted to re-offend much more often than their Caucasian counterparts (FPs or false positives).

4. Looking at FPs for African Americans relative to FPs for Caucasians, the black-box model (random forest) appeared more fair than the intrinsically interpretable model (logistic regression), thus complicating our initial assessment.

5. Returning to two key models, logistic regression and random forest, we used interpretability methods to try to sort out what was happening.

6. The logistic model hinted at a potential cause (prior arrests having less meaning for African Americans than for Caucasians); the random forest did not confirm this hint.

7. Without fully resolving the "why," we turned to bias mitigation.

8. Oversampling did not work, so to balance the false-positive rates, we were left with direct (manual) adjustment of the cutoff levels for predicting that a person will re-offend.

Note, we presented some code and output that ultimately were dead ends. This is because our purpose was not to tell a nicely edited story of what was wrong with COMPAS, but rather to take you through the entire journey of modeling, assessment, audit, and bias mitigation, as you would travel if you were the data scientist following the Responsible Data Science framework (including all of the dead ends, issues, and disproved intuitions that such a process normally entails). One noteworthy conundrum we faced was the fact that the "less fair" logistic model actually had lower FPs for African Americans than the "more fair" random forest model. Should we accept an improvement in FP rates for African Americans if this results in an even greater improvement in Caucasian rates? This is an important question, but one lying more in the realm of policy, or even philosophy, than data science.

In the end, we saw that the answers to what is fair within the COMPAS modeling task did not lie fully in the code, that not all performance criteria could be optimized simultaneously, and that attaining parity in the key false positive rate required direct adjustment of differential cutoffs for African Americans and Caucasians. While we went about these steps as systematically as possible, the specific intricacies of each particular modeling task are going to necessitate flexibility in executing an audit for teams working on other projects. In the end, we did not make the model completely "unbiased." We simply biased it differently, in a direction that we considered more fair and less likely to cause unanticipated harms once deployed.

## CHAPTER 8

Auditing for Neural Networks

We now return our focus to one of the frontiers of data science: the use of neural networks in image and text processing. As we have seen throughout this book across other examples, the promise of neural network approaches cannot be separated from the dangers that they can pose when misused. This misuse happens easily and often in spite of the absence of any malicious intent. As a reminder, we have already seen one example of how deep learning models produced résumé-review technology for Amazon that basically judged applications on the basis of whether they were male or female.

In the field of image processing, some of the examples of harm include the following:

- Use of image processing by authoritarian governments to surveil populations (e.g., with the goal of suppressing dissent or minority movements)

- Flawed facial recognition approaches employed by law enforcement falsely identifying individuals as wanted criminals

- Insufficiently trained computer vision systems for automated driving that were unable to react appropriately in a given situation due to being unable to recognize certain objects or environmental conditions

- Generation of "deepfaked" images and distributing them with the intent to cause harm (e.g., revenge porn)

- Generation of images and videos that are difficult to distinguish from the real thing (e.g., to steal identities or create believable fake online personas for misleading or trolling other individuals)

- Harvesting of pictures from the internet for uses that invade privacy (e.g., ex-spouses could readily identify and stalk new companions of the former spouse)

In the field of natural language processing (NLP), some of the examples of harm include the following:

- Creation of fake personas or content meant to mislead, corrupt, or otherwise drown out (through sheer quantity) content written by actual people

- Automated moderation tools removing benign comments or content that contains terms associated with certain styles of speech (e.g., AAVE), intricacies in tone (e.g., irony, sarcasm, etc.), or words associated with controversial content used in a different, more benign context (e.g., "looting" can indicate a pejorative characterization of peaceful protests in one context or the process of raiding another player's ship in a pirate-themed video game in a different context)

- Astroturfing of products, services, or political candidates with falsified testimonials or opinions

- Text generation models creating text that encodes and amplifies biases or harmful language within their training data

- Text classification models that discriminate against certain groups or viewpoints

The task of keeping up with the "bad guys," like the task of producing drugs to fight infections, is never-ending due to the capability of both sides to adapt to the other. The field of data science itself provides solutions to some of these problems via classification algorithms built into automatic social media moderation tools that can identify and potentially eliminate spurious or harmful posts from malevolent actors.

However, the story of "AI as a detective" to find the AI bad guys is one for another time and another book. Our focus in this book is on the well-intentioned practitioner who wants to avoid accidental harm from their own AI products.

The types of harm caused by neural networks for image processing and NLP tasks are more diverse than those caused by predictive models operating on tabular data. Nonetheless, many of the same tools and processes that we discussed in previous chapters can be adapted for projects that require neural networks. First, we review what makes neural networks different from shallow machine learning models. We follow this with a practical example of building out a facial recognition model within the RDS framework and discussing the implications of our results. We then dedicate the rest of the chapter to discussing concerns and sources of bias when working with NLP models.

Why Neural Networks Merit Their Own Chapter[1]

For machine learning tasks on tabular data, the input is most often a vector of semantically distinct handcrafted features. We can feed these to a logistic regression or a decision tree to get an interpretable output alongside whatever model we run in production. Neural networks, on the other hand, often operate on data that are not amenable to traditional machine learning techniques. Images and text are high-dimensional complex data where making precrafted features is laborious or altogether impractical.

Neural networks are a flexible class of machine learning algorithms that exhibit an uncanny ability to learn complex nonlinear relationships from large unstructured datasets. They are comprised of a large set of connections and mathematical operations that link low-level data (e.g., pixel values, words in a text, etc.) to high-level predicted output (e.g., classes of images or texts, etc.). Through highly repetitive (and computationally intensive) modifications and consolidations, neural nets "learn" a mathematical structure (i.e., connections and weights) that accurately predicts, and, as part of the bargain, learns intermediate consolidations of network elements that signal meaningful features. Although they have achieved state-of-the-art predictive performance in a wide variety of modeling tasks, they can be difficult to train and even harder to interpret due to long training times, opaque feature generation processes, and high compute costs. In this section, we lay out in greater detail the nuances of deep learning, review some applicable local and global interpretability methods, and consider how the unique elements of neural networks can complicate our goal of performing data science more responsibly.

Neural Networks Vary Greatly in Structure

The primary difference between a trained and an untrained neural network is the finalized network weights connecting neurons across layers. However, network weights aren't the only candidates for optimization in a neural network. Other structural factors of the network (referred to as *hyperparameters*), including the number of layers, the number of neurons per layer, the number of observations processed per training epoch, the learning rate for backpropagation, and the activation function used within each neuron, are all relevant to the final predictive performance of the trained network. These hyperparameters tend to increase in

[1]This section and subsequent sections in this chapter © 2021 Datastats LLC and Grant Fleming.

both number and importance as neural networks become more complex. This presents a challenge to researchers who desire to understand the effect of different architectures and training schemes on fairness, as many possible configurations of models need to be considered.

Further complicating this situation is the fact that neural networks built for different purposes require the optimization of different hyperparameters. For example, Google's popular NLP model, Bidirectional Encoder Representations from Transformers (BERT), has a significantly different architecture from UNet, a seminal network for semantic segmentation of images. (The structure for both is depicted in Figures 8.1a and 8.1b.) Though both networks consist of layers of neurons, the structure of each one is optimized for a different goal and input data type.

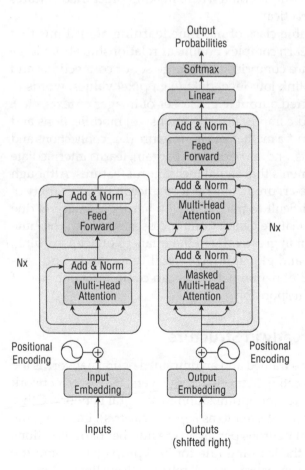

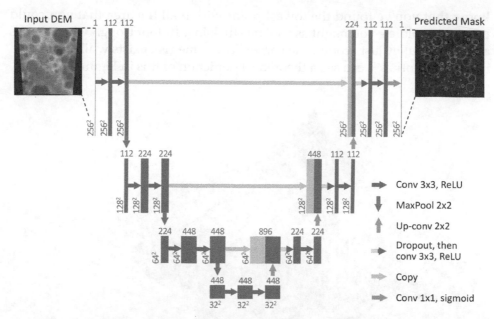

Figures 8.1a and 8.1b: Architectures of two popular neural networks. On the previous page, the transformer module from Google's BERT embedding for NLP. On this page, the UNet architecture for semantic segmentation.

Sources: Vaswani, Ashish, et al., 2017. "Attention Is All You Need," found at `https://arxiv.org/abs/1706.03762`; Silburtand, Ari, et al., 2018. "Lunar Crater Identification via Deep Learning," found at `https://arxiv.org/abs/1803.02192`. Used with permission.

Neural Networks Treat Features Differently

While neural networks can be used to generate predictions from tabular data, they are often the only option for higher dimensional data, including raw pixel values from an image, tokenized text from a corpus, or protein expressions from a proteomics assay. Manually creating features from these oftentimes unstructured data is highly unintuitive, requiring significant time investment and often leading to worse predictive performance than the automatic feature generation and selection methods used by neural networks. With these methods, neural networks generate their own abstracted versions of the raw input features implicitly during training through a generalized optimization process known as *gradient descent*.

Gradient descent is the process of iteratively adjusting the network's parameters and weights to reduce prediction error. It is best explained through a physical example. Imagine that you've been tasked with finding the lowest elevation point in a mountainous area, but you are blindfolded while doing so. Using the gradient descent methodology, you can feel the ground around you, identify which direction is lower than where you are, and take a step in that direction, repeating this process until you've stumbled upon what you presume to be the area's lowest point. However, because you are blindfolded, you don't actually know that you've found the lowest point within all the area that you could possible explore—you might as well be stuck in a 10-foot trough when there's a 500-foot valley just around the corner. The same risk exists while training a neural network. We can see a theoretical depiction of this in Figure 8.2.

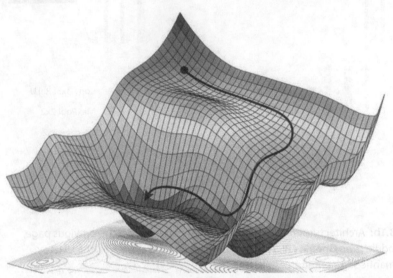

Figure 8.2: Example of using gradient descent to find the global minima. While the arrow (the gradient descent algorithm) ultimately found the global minima, it could have gotten itself "stuck" in the local minima before it curved right.

Source: Amini, Alexander, Soleimany, Ava, Karaman, Sertac, and Rus, Daniela. *Spatial Uncertainty Sampling for End-to-End Control*. arXiv preprint arXiv:1805.04829, 2018. Used with permission.

Fortunately, the AI community has developed numerous techniques for avoiding local minima in the pursuit of a global minimum. Many of these techniques rely on a concept known as *step size*, or, in our mountain descent, how far you reach with your toe when you are identifying the next place you should step. While quarter-mile steps can help explore the region, they will leave you bouncing around from one side of the valley to the other. On the other hand, 2-inch steps will leave you shuffling around the mountains for days. Neither is ideal. A better idea might be to take larger steps in the beginning and then slowly shorten your steps as you get closer to identifying the true global minimum, also known as *learning rate annealing*. "Learning rate" is proportional to the step size—larger step sizes correspond to faster learning rates. Along with learning rate annealing, several gradient descent variants exist that decrease the time to convergence; for example, Adam (derived from "adaptive moment optimization") is a popular optimizer that adaptively updates learning rates for each network parameter, rather than using one learning rate for all parameters. Furthermore, Adam adapts learning rates based on how quickly the parameters change.

Along with learning rates and optimization methods, deep learning practitioners must select a batching paradigm for their models. Gradient descent (and its variants) comes in a few different flavors: batch gradient descent, stochastic gradient descent, and mini-batch gradient descent.

- **Batch gradient descent:** During batch gradient descent, the network calculates the cost (e.g., a function of the prediction error) for all the training examples and then updates the parameters once after all observations have been seen.

- **Stochastic gradient descent:** As in batch gradient descent, the network calculates the cost for each of the training observations. However, instead of waiting until all observations have been processed to update the network parameters, it updates the parameters one observation at a time.

- **Mini-batch gradient descent:** Mini-batch gradient descent combines both of the previously mentioned methods. Instead of assessing all the data at once (batch) or one observation at a time (stochastic), mini-batch gradient descent breaks the training data up into batches, calculates the cost for each batch, and updates the network parameters after each. This gradient descent style is the most popular among AI practitioners.

Neural Networks Repeat Themselves

Neural networks tend to perform better after they have seen the entire dataset multiple times. Each time the network processes the entire dataset, it completes one *epoch*. The number of times the network processes the entire dataset, or the number of epochs it's trained for, is an important network hyperparameter to be aware of while tuning a network. In some cases, when data are highly complex, a properly constructed neural network can continue to learn after seeing the dataset hundreds of times. In other cases, when the data are relatively simple, the network might finish converging after only a few epochs (which we would notice as a static or decreasing measure of predictive performance).

As previously shown, while gradient descent and the modification of weights in the neural network occur automatically as a part of training, the results of these processes are heavily influenced by user-specified hyperparameters (i.e., factors) including the specific optimization algorithm, the batch size of the training data, and even the structure of the neural network's components (e.g., the number of layers, number of neurons per layer, etc.). Although conventional algorithms like support vector machines and random forests also have hyperparameters that can be tuned, they don't have nearly as many as neural networks. Furthermore, conventional algorithms tend to be less sensitive to hyperparameter selection, whereas neural network performance is heavily linked to network architecture. As a result, switching from conventional models to neural networks shifts the focus from feature selection to architecture modifications, making it more difficult to dissect the network's decision path. For example, it's easier to reason about the effect of adding a new variable to a logistic regression, as opposed to changing the number of convolutional layers in a network.

A More Impenetrable Black Box

Because of the high dimensionality of a neural network's input, its opaque feature selection process, and its creation of intermediate feature representations across layers, achieving model interpretability for neural networks is uniquely challenging. Consider the global interpretability methods discussed in Chapter 5, "Model Interpretability: The What and the Why," like permutation feature importance or partial dependence plots (PDP), which show the average impact that different values of a feature have on the model's predictions. These methods are applied with respect to the input features, which in an image recognition or natural language processing (NLP) task represent raw pixels, word tokens, or word embeddings. The explanations generated for these then come to describe the average importance of individual pixels or words across *all* predictions, leading to trivial explanations, such as the pixels at the center of images being the most important or the most important word of a sentence being the subject. While features like individual pixels in an image or individual words in a sentence may not have useful global meaning, they are nonetheless relevant to local predictions, leaving open the possibility of using local interpretability methods like Shapley Values, SHAP, or LIME as a result. The husky image from Chapter 5 (reprinted here as Figure 8.3) is a good example of the use of these methods for neural networks.

(a) Husky classified as wolf   (b) Explanation

Figure 8.3: LIME output for an image of a husky incorrectly classified as a wolf

Source: Ribeiro, et al., 2016. "'Why Should I Trust You?' Explaining the Predictions of Any Classifier," found at https://arxiv.org/abs/1602.04938. Used with permission.

Beyond local interpretability methods, the unique characteristics of neural networks have presented opportunities for the development of neural network–specific interpretability methods. We list the four main categories of these next, along with references for external material for interested researchers to pursue.[2]

---

[2]Readers interested in a deeper dive into each of these types of interpretability methods should read Xie, et al. (2020), "Explainable Deep Learning: A Field Guide for the Uninitiated," arxiv .org/abs/2004.14545.

Baseline Methods

Baseline methods are local interpretability methods that calculate how much individual feature values, relative to a baseline of all-black pixels or random noise in an image, or padding or random characters in text, contribute to a particular prediction. This contribution is typically visualized as a heat map of the individual values of the input (i.e., activations) that most influenced the label assigned to the prediction. The most widely used of these methods include Integrated Gradients, DeepLIFT, and Expected Gradients. For example, the "Expected Gradient Attributions" pane in the killer whale prediction (see Figure 8.4) tells us that the pixels in the center of the image are those that contribute most to its identification. At the time of writing, implementations for these methods exist in packages like *Captum* for PyTorch and *tf-explain* for TensorFlow/Keras. The documentation pages for both packages contain excellent hands-on tutorials for applying these methods in practice. Figure 8.4 depicts heatmap plots for two baseline methods alongside the original image.

Figure 8.4: Heat map of integrated gradient and expected gradient attributions depicting pixel activations, with brighter pixels most influencing the classification label, "killer whale," for the original image.

Source: Sturmfels, et. al., "Visualizing the Impact of Feature Attribution Baselines," Distill, 2020, https://distill.pub/2020/attribution-baselines/. Used with permission.

We discuss one of these methods, Integrated Gradients, in a practical example, later in the "Interpreting Our Models: Why Are They Unfair" section of this chapter.

Representation Methods

Representation methods are global interpretability methods that visualize the structure of the network or how it functions. At the highest level, this includes generating a graph network of the internal structure of the neural network, including the layer structure and types. At the time of writing, numerous tools are available for visualizing neural network structures as a network graph, though Tensorboard is the most popular (and is used in our example in this chapter).

Representation methods also encompass visualizations of activity within individual network components, such as activations within particular neurons or representations for more complex concepts that the network learned from the data during training. The ConceptSHAP image from Chapter 5 (reprinted here as Figure 8.5) depicts the "concepts" learned by an image recognition network trained on a dataset of wild animals. The concepts are abstract higher-level features learned by the neural net from large numbers of individual pixel values, or tokenized words in NLP tasks, over many cases. These concepts often (but not necessarily) correspond to obviously recognizable patterns (e.g., the stripes in Concept 16).

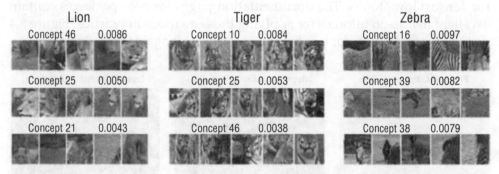

Figure 8.5: Depiction of ConceptSHAP output for a Convolutional Neural Network (CNN) (Yeh, et al., 2019). The thumbnails are examples of the numbered "concepts" most associated with certain image classes.

Source: C.-K. Yeh et al., "On concept-based explanations in deep neural networks," arXiv preprint arXiv: 1910.07969, 2019.

Distillation Methods

Distillation methods are global interpretability methods that approximate the functioning of an entire neural network via a simpler interpretable model. Researchers have proposed several methods, including using decision trees, rule-based models, graph networks, or causal models, to approximate a wide variety of neural networks. This variety of methods and use cases limits the generality of distillation methods. For example, decision-tree or rule-based models could not be applied at the pixel level to image analysis. Moreover, these methods are not yet widely implemented in open source software packages, remaining either theoretical constructs or difficult-to-adapt code built specifically for a given research paper.

NOTE Model distillation does not necessarily require that a neural network be distilled into a simpler, interpretable model. Rather, a neural network can be distilled into another, smaller network as well. This is quite common in practice, as it allows for the creation of a network that trains much more quickly, predicts more quickly at inference time, and requires less storage than the original model while maintaining much of its predictive performance. In this context, model distillation is often referred to as *knowledge distillation, knowledge transfer*, or *network pruning*. Relevant concepts to read about include *student-teacher networks* and *the Lottery Ticket Hypothesis*. Walk-throughs are available online for implementing custom distillation methods in both PyTorch and TensorFlow.

Intrinsic Methods

Intrinsic methods are local interpretability methods that are integrated into certain neural networks, making them intrinsically interpretable by default. So long as a particular intrinsically interpretable network structure fits the needs of the task, intrinsic methods can be, by far, the easiest of the neural network–specific interpretability methods to leverage. For example, transformer-based models for NLP tasks use a method called *attention* (or *self-attention*), which for our purposes can be thought of as a means for the network to look at all input steps in a sequence (e.g., words in a sentence of text) simultaneously, rather than one by one, or only a given number of steps at a time, as is common in other recurrent neural networks (RNNs). By "attending" to all the elements of a sequence simultaneously, the network learns to understand which of the elements of the sequence are most important. Producing an explanation for what the network "focuses on" as most important within a given sequence then requires nothing more than finding and reviewing this attention mechanism that the model is already using![3] Figure 8.6 shows an example of attention being used within a convolutional neural net (CNN).

A woman is throwing a <u>frisbee</u> in a park.   A dog is the dog is actually lying down.

Figure 8.6: Example of how a CNN can "attend" to the primary subject of captioned text

Source: From Xu, Kelvin, et al., 2015. "Show, Attend, and Tell: Neural Image Caption Generation with Visual Attention," found at `https://arxiv.org/abs/1502.03044`. Used with permission.

---

[3]There has been much discussion over whether a visualization of a network's attention is a useful explanation for a model. Readers interested in learning more about the constraints of attention for uses of model interpretability should read Wiegreff and Pinter's (2019) paper "Attention Is not not Explanation."

Beginning a Responsible Neural Network Project

To demonstrate how auditing can work for neural network approaches, we will build several gender classification models on the FairFace face image dataset. Among other things, we want to learn how skin tone (approximated by labels for race) and dataset balance across race groupings influence both the overall and per-group predictive performance of the gender classification model. We will attempt to address any disparities in per-group predictive performance to improve the predictive fairness across different race and gender subgroups within the final model. As in Chapter 7, "Auditing a Responsible Data Science Project," our experiments are structured within the RDS Framework. As always, the code for this chapter is available in the repositories at `www.wiley.com/go/ responsibledatascience` and `www.github.com/Gflemin/responsibledatascience`.

Justification

Facial image processing plays a major role in government surveillance, border processing, and law enforcement. We can explore an application of this in a hypothetical security screening example. Most of us think of security screening in the context of baggage and identity checks at airport security checkpoints. However, there are a myriad of other venues where security screening is conducted—rail transportation, entry to concerts, museums, sporting events, and the like. These events often do not conduct identity checks, and the time and resources available for an individual screening may be extremely limited. This limits their effectiveness. At times, for example, mass transportation agencies have considered implementing security checks and given the idea up as impractical—the flow of people per minute is too high to permit screening of all passengers.

In many cases, screening of just a small proportion of passengers can play a key role—higher-risk people have a higher risk of being screened, and potential terrorists would see that a security protocol is in place. However, in such cases, it is essential that the screening be as random as possible—terrorists should not be able to discern evident patterns, and security agents (who might be compromised) should not have the discretion to pick and choose. Being "random" does not require that each individual has a 50/50 chance of being selected, or even the same probability of being selected as all other individuals. An algorithm can weight different factors, such as age, gender, time of day, current threat level, resources available, etc., setting the probability of being screened accordingly for each individual and providing yes/no screening signals for each person reviewed. Here we examine the use of an AI algorithm for gender identification to provide that component of the screening selection randomizer. We emphasize that the prediction is not "screen or don't screen," but male or female. The ultimate algorithm that determines "screen or don't screen," lacking individual level training data on "terrorist or non-terrorist," will be one that is human-specified. Our AI portion relates only to the gender classification aspect, which is used as an input to the ultimate algorithm.

What is the goal of the project?

The project's goal is to develop and assess an algorithm that can take images from security cameras and tag them according to gender. The results would then be used, along with other factors, in a randomizing algorithm to determine whether an individual should be subjected to security screening. This security screening might be the only such screening used, or it might be supplemental to other individual screenings. For example, individuals waiting in a queue to enter a museum might be photographed as they passed a certain point and then either selected or not selected for screening. Individual-specific factors, such as age or gender, as well as systems issues (e.g., threat level or resources available), would determine whether a person is to be screened.

Achieving equality or near-equality in predictive performance for predicting gender across protected groups (i.e., predictive fairness) is important within this example for several reasons, including the following:

- An algorithm that errs more often for certain groups will be judged less effective and could justifiably lead to public criticism and accusations of unfairness.

- An algorithm that errs more often for certain groups will be judged less effective and will be less valuable commercially.

- An algorithm that errs more often for certain groups is fundamentally less fair to those individuals.

- An algorithm that consistently underperforms for certain groups could cause members of these groups emotional duress if they think that the result will be discriminatory over-screening (especially if the screening managers interpret a "not sure" result from the algorithm as a signal, dramatically boosting the selection probability as a result).

In our project, we explore how issues of fairness can occur in image classification tasks, and how to identify them by using the Responsible Data Science (RDS) Framework. We look at improving cross-group predictive fairness by ensuring dataset balance and, if that is insufficient, by over-sampling images from classes where the model performs.

To train our model, we need data. We do not have access to the same data that the surveillance system would operate with because the system has yet to be created. We will use the FairFace dataset instead.[4]

---

[4]Kärkkäinen and Joo, "FairFace: Face Attribute Dataset for Balanced Race, Gender, and Age," preprint, Computer Science, Computer Vision and Pattern Recognition, Submitted Aug. 14, 2019, arxiv.org/abs/1908.04913 (paper) and github.com/joojs/fairface (data).

What are the expected benefits of our project?

The project's benefit is the development of an algorithm that can feed useful data to a random selection screening algorithm. Random secondary screening lowers the cost of screening and makes it feasible to add security to large volume public venues where it is now impractical. It also enables screening agencies to add redundancy to existing high-stakes full screening (e.g., for air travel). Moreover, our work helps quantify the potential for a hypothetical facial recognition model to discriminate against certain groups, as well as measure the efficacy of bias mitigation techniques, should issues of discrimination be found.

What ethical concerns do we consider relevant to our project and how do we plan on addressing them?

1. **Misuse**—As with any other facial recognition model, this model has the potential to be repurposed for harmful uses outside the initial project scope. For example, the secondary screening selection project itself, which this model is a part of, could potentially be misused by screeners who could figure out how to adjust the proportion of women directed to secondary screening. This is more than a theoretical issue, as witnessed by the number of lawsuits alleging sexual harassment by security screeners.

2. **Misrepresentation**—Though the FairFace facial recognition dataset is large and includes a diverse group of faces, it nevertheless falls short of capturing a diverse enough set of the global population to be accurate across all contexts. For example, the dataset does not include labeled images of indigenous peoples. FairFace also does not include many images of individuals wearing a face mask or other face-occluding headwear (a major issue during the 2020–2021 coronavirus pandemic). In a real-world scenario, to optimize performance and fairness, datasets like FairFace ought to be augmented with additional images drawn from the relevant population demographic of the area and time period.

3. **False Confidence**—We attempt to quantify and improve predictive fairness within our project. However, even if we are able to mitigate all of the disparities in predictive performance discovered between groups, it still does not necessarily mean that our model is fair or that we have fulfilled all of our responsibilities as responsible data scientists. Bias mitigation does not address concerns around procedural fairness, including whether the data were gathered ethically (i.e., with full consent and awareness of subjects), or whether the specific task that the model is planned to be used for is ethical. We cannot let achieving or improving predictive fairness within our models give us false confidence that the entire modeling pipeline that we're working through is fair, or that the outcomes it produces when deployed in the real world are fair.

Have other groups attempted similar projects in the past, and, if so, what were their outcomes?

Projects completed by other researchers in 2019 have laid substantial groundwork for understanding gender classifier performance across groups, finding that different deep-learning architectures did consistently better across certain gender-race groups.[5] These models were most accurate in classifying the gender of Middle Eastern males and Latina females, whereas Black females were hardest to predict. Representation imbalances in the model's training data widened the gap in performance. We expect to see similar results in our work when comparing leave-one-race-out models to balanced models.

Have we anticipated and accounted for future uses of our project beyond its current use?

Only somewhat; see the previous section titled "Misuse." Given that we are helping to build a somewhat new technology (i.e., the secondary screening random selection algorithm), one that would be used by government security agencies, we should be vigilant about prospective future uses of the technology and invite the agency commissioning it to formulate appropriate regulations governing its use.

Moving Forward

Stepping through this project will provide a useful tour of issues to consider in image processing tasks.

1. First, we develop an understanding of the challenges intrinsic to image recognition tasks and how these challenges are aggravated by the use of single aggregate performance metrics.

2. Second, we demonstrate how data scientists can audit their neural networks to identify disparate treatment between groups and mitigate a portion of this bias by ensuring dataset balance across groups and oversampling on poorly performing classes.

3. Finally, the code provided for this project serves as a basis for developing a general framework for tracking the results of neural network fairness experiments in PyTorch and visualizing the results of these in Tensorboard.

Compilation

The FairFace dataset was created by manually extracting faces from the Yahoo YFCC100M dataset and crowdsourcing labels through Amazon Mechanical Turk (see Figure 8.7). The resulting dataset represents approximately 100,000

---

[5]Krishnan, Almadan and Rattani, "Understanding fairness of gender classification algorithms across gender-race groups," Sep. 2020, arxiv.org/abs/2009.11491.

cropped and centered face images that are approximately balanced by race and gender. The data was downloaded from the FairFace GitHub page and stored in a mounted data directory on a Linux server with access to GPUs. As with Chapter 7, we version-controlled our project on GitHub, maintained documentation in a README, and have the code available for reader use within a Collab notebook.

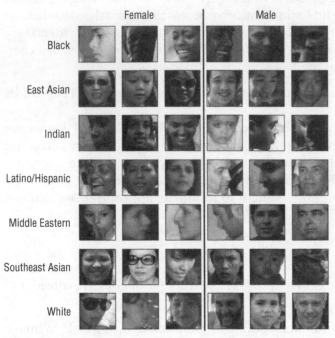

Figure 8.7: Sample of FairFace images from each race-gender combination

Unfortunately, there is not yet a readily available Python or R tool for creating computer vision datasheets. However, if making a datasheet from scratch, we recommend including, at a minimum, a visual sample of images along with a summary table on the number of image classes, the number of images overall, and the dimensions of the images. This is in addition to the standard suite of information we would expect from a datasheet: how the data was gathered, whether it is static, what sort of transformations were applied to it, and relevant ethical concerns when using the data, among other things. We provide a data breakdown by race and gender in the "Preparation" section when we split the data into train, test, and validation sets. As with the COMPAS example that we introduced in Chapter 6, "Beginning a Responsible Data Science Project," we refer to all racial and gender groupings in our discussions using the same terminology as the datasets being discussed to ensure clarity. Table 8.1 presents some summary information about the FairFace dataset that will be relevant for our analysis.

Table 8.1: A Minimal Summary Table of the FairFace Data

N	97,698 images (faces)
Image Size	224 × 224
Races	Black, White, East Asian, Southeast Asian, Latino/Hispanic, Indian, Middle Eastern
Genders	Male, Female

Along with Table 8.1, we recommend documenting the intended use for the data on the datasheet, and we point readers to the FairFace whitepaper for more information on the dataset creation process.

Tracking Experiments

Another core component of effective compilation for computer vision projects is experiment management. We define an *experiment* as a single training and testing configuration, and we track each of these experiments using a Python package, *yacs*, that outlines system, data, and structural information about the network. By meticulously tracking our experiment parameters, we ensure the reproducibility of our work, which is essential for responsible data science.

Figure 8.8a shows our default network parameters, defined using the *yacs* `ConfigurationNode` class. To create a new experiment, say, to train on a different population subset, we overwrite parts of the experiment via a YAML file (see Figure 8.8a and Figure 8.8b).

Each time an experiment is run, a timestamped run folder is added to an experiment folder, and the tensorboard outputs are saved temporarily for future reference. These are viewable within any modern web browser and appear as variants of the output shown in Figure 8.9.

For consolidation purposes, at the end we retain model weights and metrics only for the latest run, which is made feasible by our relatively fast training times (~25 minutes). Creating timestamped metric files is an easy addition if a user wants to track metrics and models for all runs. The system guarantees that all code runs will correspond to a timestamped run of a tracked experiment.

Experiment tracking, the visualization of performance metrics, and the automatic generation of model cards is available for Keras and Tensorflow models as part of Google's recently released *Model Card Toolkit (MCT)* package. Figure 8.10 shows an example of a model card produced by this package. Unfortunately, at the time of writing, no functionality within the *MCT* package allows for PyTorch models to be used, nor is there a suitable package within the PyTorch ecosystem that can serve as a substitute. Therefore, if you use PyTorch, you need to create an audit report manually.

```
1   import os
2   from yacs.config import CfgNode as CN
3
4   DATA_DIR = '/data/fairface'
5
6   _C = CN()
7   _C.EXP_NM = 'default'
8   _C.EXP_DIR = 'experiments'
9
10  # training params
11  _C.TRAIN = CN()
12  _C.TRAIN.EPOCHS = 15
13  _C.TRAIN.MEAN = [0.4927, 0.3667, 0.3144]
14  _C.TRAIN.VAR = [0.2095, 0.1814, 0.1710]
15  _C.TRAIN.CHKPNT_DIR = 'checkpoints'
16  _C.TRAIN.SAVE_CP = False
17
18  # dataloader params
19  _C.DATALOADER = CN()
20  _C.DATALOADER.N_WORKERS = 4
21  _C.DATALOADER.BS = 32
22
23  # model params
24  _C.TRAIN.MODEL = CN()
25  _C.TRAIN.MODEL.N_CLASSES = 2
26  _C.TRAIN.MODEL.ARCH = 'resnet18'
27  _C.TRAIN.MODEL.PRETRAINED = True
28
29  # optimizer params
30  _C.TRAIN.OPTIMIZER = CN()
31  _C.TRAIN.OPTIMIZER.LR = 0.001
32  _C.TRAIN.OPTIMIZER.MOMENTUM = 0.9
33
34  # learning rate scheduler params
35  _C.TRAIN.LR_SCHEDULER = CN()
36  _C.TRAIN.LR_SCHEDULER.STEP_SIZE = 7
37  _C.TRAIN.LR_SCHEDULER.GAMMA = 0.1
```

```
1   EXP_NM: baseline-black
2   DATASETS:
3     TRAIN:
4       CSV_PATH: /data/fairface/fairface_label_train.csv
5       RACES:
6         - east_asian
7         - indian
8         - white
9         - middle_eastern
10        - latino_hispanic
11        - southeast_asian
12    TEST:
13      CSV_PATH: /data/fairface/fairface_label_train.csv
14      RACES:
15        - black
```

Figures 8.8a and 8.8b: Relevant portions of the code to define network parameters in *yacs* and new experiments within a YAML file

We track several fairness metrics across each experiment, with a focus on improving parity in these metrics across groups. For each experiment, we calculate and compare metrics for accuracy and false positive rate (FPR). We need not focus on the false negative rate (FNR) because it is a mirror image of FPR and contains the same information (see the later section, "Per-Group Metrics: Unusual Definitions of 'False Positive'"). As there does not appear to be any reason to assume misclassifying men as women is more harmful than classifying women as men, we primarily aim to minimize overall error rate and/or minimize FPR. To help achieve model interpretability, we use Integrated Gradients with Noise Tunneling—a variant of Integrated Gradients that reduces noise within the final estimates. Our goal for predictive fairness within this example is to identify the methods that can help improve predictive fairness for the race feature relative to a reasonable baseline model, rather than attempting to meet a specific parity metric.

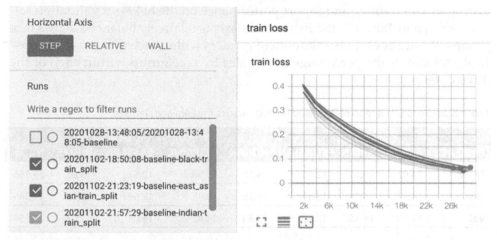

Figure 8.9: Tensorboard output from FairFace experiments

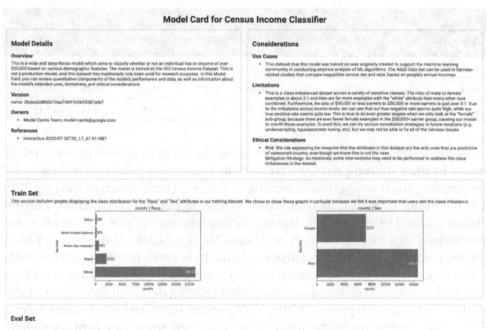

Figure 8.10: Example model card output from Tensorflow's Model Card Toolkit (MCT) package

Source: Mitchell, Margaret, et al. "Model Cards for Model Reporting." Proceedings of the Conference on Fairness, Accountability, and Transparency, Jan. 2019, pp. 220–29. `arxiv.org/abs/1810.03993`, doi:10.1145/3287560.3287596. Used with permission.

Preparation

Because the data are already presplit into training and holdout sets, we opt only to divide the training data into a training set (80 percent) and, for model tuning, a test set (20 percent). We use the test set to select optimum model parameters during model training and report performance on the held-out validation set.

As shown in Table 8.2, the FairFace dataset is relatively balanced across race groups. What about the breakdown of genders within each of the race groups? Table 8.3 shows the percentage of females by race group within each of the three dataset splits.

Table 8.2: Cross-Tabulation of Race and Gender Across the FairFace Dataset

FAIRFACE	BLACK	EAST ASIAN	SE ASIAN	INDIAN	LATINO/ HISPANIC	MIDDLE EASTERN	WHITE	N
Train	14.07	14.17	12.40	14.19	15.50	10.61	19.06	69,395
Test	14.23	14.14	12.61	14.26	15.05	10.69	19.02	17,349
Val	14.20	14.15	12.92	13.84	14.82	11.04	19.03	10,954

Table 8.3: Percentage of Observations in Each Race Grouping Who Are Women

FAIRFACE	BLACK	EAST ASIAN	SE ASIAN	INDIAN	LATINO/ HISPANIC	MIDDLE EASTERN	WHITE	% FEMALE TOTAL
Train	50.31	49.76	48.00	47.72	50.00	30.65	47.26	46.86
Test	49.62	50.88	48.08	48.95	51.21	31.86	47.74	47.49
Val	48.65	49.87	48.06	50.33	51.14	32.75	46.19	47.12

Because other facial recognition projects are likely to exhibit greater imbalances in their training data, we created an alternative unbalanced dataset by resampling the training data according to the racial breakdown of the July 2019 United States Census data (76 percent White, 13 percent Black, and 6 percent Asian—a total of 95 percent). The remaining 5 percent of the Census races are comprised of American Indian or Alaska Native, Native Hawaiian or Other Pacific Islander, and Other. Because we do not have corresponding race labels for these races in the FairFace dataset, they are not included in the analysis, making the final racial breakdown of our resampled training data slightly different from that of the Census (80 percent White, 13.68 percent Black, and 6.31 percent Asian). However, the relative proportions of the three race groups are kept consistent. For example, although the Census has 76 percent White people and 13 percent Black people, which differs from our 80 percent and 13.68 percent, both have a ratio of approximately 5.8 White people for every Black person in the dataset.

NOTE   In facial recognition tasks, images are encoded in the visible light spectrum, typically by three color channels or bands—red, green, and blue. Other tasks that use computer vision, like geospatial analysis, use additional channels of visual information. These additional channels can necessitate the use of feature selection methods, but those methods are not applicable to this gender classification example.

During the training and testing stages, we load the images in batches from disk using the *Pillow* package, transform them into tensors (i.e., a multidimensional matrix of numbers to facilitate processing of the data), and normalize the color channels to match the dataset that the model was pretrained on. During the training stage, we also randomly flip each image in the batch horizontally (using the torchvision transformations module) to improve the network's invariance to affine transformations.[6] Transformations like this during the training process increase overall training time, so for our experiments we stick with just this one transformation. In a production scenario, we recommend experimenting with different transformation combinations, including cropping, stretching, or adding color filters to the images to improve the model's overall predictive performance. We do not perform this transformation during the prediction phase (or the *inference phase*, as many deep learning practitioners prefer to call it). However, some researchers suggest aggregating the predictions across multiple transformations of an image to produce a final prediction.

Having prepared the data and established transformations for the training and test phases, we are ready to begin modeling.

Modeling

The first step in the modeling process is selecting an architecture to train. For nearly all computer vision projects, we start with a pretrained model to speed up the training process; here, we'll fine-tune a ResNet18 model that was pretrained on the ImageNet dataset. ResNet18 is a variant of the popular residual network for deep learning in computer vision. The network's main feature is a residual block that passes information from earlier in the network to later network parts through what's known as a *skip connection*. Skip connections effectively enable the network to recover lost information that can be combined with deep feature embeddings to create a richer learning representation, increasing the predictive performance of the network.

Along with selecting the architecture, we need to select a loss function. Because gender classification in this example is a binary prediction, we use the standard log-loss function to train our models. All functions related to training, testing, and tracking network performance are contained inside of a convenient `Trainer` class.

---

[6]See the Pytorch documentation: `pytorch.org/docs/stable/torchvision/index.html`.

We attempt in our modeling to mimic the real-life situation in which a data scientist is building a gender classification algorithm on two datasets: one that is balanced (approximately equal numbers across groups), and one that is unbalanced (which we already know in this case; in the real world, we must discover ourselves whether the data are balanced. While a random sample of face data would ordinarily yield an unbalanced sample (as so much of the available facial recognition datasets available overrepresent the faces of White males), FairFace is already quite balanced. To approximate the imbalance that prevails in the real world, we fit two separate models: a balanced model fit on a random sample from the FairFace data, and an unbalanced model that is structured to reflect the diversity (or lack thereof) within the July 2019 United States Census data. This "census model" is created by training a separate ResNet18 model on the resampled census data that we introduced in Table 8.4, which shows the results of the first training experiment and the associated breakdowns in racial and gender categories. We refer to these models as the "census model" and the "balanced model" moving forward.

Each of the models predict the probability of a positive gender classification, which in this case corresponds to a face having the "Female" gender label. See Table 8.4.

Table 8.4: Validation Performance for the Models Built on the Census and Balanced Datasets

	CENSUS MODEL	BALANCED MODEL
Accuracy	90.08%	91.19%
True Positive Rate (TPR)	90.31%	90.80%
False Positive Rate (FPR)	10.17%	8.36%

For example, we interpret the TPR for both models as the probability of correctly predicting the gender of a face, given that that face is labeled as being female. While the balanced model does perform better than the census model across all of the overall performance metrics listed, both models actually seem to perform quite well. However, we know by now that we need to audit each of these models more deeply, as overall performance metrics might hide deeper disparities in per-group performance.

POSITIVES VS. NEGATIVES

In classification datasets up to this point, there has been a natural division between cases of special interest, typically classified as 1s, and other cases, typically classified as 0s. In the previous chapter, we looked at recidivists versus non-recidivists, where the consequences of misclassification were very different for 1s versus 0s. In this chapter, no particular difference exists between misclassifying males versus females, and no special interest, *a priori*, attached to one or the other (though later we see that there is public concern over the greater difficulty models have in classifying females). We arbitrarily designate females as 1s and males as 0s.

Auditing

To begin the audit, we first delve into per-group performance to see if the disparities in model performance are attributable to poorer performance across specific protected groups. This mirrors the work that we did for the COMPAS example in Chapter 7 in calculating metrics across protected groups for race, as the overall performance metrics ended up hiding more concerning disparities in performance within the model across racial groups once we examined the results more closely.

Per-Group Metrics: Overall

Figure 8.11 depicts the classification accuracy of the model broken down into each of the protected groups corresponding to the levels of the feature, race.

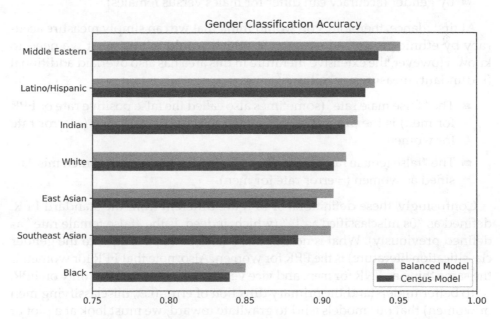

Figure 8.11: Plot of accuracy metrics across protected groups within each of the two models

A cursory examination of this plot shows that we have already uncovered evidence of significant bias within both the census and balanced models.

Specifically, we can see that, while there are disparities in accuracy between the non-Black groups, both models experience a much larger drop in accuracy when predicting Black faces compared to non-Black faces. So far, the performance profiles of both of our models are in line with the biased commercial models explored by Joy Buolamwini and her team in the Gender Shades report in 2018. This a dangerous result—either model, if deployed, would err notably more often in identifying the gender of Black faces versus faces of people from other racial groups.

What about errors in classifying males versus females? Buolamwini and other researchers in facial recognition have found that existing models are more likely to misclassify women than men as well, so we will want to keep an eye out for that in our work here.

Per-Group Metrics: Unusual Definitions of "False Positive"

There are two dimensions across which this model can make errors that result in unfairness:

- By ethnic group (accuracy can differ for different groups)
- By gender (accuracy can differ for males versus females)

At first glance, therefore, you would think that we can simply measure accuracy by ethnic group and by gender, which would tell us what we need to know. However, the extensive literature in this area has also overlaid additional (redundant) measures, as follows:[7]

- The "false male rate" (sometimes also called the false positive rate or FPR for men) is the proportion of women misclassified as men (= error rate for women).
- The "false female rate" (FPR for women) is the proportion of men misclassified as women (= error rate for men).

Confusingly, these definitions of FPR are different from the standard FPR, defined as "0s misclassified as 1s" (which, indeed, is the "false female rate" as defined previously). What is nonstandard (and perhaps unique to the gender classification literature) is the FPR for women. Also, note that FPR for women is the same thing as FNR for men, and vice versa, so we need to focus only on FPR.

To better understand the primary direction of error (i.e., misclassifying men or women) that our models tend to gravitate toward, we must look at a plot of FPR for each race and gender pair (see Figure 8.12).

---

[7]Readers can learn more in NIST's "Face Recognition Vendor Test (FRVT) Performance of Automated Gender Classification Algorithms" (2015) by Ngan and Grother, published by the National Institute of Standards and Technology and available at nvlpubs.nist.gov/nist-pubs/ir/2015/NIST.IR.8052.pdf. These metrics were used by Buolamwini et al. in their "Gender Shades" work.

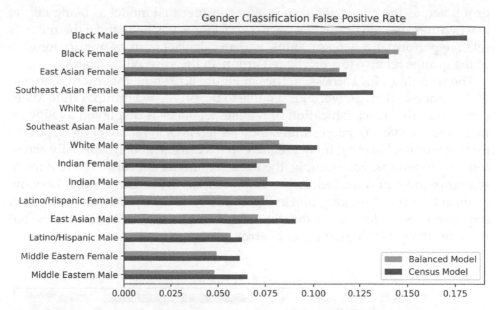

Figure 8.12: Error rates for race and gender groups within each of the two models. The misclassification of Black women as Black men is plotted as the FPR for Black males, for example.

As expected from the plot of per-group accuracy in Figure 8.11, both of the models reach the highest rates of error when attempting to classify the gender of both Black Male and Black Female faces. (In reviewing the plot, keep in mind that error, as noted previously, is tracked as FPR. FPR for males is the proportion of females misclassified as males, and vice versa for females.) Interestingly, females from every non-Black race group are predicted with higher rates of error than males from the same group, regardless of the overall error rate within the group. This result is similar to what Buolamwini and other researchers have found in their work; facial recognition models don't work as well at accurately classifying the gender of female faces. This might indicate that there is greater variety within female faces than male faces, at least for the set of female faces and photographing conditions examined within the FairFace dataset. For example, similarly framed and lit pictures of women might nonetheless exhibit more variation than pictures of men due to a greater variety of hair lengths, styles, and colors. In addition, a substantial proportion of men have facial hair, which is a nearly perfect predictor for them.

Fairness Metrics

Because we are concerned with maximizing the predictive fairness of our models, we must focus on the relative performance that they achieve across each of the protected groups. If the model performs distinctly better or worse on one group versus the others, then we cannot consider that model as being fair (at least with respect to predictive fairness). To more easily analyze the model's relative performance across groups, we can calculate fairness metrics for each of the groups relative to a privileged group, in this case White Males.

The resulting FPR fairness metrics in Figure 8.13 show that more than half of the groups achieve lower FPR relative to the privileged group, White Males (recall that the misclassification of females as males is displayed as FPR for men, and vice versa). Interestingly, these differences in relative FPR appear to increase for the balanced model relative to the census model, especially across the female groups. For example, the balanced model appears to have a much higher relative FPR for East Asian Females than the census model. Looking again at the overall accuracy plot in Figure 8.11 reveals why: the balanced model improved predictions for both East Asian Females and for White Males, but more for the latter. Thus, the gap in error rates expanded.

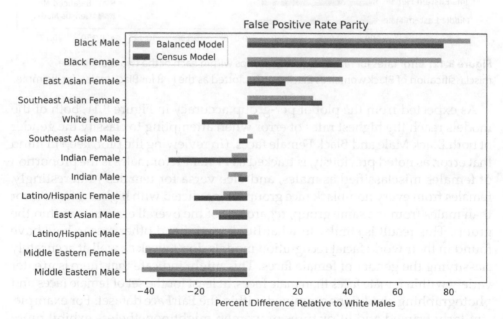

Figure 8.13: Comparison of fairness metrics as percent difference in FPR from privileged group White Males

We have now come face to face with a dilemma that data scientists can't solve on their own on their own, similar to the dilemma we faced with the COMPAS data. Is it worth improving the performance of predictions for one protected group if doing so improves predictions even more for the privileged group, thus increasing predictive unfairness within the model?

We normally take improved model performance without question, but the situation becomes more complicated if that improvement further aggravates issues of fairness. Decision-makers and other nontechnical stakeholders must weigh in on deciding a course of action for this situation, as the best answer depends on the following:

- The business or organizational context of the problem and the gravity of the consequences of any decisions (For example, is a court handing down a sentence? A bank approving a loan? An automated system choosing to serve a specific ad or not?)

- The importance of predictive fairness versus overall model accuracy

- The potential political or reputational ramifications of unfair predictions or outcomes

- The ability to "correct" biased classifications within the model (e.g., by setting classification cutoffs at different levels for different groups). This may not be possible in all contexts.

In the recidivism example that we considered in earlier chapters, the discriminatory harm suffered by a protected group (i.e., Black defendants) was serious and consequential. Black defendants were much more likely to be misclassified as recidivists than White defendants—an error that resulted in higher bail, longer sentences, and tougher parole conditions. Achieving predictive fairness was, therefore, of great consequence, as the cost of an incorrect classification made gaps in predictive performance between protected groups all the more unjust. Improved predictions for all groups (or *only* for other groups) would not have fully mitigated this issue. However, we had the option of adjusting classification cutoffs to achieve parity.

Compared to the recidivism and associated cash bail decisions being made by the COMPAS model, the harms from misclassification in the facial gender classification problem at hand are more diffuse and the impact on individuals is less clear. Moreover, a glance at Figure 8.13 shows that adjusting the classifications as part of the modeling process to improve overall parity would be a complicated optimization problem. Attempting to do it manually would be somewhat like a game of Whack-a-Mole: improving parity for one group would worsen it for others, similar to what we have already seen occur when we improved overall accuracy by switching from a balanced model to an oversampled model.

Questions of the right trade-off between predictive fairness and predictive performance aside, our results appear to mirror the results achieved by the authors of the FairFace dataset whitepaper: impressive performance on Middle Eastern faces and Latino/Hispanic female faces, and poor results on Black faces even after creating a more balanced model. Can the application of interpretability methods help reveal to us why this might be occurring?

Interpreting Our Models: Why Are They Unfair?

Neither the census nor the balanced models was able to solve the primary issue impacting predictive fairness: the large increase in error for classifying the gender of Black faces relative to other groups. Perhaps the models leverage different (and likely incorrect) facial features when predicting the gender of Black faces. To explore this possibility, we used the Integrated Gradients functionality in Captum to produce per-pixel attributions for the final gender classification across a sampling of correctly and incorrectly classified faces from Black Males, Black Females, White Males, and White Females.

Because the learning is imperfect, the resulting visualizations highlight *not* just the correct elements of the image, but also other areas that the neural net thought might be important but really weren't (e.g., parts of a flat background). To improve the quality of each of the outputs, the NoiseTunnel attribution method within Captum was used to generate a distribution of 10 Integrated Gradient outputs for each image, with added random noise. The added random noise is then averaged, which smooths over the spurious learning areas, leaving the high-signal "true" learning areas in sharper focus. An image of all black pixels was used as the baseline image for each of the Integrated Gradient calculations.[8]

Figure 8.14 shows the Integrated Gradients with Noise Tunneling results for one falsely classified image (i.e., the two leftmost columns) and one correctly classified image (i.e., the two rightmost columns) for Black Males, Black Females, White Males, and White Females. All predictions and Integrated Gradient with Noise Tunneling outputs were made from the balanced model, as this is the model that showed the most promise so far. The results appear to be generally consistent across each of the groups—facial hair is an important indicator for both Black and White Males, and the model appears to identify as most important the parts of the face that we would expect it to in determining gender (e.g., the area around the mouth, hair, etc.). From these images and from others that we generated (viewable on GitHub), we also find that the model appears to assign relatively similar importance across similar regions of the face for both Black and White faces.

What is *not* clear from these or the other interpretability method outputs that we examined (GradientSHAP and Integrated Gradients without Noise Tunneling) is a consistent pattern in the false positives within each of the groups. If we could find that false positives for one group, say, Black Men, were associated with consistently different Integrated Gradient outputs than White Males, we would likely be able to better understand why the model has a harder time accurately classifying gender for the faces of Black Men. Unfortunately, we see

---

[8]An all-Black baseline image may not have been optimal. Readers interested in learning more about Integrated Gradients and how the choice of the baseline image can affect the quality of outputs should click through Sturmfels et al.'s (2020) interactive article, "Visualizing the Impact of Feature Attribution Baselines" on Distill.pub.

no such pattern in the images. The Integrated Gradients outputs don't provide as much insight into this as we initially hoped, with no discernibly distinct pattern in the false positives for Black faces. We explore some of the possible reasons why this might be the case in the "Wrap Up" section of this chapter, however, for now we press on to attempting to mitigate the bias that we have seen so far within both of our models.

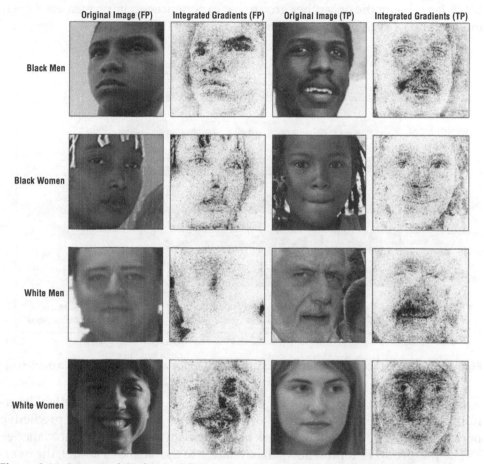

Figure 8.14: Integrated Gradients with Noise Tunneling results for a sampling of Black and White faces; incorrect classifications on the left and correct classifications on the right.

Bias Mitigation

As in Chapter 7, an initial effort is made here at mitigating the bias discovered within our model(s) to achieve predictive fairness. In this case, we attempt to mitigate the biases in our models against Black faces by fitting a new model on a subset of the FairFace data where Black faces are over-sampled.

Because dataset balance alone does not appear to mitigate the bias associated with predicting the gender of Black faces, we turn to over-sampling Black faces. We accomplish this over-sample simply by creating a new model that visits Black faces twice per epoch during the training process. We compare the performance of this over-sampled model with the balanced model first across per-group accuracy shown in Figure 8.15. Oddly enough, the greatest change in accuracy is with respect to an improvement for East Asian faces, with the improvement for Black faces being the only other group that experiences an improvement (albeit more minor). Obviously, we need to delve deeper!

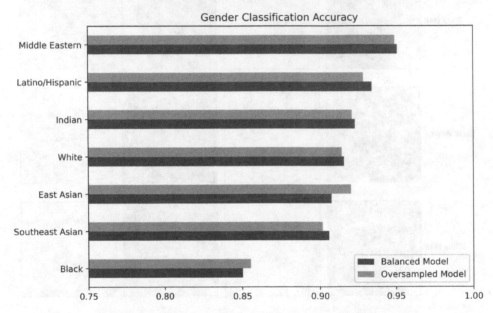

Figure 8.15: Plot of accuracy metrics across protected groups within each of the two models

Per-group FPR metrics (see Figure 8.16) ought to help us to better determine whether over-sampling Black faces decreases the disparity in predictive performance between White and Black faces originally seen in the balanced model.

The per-group FPR plot shows that, relative to the balanced model, the over-sampled model achieves slightly lower error rates on Black faces, lower error on most male faces from other race groups, and higher error on most female faces from other race groups. Perhaps most notably, the over-sampled model is roughly 50 percent more likely to misclassify Middle Eastern Females as males relative to the balanced model. Regardless, at this point it is still unclear whether the over-sampled model made a meaningful difference in the overall predictive fairness of the model. What remains clear is that misclassification of Black faces remains high.

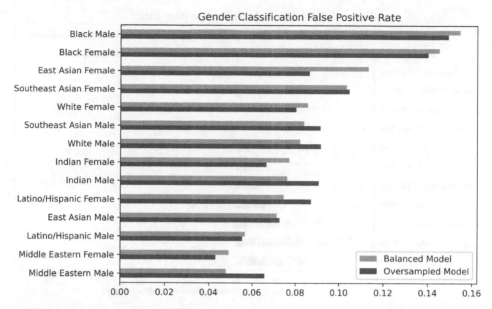

Figure 8.16: Plot of FPR metrics across unique race and gender groups within each of the two models

The plot of fairness metrics for FPR in Figure 8.17 places these measurements in comparison to the privileged group, White Males. The over-sampled model improves FPR parity for Black faces significantly, and boosts it for most other groups as well. However, we don't want to put too much stock in this. The main reason for the parity improvement is the worsened false positives for the privileged group, White Males.

Perhaps this doesn't matter because they are the privileged group? Recall that our original designation of a privileged group in this problem was *technical* in nature—a necessary part of the process of checking a model's predictive fairness. Hardly any tangible benefits of an accurate gender classification accrue for the individuals being screened, whose probability of being selected is unknown to them. Rather, the overall benefit is to the screening system itself—that it receives good data as to gender for inclusion in the randomizing algorithm. Plus, there is general "good will" benefit to those implementing the system that the system is not biased in its errors. Hence, the worsened false positives for White Males is of some concern.

Wrap-Up

The audit of our facial recognition models reveals substantial discrepancies in model performance in two respects.

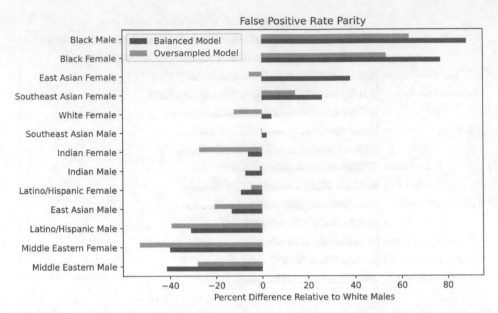

Figure 8.17: Comparison of fairness metrics as percent difference in FPR from privileged group White Males

1. The gender of Black faces were classified less accurately than the gender of White faces.

   ▪ When comparing within individual race groups, female faces were almost universally classified less accurately than male faces.

This was true both for the model in which the data was balanced across groups and in the model where the data were over-sampled to increase the proportion of the group (Black faces) that the models performed worst on. Of the three models, the over-sampled model achieved the lowest error rate relative to the other models in accurately classifying the gender of Black faces.

Although the over-sampled model did improve predictive fairness relative to the other models, it still falls far short of reaching a reasonable parity threshold for predictive fairness. After all, relative to White Males, the error rate for groups within the over-sampled model was anywhere from almost 50 percent less than to almost 60 percent higher. Moreover, the absolute performance metrics achieved by our model(s) still fall short of the metrics other researchers have recorded for commercially available models. For example, while the balanced model achieves an overall accuracy of 91.19 percent, the 2018 version of Microsoft's facial recognition algorithm achieved an overall accuracy of 99.52 percent.

Given the substantial relative performance gaps remaining within our model and the absolute performance gaps with other models, we suspect that there may be more foundational problems with the model or the data. We did a manual analysis of all of the false positives for the White Female category and it revealed that almost all of the false positive images were due to exaggerated facial expressions, the image not being head on, difficult facial lighting (e.g., varying degrees of light and shadow; see the FP example for White Women in Figure 8.18), or the image subject being very young or very old. If the false positives in other groups happen to exhibit similar issues, then our (relatively) low model performance might well be more due to data quality and quantity constraints than any true difference in per-group performance.

Regardless of whether this issue is present for other groups, additional steps that we could take at this stage include increasing the size of the training data, switching to a more effective model architecture, and/or fine-tuning the hyperparameters of the ResNet18 model that we used. After making those modifications, other bias mitigation techniques besides over-sampling could be used to further improve predictive fairness within the model.

CALLS FOR FACIAL RECOGNITION'S HEAD

The goal of attaining perfect predictive fairness might remain elusive in the case of facial image processing for individuals with darker skin, due at least in part to the fact that cameras and photographic techniques are geared primarily toward capturing lighter-skinned faces.[9] Several major tech companies offer gender classification products, which naturally attracted the attention of researchers in algorithmic fairness. As a result of being publicly criticized by these researchers for achieving poor results, these companies spent considerable time improving the performance of their models, which were inaccurately classifying the faces of darker-skinned people, especially Black people. As noted previously, Microsoft managed to reduce the overall error rate of its model below 0.5 percent, but it still had higher error rates for females than for males, and for Black people than for White people. The error rate for Black Females remained at 1.52 percent, while it was reduced to near 0 for White Males.[10] Though the remaining error for Black Females may be small in absolute terms, it represents a *massively* increased error rate relative to other groups.

Sometimes, this disparate treatment between groups is relatively inconsequential. In our gender classification exercise, the impact of this discriminatory model behavior on individuals was modest. In other facial recognition settings where individual identities are predicted, the impact has been much more significant and harmful. The use of facial recognition software by police to identify and arrest people is one example that has attracted much public attention. At the time of writing, at least three people within the United States, all Black men, have been mistakenly arrested and charged with a crime after being misidentified by facial recognition software. And these are just the cases that are public knowledge.

---

[9]See this article by Dr. Sarah Lewis in the *New York Times* (www.nytimes.com/2019/04/25/lens/sarah-lewis-racial-bias-photography.html), or Roth, Lorna, "Looking at Shirley, the Ultimate Norm: Colour Balance, Image Technologies, and Cognitive Equity," Mar. 2009.
[10]These results were published in Deborah Raji and Joy Buolamwini's (2019) paper "Actional Auditing: Investigating the Impact of Publicly Naming Biased Performance Results of Commercial AI Products," less than a year after they had published "Gender Shades."

> Due to these issues with bias and facial recognition, an influential industry group (the U.S. Technology Policy Committee of the Association for Computing Machinery) issued a letter in June 2020 on facial recognition (FR) that "urges an immediate suspension of the current and future private and governmental use of FR technologies in all circumstances known or reasonably foreseeable to be prejudicial to established human and legal rights."
>
> The group also called for additional laws and regulations to address the practice. Numerous data science practitioners have also called for it to be banned outright, noting that the poor model performance aggravates issues of systemic racism. Whatever direction this debate takes, data scientist practitioners and managers must be extremely vigilant in overseeing facial image processing work and be cognizant of the fact that even the most well-resourced, technically talented companies *still* are building facial recognition models that are incapable of dealing with darker-skinned faces as accurately as lighter-skinned faces, despite the considerable efforts they have made to address this issue.

Auditing Neural Networks for Natural Language Processing

Auditing is just as relevant for NLP applications as it is for image recognition. After all, much reporting has occurred in recent years on biased models for resume screening, sentiment analysis, translation, chat bots, and text generation applications that would have benefitted from further auditing. Some stories have even penetrated into mainstream news, including the intentional Nazification of Microsoft's Tay AI chatbot and the propensity of OpenAI's GPT-2 and GPT-3 text generation models to generate racist, sexist, or other harmful answers when the user provides certain prompts. Awareness of these issues is a good first step, but as practitioners and/or data science managers, we must know how to identify and mitigate these issues in our own work. How do we go about doing that for NLP models?

Identifying and Addressing Sources of Bias in NLP

From what it constitutes to how to diagnose and mitigate it, the subject of bias in NLP remains a heavily contested issue. Here's an indicative example: one team of researchers, after analyzing 146 other research papers on bias within NLP tasks, concluded that, in addition to authors using multiple mutually incompatible definitions of bias (often within the same paper), many papers did not indicate any definition of what that bias actually is or why it is important to consider.[11] Fortunately, the language and lessons that we have learned throughout this book to describe bias in a tabular and image data context are applicable here as well.

For example, take the diagram from Figure 5.3 in Chapter 5 (repeated as Figure 8.18 here) depicting how information about the real world is filtered down within each step of the modeling process:

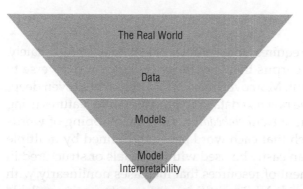

The Real World

Data

Models

Model
Interpretability

Figure 8.18: Flow and narrowing of information within modeling tasks

As in Chapter 5, we can identify relevant bias sources within each of these levels.

The Real World

Associations between words and concepts, which are oftentimes overly simple, negative, or untrue, are built directly into the structure and standard usage of languages. For example, words indicating gender like *man* or *woman* are often associated with words like *strength* and *soldier*, or *caring* and *nurse*. Specific words might be used most often in specific phrases or have entirely different meaning, depending on the context in which they are used. These differing contexts also include the medium that the language is used in, as the norms for language can vary, depending on whether it is written or spoken, presented as formal or informal, or used in public or in private. We could go even deeper—language can change depending on perceived gender, age, or other apparent characteristics of the speaker and the person being spoken to (or vice versa). For example, an adult might discuss a particular topic with another adult using different speech patterns than they would if they were discussing the same topic with a child.

---

[11]Blodgett, Su Lin, Barocas, Solon, Daumé III, Hal, and Wallach, Hannah, "Language (Technology) is Power: a Critical Survey of 'Bias' in NLP," preprint, May 28, 2020, Computer Science, Computation and Language, https://arxiv.org/abs/2005.14050.

Humans, by virtue of our many flaws and foibles, have encoded bias into language through multitudinous levels of subtle association and implied meaning. Addressing bias at this level requires societal changes that are beyond the scope of any one individual group to influence. Instead, teams ought to keep in mind that much of what manifests as bias or unfairness within an NLP modeling context is a magnification of the biases in how our language is used in the real world, and be prepared to adjust their data and models accordingly.

Data

Training accurate NLP models requires large volumes of text data. Unfortunately, the creation of a custom text corpus that is sufficiently large and diverse to solve a nontrivial task is difficult. Moreover, most NLP approaches (even deep-learning–based ones) require the raw text data to be processed into features using approaches like the generation of *word embeddings* (i.e., the mapping of words to vectors of real numbers such that each word becomes defined by multiple real-numbered features that can easily be used within models or structured in some other way)—an investment of resources that increases nonlinearly with the data's size. Typically, this leads NLP practitioners to turn to freely available text corpuses or pretrained word embeddings from models like BERT, GLoVE, or word2vec that are generated from text data scraped from all over the internet.

Unfortunately, these data encode many of the linguistic quirks that we identified in the previous subsection. Because much of the conversation on the internet occurs anonymously, and because people under conditions of anonymity tend to make extreme and offensive statements that they would otherwise self-censor, text corpuses and word embeddings made from these data inherit the same toxicity and negative associations.

The authors of OpenAI's GPT-3 paper, in describing the gravity of the problem, perhaps put it best: "internet-trained models have internet-scale biases."[12]

To be clear, this is not an issue limited only to data gathered from the internet. Biased associations between words or phrases used in all forms of communication typically make it into text data as well. One of the most oft-cited examples of this is how words indicating gender and words indicating gender-stereotyped roles or descriptive characteristics appear "next to each other" after the data is processed into word embeddings. Some of this bias reflects unfairness and an ill-informed opinion, while some of it is bias only in the technical sense of "imbalance" and reflects current reality in a given culture. Much of this real-world bias is benign and not something we ordinarily notice. Social media discussion of baby showers is typically dominated by women, and neither men

---

[12]Brown, Mann et al., "Language models are few-shot learners," 2020, arxiv.org/pdf/2005.14165.pdf.

nor women are likely to have an issue with a model that identifies this association. However, a model that produces an association between "CEO" and "Man," even if it reflects a real-world reality (albeit an unjust one resulting from the historical exclusion of women from the workplace), is certainly more problematic. Our goal is to achieve the right balance between cleansing all hint of bias, benign or not, and focusing strictly on specific manifestations of unfairness.

Fortunately, there already exist effective bias mitigation approaches for text data. These approaches fall into two primary groups: data augmentation and debiasing word embeddings. While these methods have been explicitly tested and presented in the context of reducing gender bias, they ought to be applicable to arbitrary sources of bias.

In the context of a dataset containing a large degree of gender bias, these methods proceed as follows.

Data Augmentation

Data augmentation creates a copy of the old dataset, randomizes the gender of all gendered words within the dataset, and unifies the new (gender randomized) dataset with the old dataset. It finishes by anonymizing all proper nouns (e.g., gendered names like Mary or Matthew with unique identifiers like "M1" and "M2".) Any model trained on the unified data now deals with a more equal distribution of gender.

Debiasing Word Embeddings

Concepts like gender are approximated by a single number or set of numbers within word-embedding vectors. If these numbers are outright removed or set to zero across all observations (i.e., effectively removing them), then the word embeddings will no longer account for gender and are debiased. While gender could still be inferred from more subtle relationships between the remaining word embedding features, methods in this category ought to prevent models from accounting for gender explicitly.

Needless to say, neither this approach nor data augmentation will work in predictive modeling tasks where gender identity or proper names are important and valid predictors.

Models

Models trained on biased data generally reproduce and amplify those biases, and NLP models are no different. Bias in NLP models has most often been noted as an issue with text generation models like GPT-3 or in chatbots, which have been shown to make offensive statements across a variety of topics.[13] In other tasks like sentiment analysis or next-word prediction, current approaches are also prone to predictions that rely on spurious relationships within the word embeddings the model was trained on. While researchers have proposed the use of in-processing methods, including adding some sort of fairness penalty or constraint to the model and adversarial debiasing, there are not yet any widely available tools for leveraging these techniques.

Model Interpretability

Modern NLP models are based on neural network approaches and as such are impossible for humans to directly interpret and understand. And, as we by now know, model interpretability is critical; not knowing how a model makes its predictions is one of the primary reasons that harmful predictions are able to be made in the first place. This necessitates the use of interpretability methods to bridge the gap, providing both practitioners and users insight into features that the network might rely on and explanations for individual predictions. Fortunately, all of the neural network–specific interpretability methods that we discussed earlier in this chapter in the "A More Interpretable Black Box" section are applicable to neural networks for NLP. At the time of writing, baseline methods (e.g., Shapley Values, Integrated Gradients, etc.) and intrinsic methods centered around visualizing attention and masked word prediction are most popular.

> **NOTE** At the time of writing (and in the opinions of the authors), Google's Language Interpretability Tool (LIT) is the best tool for leveraging interpretability methods for NLP in a practical setting. This link contains a good introduction to the tool and links to demos: `ai.googleblog.com/2020/11/the-language-inter-pretability-tool-lit.html`.

Summary

Just as the use of deep-learning neural nets in image and text processing is rapidly advancing, so, too, are the challenges of keeping the practice of AI in this area responsible and ethical. The scope of these challenges is huge, and we could do little more than scratch their surface within this chapter.

---

[13]Readers interested in examples of this should read the excellent "How to Make a Chatbot That Isn't Racist or Sexist" article on MIT Technology Review: `https://www.technologyreview.com/2020/10/23/1011116/chatbot-gpt3-openai-facebook-google-safety-fix-racist-sexist-language-ai/`.

We began by laying out a number of the harms that poorly constructed or maliciously used neural networks can cause. Next, we walked through a case study of predictive fairness in a more traditional prediction context: the gender classification of faces. In that example, we saw how balancing across groups and over-sampling data for low-performing groups improved performance but did not eliminate disparities in predictive performance across racial groups or between males and females. The improvements in accuracy that commercial gender classification algorithms have attained, plus the length of time it has taken to achieve them, point to both the feasibility of improving predictive parity far beyond the level we were able to achieve and the amount of work it takes to get there. We also noted that image recognition, in general, has become extremely controversial, with some groups suggesting that facial recognition applications specifically ought to be banned.

In passing, we recognized that much of the harm from the use of deep-learning models in image and text processing can be countered by the "policeman role" of AI—using classification algorithms to identify fake postings, fraud, deception, etc. Our focus, however, has always been the use of the Responsible Data Science framework to help the practitioner avoid unintentional harm in the first place—harm that might result from image and text processing classification and prediction algorithms.

9

Conclusion

AI, and data science more broadly, bring the promise of seemingly unlimited good. After all, the ability to ingest any set of arbitrarily sized, minimally structured data and to produce predictions or explanations for these data is applicable to almost every domain. Our societal attention often focuses on the revolutionary future applications of this potential: cars that drive themselves, computers that can hold natural conversations with humans, precision medications tailored to our specific genomes, cameras that can instantly recognize any object, and software that can automatically generate new images or videos. However, we often forget that AI and AI-augmented methods already greatly empower us in the present. Authoritative information on almost any topic can now be accessed with the tap of a finger. Detailed photographs and video can be taken in near-complete darkness. Media and advertising platforms make startlingly accurate recommendations for the content or products that are most likely to appeal to us. Government services (ideally) become more cheap, effective, and fair. Whether we recognize it or not, these AI methods make an increasingly large number of decisions about our lives. These rapid, accurate decisions are often helpful: fraudulent credit card use is stopped in its tracks, home loan approval arrives quickly, and automatic content moderation removes illegal content before it is ever seen by a human. However, when these decisions are wrong, we are all too often left without appeal or recourse.

Conversations about the benefits of AI too often ignore the long, ongoing history of harms, both intended and unintended. These critiques began at the dawn of statistics as a modern science and are now re-emerging as a result of the oft-unfulfilled, grandiose promises of the applications of AI and data science that grew out of it. Even if we were to discount the numerous cases where AI methods were deliberately developed or appropriated by malevolent actors or state agencies, in ways intended to deceive, con, incite, oppress, or suppress, we still are forced to reckon with this sobering reality:

Good intentions and technical excellence alone are not enough to prevent our models from causing harm.

This fact should not come as a shock. Despite the ubiquity and broad application of AI, the goals of individual AI models are, so far, always narrowly defined. Predict a binary "yes" or "no." Calculate a risk score. Produce the most probable label for the class of an image. Reduce the dimensionality of a set of data and display it as a plot. Estimate the next element in a time sequence. In each case, we narrow a complex, multifaceted set of relationships down to a smaller subset for the AI to focus on. This is unavoidable. AI methods require information about the world to be provided in a form that they can ingest and use to produce outputs that are sufficiently accurate and understandable to humans.

Our contributions to this process as the humans in the loop are critical, and are perpetually overlooked. We are the ones who determine which information about the world ought to be encoded as data, how it should be encoded, what the model's goal should be, and whether certain modeling results are acceptable or not. By the time the data make it into the model, it has our fingerprints all over it. Regardless of whether we acknowledge it or not, bias within these models unavoidably becomes a feature.

Unfortunately, this laser-like focus of an AI model in optimizing a particular function is too often a trait that we, as data science managers and practitioners, adopt ourselves, blinding us to everything prior to or beyond the technical elements of our work. We do this at great peril both to ourselves and to the groups that we aim to serve. Nothing about building an accurate model requires us to question whether we used the correct data, or whether our data are unbiased. Nothing about building an accurate model requires us to ask whether a modeling task is ethical, or whether a model is able to generalize well to new data. Nothing about building an accurate model forces us to ask whether the model's predictions are equally accurate across groups, or whether the real-world consequences of these predictions differ meaningfully across groups.

These are not hypothetical concerns for the future, nor are they theoretical. Recent history has shown the risks of ignoring the broader context of our models beyond metrics and code. These models may magnify already existing biases in the data and manifest them at scale in the real world. The harms caused by these biases constitute a real and present problem, especially for the most vulnerable and disadvantaged members of our societies. We covered many examples of this in the book, but still did not mention many others. A model intended to estimate severity of kidney dysfunction systematically underestimated kidney function for Black patients. Another intended to make the selection of employees more efficient and objective ended up reflecting and intensifying existing bias against women.

Surely, we can do better.

How Can We Do Better?

We should all be familiar with cases similar to those that we have covered within this book. Every week seems to bring new media stories about the harm, or potential harm, that AI can cause. By the time of this book's publication, other stories about harmful AI will have come to the fore. In our positions as managers of data science teams or as data science practitioners, what can we do to detect and mitigate these harms within our own work? How far must we go beyond the typical work of a data science project to ensure that our own projects are done responsibly?

The Responsible Data Science Framework

Doing data science responsibly requires us to broaden our perspective beyond the code or metrics involved in building our models. The primary work involved in adopting this broader perspective is not in learning anything new, but rather in thinking more deeply about and reframing the work that we already do. Whether we recognize it or not, we already make decisions about these broader factors all the time—through making decisions about what information ought to be encoded as data, whose voices are heard within a project, how the impact of the project is measured, and all manner of other factors. Our primary work within this book has been in highlighting each of these overlooked factors, showing why they deserve the same conscious, deliberate focus that we place upon the technical steps within our modeling pipelines.

The Responsible Data Science (RDS) framework is a more systematic and simple means of adopting this broader focus. Each of its steps directs our attention to the oft-overlooked nontechnical factors in our projects, occasionally having us think more like sociologists, anthropologists, and economists. Our work has to include consulting with diverse groups to understand whether a particular modeling task is appropriate. It must involve consideration of the possible harms of our model and understanding how our model's predictions impact individuals and groups in the real world after it is deployed. These are all parts of the broader nontechnical factors in our projects that are too often overlooked. At the same time, paying attention to the broader context of our project will also enhance its chances of success: Gartner contends that 80 percent of data science projects fail, often due to overconcentration on narrow technical goals. That rings true in our experience.

And yet, there remain issues on the technical side of conventional data science work that the adoption of this framework also helps to address. Fundamentally, these issues come down to data science and the development of AI too often being treated as an experimental ad hoc pursuit more suited to a research or academic environment. While this sort of mindset makes sense within a certain small set of work contexts, it is poorly suited to the many environments where AI models are designed for deployment and make all manner of consequential decisions in the real world. In these contexts, the development of AI models requires a much higher level of precision and oversight than it typically receives. In scenarios where predictive models are going to be deployed in the real world, data scientists must emulate the conventional processes for software development and engineering. The RDS framework helps enforce increased technical rigor through the following:

▪ Comparing multiple models across multiple performance metrics

▪ Building more comprehensive, more transparent documentation

▪ Highlighting the importance of model interpretability

▪ Requiring the comparison of model performance across groups (if relevant)

Just as pilots and surgeons have checklists to ensure all potential problem areas are covered before proceeding, the RDS framework establishes a formal process to help ensure that models are fair and unbiased. Just as mechanics and engineers employ diagnostic steps to identify problems with machinery, the framework sets out procedures to investigate the presence and nature of bias and unfairness in models.

The audit process developed within the framework helps make this checklist orientation concrete. We repeat it here for emphasis:

1. Quantify and visualize the predictive performance across protected groups for each of the models.

2. Quantify and visualize the predictive error across protected groups for each of the models to explore failure cases for the models.

3. Decide upon appropriate fairness metrics for the task and calculate them for each of the groups with respect to one or more protected features.

4. Compare fairness metrics across groups within each model to determine whether unfairness is a problem.

5. Leverage interpretability methods to better understand important features, global and local feature impacts, as well as possible sources of unfairness in how the model leverages the underlying features.

6. Apply preprocessing and postprocessing techniques to mitigate bias if large amounts of it are discovered. If model predictions are to be modified, model architects and organization decision-makers need to be consulted.

Maybe it doesn't make sense in your specific work context to adopt a whole new framework for doing data science, especially if you and your team have already evaluated many others. Perhaps you find the idea of adopting a new data science framework to be overkill or burdensome. Fortunately, the RDS framework does not need to be adopted wholesale; any of its individual components ought to be useful. In the following two sections, we offer the most important takeaways for data science managers and data scientists seeking to do data science more responsibly.

Doing Better As Managers

Data science has long since moved beyond the ad hoc development of a model to address a particular situation. It has become a process embedded in the way that organizations do business. As a data science team manager, you are responsible in large part for the team's culture, composition, and other nontechnical elements that are nonetheless critical to the team going about doing their work responsibly. You can start by ensuring that teams are diverse, not just in terms of race, gender, sexual orientation, etc., but in other respects such as nation of origin, professional background, personal interests, age, etc. Diverse teams tend not only to be more productive and creative, but also less likely to fall into groupthink, and more likely to identify moral or technical issues with models. You can also work to involve all the project's stakeholders, and do what you can to ensure that the set of stakeholders includes those who will be affected by a model's deployment.

In checking in with data science technical teams and reviewing their work, keep in mind the project's overall objectives and that improving individual model performance metrics is not necessarily the only relevant factor in achieving these objectives. Solicit feedback often, and encourage a culture of openness and thinking critically about the benefits/harms of the team's work. If the potential for serious reputational or legal harm develops, be prepared to put the case to senior management that revenue hits from modifying products or pulling them from the market are often counterbalanced by future goodwill, increased trust, and a better organizational reputation.

It is true that much of the benefit of an ethical approach to data science is invisible: the bad things that don't happen. Nonetheless, having a reputation for practicing data science responsibly and ethically can be a bonus when it comes to recruiting more data scientists, which, in turn, enhances that capability for practicing data science responsibly.

Doing Better As Practitioners

As a data science practitioner, you ought to understand that the process of doing data science and AI modeling does not begin with the model, or even with the data upon which it is trained. Decisions about how the modeling task is framed, what purpose the model is intended to serve, who is consulted in its creation, and which information ought to be recorded as data all indelibly influence the steps later in the modeling process where we tend to focus most of our efforts. Each team member should consider whether a particular modeling task is ethical, the proposed data are comprehensive (and ethically acquired), and whether the model or methods are at a high risk of misappropriation for potentially harmful uses in the future.[1] Basically, strive to ensure your project reaches a high degree of procedural fairness.

On the technical front, you can first ensure that you understand well how and why your models generate predictions. We have suggested tools and processes to help accomplish this. The challenge is greatest when black-box models are used because they reveal no information about relationships between predictor variables and outcomes and are typically judged simply on the basis of whether they make accurate predictions. To better understand relationships in the data, you should explore one of the following options:

- Using models that are intrinsically interpretable, for example, logistic regression, where the predictor coefficients provide direct information about how features relate to outcomes
- Applying interpretability methods after the fact to black-box models to better understand how features relate to outcomes

Regardless of whether an intrinsically interpretable model is chosen as the final model, you should always attempt to fit one for comparison if the modeling task allows for it. Getting a good sense of the final model's relative performance requires comparing it with alternative models over multiple resamples, including with a baseline featureless model and an intrinsically interpretable model, as

---

[1]The questions in the "Datasheets for Datasets" paper (https://arxiv.org/abs/1803.09010) and the Ethical Considerations section of the "Model Cards for Model Reporting" (https://arxiv.org/abs/1810.03993) provide good inspiration for considering these issues more comprehensively.

well as with an estimate of the optimal model performance. And, to be clear, these performance comparisons should happen over multiple metrics! While one metric might be most suitable for your modeling task, too much focus on a singular modeling metric can blind you to other interesting or useful relationships within the data that other metrics could help to reveal. The results of these comparisons should provide justification for your work (e.g., "look how much better our method does than all of these other alternatives"), and you should document them as clearly and transparently as possible for the benefit of other team members and external parties.

Achieving good overall predictive performance is no doubt important. Without good predictive performance, the whole promise of AI evaporates, and the harms it can cause actually magnify. However, once you have achieved a generally well-performing model, adding tiny increments of overall predictive power becomes less important than, say, exploring the performance of your model across groups, as large differences in per-group performance are a key indicator of bias sneaking into a model. These differences should be explored relative to one another on both an absolute and a relative basis, as small differences in absolute metrics are often much more stark when compared on a standardized basis. If bias is discovered, you should make attempts to mitigate it and achieve predictive fairness, documenting these attempts where possible.

Finally, your responsibilities as a data science practitioner or as the data science team's manager do not cease upon the delivery of modeling results or the model's deployment. The real-world outcomes of the model could be unexpectedly harmful (or unexpectedly good), and these outcomes could vary greatly between different groups. Practitioners and managers should adjust and improve their monitoring procedures so that they reflect not just best practice from a technical or social responsibility standpoint but, more broadly, a unified system of responsible data science.

A Better Future If We Can Keep It

In the future, the potential of AI methods will continue to improve and grow in scope. Public scrutiny and regulation for these approaches will grow in lockstep. It is our hope that, at some point in the future, people will look upon the successes and failures of AI and data science over the past few decades as occurring during a sort of AI Wild West—a period flush with lucrative opportunities and boundless potential that was, nonetheless, rife with abuse, fraud, and shoddy workmanship. In this better future, these issues will, hopefully, be seen as a relic of the times.

Laws and regulations will address some of these issues and move us toward that better future. Legislators and regulators around the world are showing greater interest in holding tech companies accountable for their mistakes. However, technology is like water running downhill—it will eventually find its way around regulatory obstacles that were built to serve a given point in time. Consider landline telephones in the early twentieth century: The complex tax and regulatory structure that governs landlines to this day evolved over time, beginning in 1934 when the Federal Communications Commission (FCC) was established to control ATT and other monopolies. Its scope can be seen from a quick glance at a landline bill, which would require a visit to grandparents or a museum for most data scientists now. Landline bills require multiple pages to list the various taxes, adjustments, and services required by law. These regulations are now largely irrelevant, as wireless service and other forms of digital communication have largely replaced traditional landlines. And so continues the game of regulatory cat and mouse.

Laws and regulations might address some of the egregious problems of today, but they might also introduce unwanted complexity, create new incentives for circumventing laws, and provide us with a false sense that the problem can be solved without any effort of our own. We might conclude that the problem isn't *our* responsibility to solve, despite the fact that we are often the ones who did the work that caused the problem in the first place. As data scientists and data science team managers, we should not rely solely on regulation and laws to address the ethical failings of the models that we ourselves produce. We have to avoid the Scylla and Charybdis of a "legal solution" to the problem brought on by doing either of the following:

- Shifting all responsibility to the lawyers ("not my department")
- Becoming quasi-lawyers ourselves, focusing in detail on the delineated risks of today but forsaking the larger picture

Rather, we as data science professionals must practice responsible data science ourselves, based on the fundamental goals of avoiding bias and unfairness, and embrace accountability for our work to keep the possibility of this better future a realistic one.

Index

A

accuracy, 183
Amazon resume screener, 100
Ames housing data, 108
Apple credit card, 57
association rules, 42
astroturfing, 226
ATT, 272
attention, 235
AUC, 31
audit process, 174
Audit reports, 95
Auditing COMPAS, 200
Auditing phase, 96
auto, 44
Azure Transparency Notes, 149

B

baseline methods of interpretability, 233
behavioral manipulation, 52
benchmarker function, 132
BERT, 228
best practives, 139
bias mitigation, 87
bias mitigation, 185
bias mitigation, 213

bias-variance tradeoff, 104
bias-variance tradeoff, 22
black, 39
black-box baseline, 124
black-box methods, 14
boosted trees, 41
bootstrap, 40
Boruta algorithm, 127
Broward County data, 141
Buolamwini, Joy, 248

C

California Consumer Protection Act (CCPA), 65
Cambridge Analytica, 52
Cambridge Analytica, 85
Captum, 233
cardiomyopathy, 57
CCPA (California Consumer Protection Act), 65
CelebA (Faces Attributes data), 78
Census racial categories, 159
checklists, 268
China, social credit, 51
classification thresholds, 218
Clearview AI, 78
clustering, 41

clustering, 23
CNN (convoliutional neural net), 19
CNN (convolutional neural network),
    44
collaborative filters, 42
Communities and Crime data, 140
COMPAS algorithm, 58
COMPAS data, 140
COMPAS model, 187
Compilation stage, 94
ConceptSHAP, 118
ConceptSHAP, 234
conditional use accuracy, 183
Confusion matrix, 28
confusion matrix, 182
convolutional neural net (CNN), 19
convolutional neural network (CNN),
    44
cost function, 34
Cost of Interpretability (COI), 196
credit scoring, 10
credit-scoring, 124
crime prediction, 151
Crime Similarity System (CSS)., 153
criminality in facial images, 8
CRISP-DM (Cross-Industry Standard
    Process for Data Mining), 76
cross, 33
cross validation, 20
Cross-Industry Standard Process for
    Data Mining (CRISP-DM), 76

D
DAG (directed acyclic graph), 143
Darwin, Charles, 7
data augmentation, 261
Datasheets, 94
datasheets, 146
debiasing word embeddings, 261
decile lift chart, 29
decision tree, 37
decision trees, 14
deep fakes, 6
deep learning, 43

deep learning, 18
deepfakes, 50
DeepLIFT, 233
demographic parity, 183
directed acyclic graph (DAG), 143
discriminant analysis, 13
distillation methods of interpretability,
    234
DNN (deep neural network), 43
DoD's Ethical AI Principles, 68
doorbell cameras, 60
drake workflow automation tool, 143

E
epoch, 231
Equal Credit Opportunity Act, 64
equalized odds, 183
Equivant, 141
error function, 34
error rate equality, 183
ethical concerns in project, 152
eugenics, 7
Expected Gradients, 233

F
Facebook, 52
Faces Attributes dataset (CelebA)
    data, 78
facial recognition, 78
facial recognition, 258
FactSheet Project (IBM), 149
Fair Credit Reporting Act, 63
FairFace image dataset, 236
fairness in machine learning, 87
fairness intervention, 87
fairness metrics, 181
fairness types, 175
false alarm rate, 182
false negative rate, 182
false positive rate, 182
feature importance, 127
feature selection, 126
feature selection, 20
featureless model, 123

Federal Communications Commission (FCC), 272
fidelity of models, 107
file and folder structure, 144
Fisher, R.A., 7
FNR - False Negative Rate, 183
FPR - False Positive Rate, 183
Frameworks for responsible data science, 89
functionalized code, 131

G
gains, 28
gains, 31
Galton, 39
Galton, Francis, 7
GAM (generalized additive model), 122
GDPR, 62
GDPR, 65
GDPR, 9
Gebru, Timnet, 146
gender identification, 236
Gender Shades, 84
Gender Shades, 248
generalized additive model (GAM), 122
German Credit data, 102
German Credit data, 124
global interpretability methods, 107
GNU Make workflow tool, 142
Goldman Sachs credit card, 57
Google Facial Expression Comparison data, 78
GPT-3, 260
gradient descent, 229

H
healthcare risk scoring, 56
heatmaps, 233
holdout data, 33
holdout samples, 20
husky/flute classification example, 122

husky-wolf classification, 232
hyperparameters, 227

I
ICE plots, 108
image recognition, 236
ImageNet, 46
immigration enforcement and AI, 59
impact statement, 94
impact statement, 145
Integrated Gradients, 233
interpretability, 35
interpretability method critiques, 119
interpretability of models, 100
interpretability of models, 87
interpretable baseline , 124
intrinsic methods of interpretability, 235

J
Jekyll and Hyde, 5
Justification stage, 94

K
k-nearest neighbors, 14

L
language interpretability tool (LIT), 262
learning rate annealing, 230
legal issues in AI, 62
lift, 28
lift chart, 28
LIME (locally-interpretable model explanations), 116
linear regression, 35
lion/tiger/zebra example, 118
loan data, 28
local interpretability methods, 113
locally-interpretable model explanations (LIME), 116
logistic regression, 13
logit, 13

loss function, 34
loss function, 245

M

maximum disparity, 184
microtargeting, 54
microtargeting, 6
missing predictors, 38
Mitchell, Margaret, 147
model card, 147
Model Card Toolkit (Google), 149
Modeling stage, 96
multi-arm bandit, 53

N

naive (featureless) model, 123
naive Bayes, 16
nearest neighbors, 41
negative predictive value, 183
neural nets, 17
neural networks, 43
neural networks, 227
NeurIPS, 145
Noise Tunneling, 242
NoiseTunnel interpretability and
    fairness package, 87
nonlinear relationships, 109
Northpointe, 141

O

objective function, 34
odds, 13
odds ratio, logistic regression, 103
optimal performance baseline , 124
Optum health, 4
outcome fairness, 176
overfitting, 33
overfitting, 21
overfitting and underfitting, 104
oversampling, 214

P

parity threshold, 184
Parscale, Brad, 53

PDP plots, 108
Pearson, Karl, 7
permutation feature importance, 108
permutation feature importance, 208
Personal Information Protection and
    Electronic Documents Act, 65
Pillow package, 245
pipeline for modeling, 143
postprocessing, 185
precision, 183
predictive fairness, 176
Preparation stage, 95
preprocessing, 185
Principles of responsible data science,
    91
privileged group, 184
procedural fairness, 176
Propublica, 141
protected feature, 180
protected group monitoring, 149
protected groups, 139
protected groups, 178

R

random variability, 131
rare class, 28
RDS framework stages, 137
RDS workflow, 193
Receiver Operating Characteristics
    curve, 31
recidivism, 58
recidivism data, 140
recidivism model - COMPAS, 187
recipe package, 160
recommender systems, 42
recommender systems, 23
recurrent neural network (RNN), 45
regression, 10
representation methods of
    interpretability, 234
reproducibility, 146
resampling, 131
residuals, 113
Right to Privacy, 65

RNN (recurrent neural network), 45
robodebt scandal (Australia), 67
robust models, 106
ROC curve, 31

S
saliency map, 122
scraping data, 78
sensitivity, 29
sensitivity, 183
Shapley values, 114
Sherlock Holmes, 8
skip connection, 245
SMACTR audit algorithm, 93
smile detection, 148
social credit in China, 51
specificity, 29
specificity, 183
Student Performance data, 35

T
TDSP (Team Data Science Process), 76
Team Data Science Process (TDSP), 76

tensorboard, 234
tf-explain, 233
threshold optimization, 218
tidymodels, 160
training and test data split, 126
Trump campaign, 53

U
Uighur profiling in China, 81
UNet, 228
Unsupervised algorithms, 47
unsupervised learning, 22

V
validation data, 33

W
wisdom of the crowd, 16
wolf/husky classification example, 116
wolf-husky classification, 232

Y
yacs package, 241

RNN (recurrent neural network), 45
robodebt scandal (Australia), 47
robust models, 106
ROC curve, 81

S

saliency map, 172
sampling bias, 75
sensitivity, 29
sensitivity, 182
Shapley value, 114
Sherlock Holmes, 5
skip connection, 245
SMACTR model algorithm, 69
smart detection, 146
social credit in China, 51
specificity, 29
specificity, 182
Student Performance data, 33

T

TDSP (Team Data Science Process), 76
Team Data Science Process (TDSP)

tensorboard, 281
tt-explain, 253
threshold optimization, p. 218
tidymodels, 160
training and test data split, 120
Trump campaign, 53

U

Uighur profiling, in China, 51
UNet, 228
unsupervised algorithms, 43
unsupervised learning, 22

V

validation data, 5

W

Wisdom of the crowd, 16
wolf/husky classification example, 116
well-known classification, 232

Y

visualization, 251